BULLYCIDE
Death at playtime

An investigation by

Neil Marr and Tim Field

2001

Published in Great Britain in 2001

Success Unlimited
PO Box 67, Didcot, Oxfordshire OX11 9YS, UK

© Neil Marr and Tim Field 2001

The right of Neil Marr and Tim Field to be identified as the authors of this work has been asserted by them in accordance with the Copyright, Designs and Patents Act 1988.

British Library Cataloguing in Publication Data
A catalogue record for this book is
available from the British Library.

ISBN 0 9529121 2 0

Typeset using FrameMaker® in Helvetica 11 point.

All brand or product names are trademarks or registered trademarks of their respective companies or organizations.

Printed in Great Britain by
Wessex Press, Wantage, Oxfordshire.

To

Skovia who made it possible

Steven who made it necessary

and

all those now without a voice

*"I have said a prayer to God. Why do I have to
live like this? If I do I must kill myself."*
Steven Shepherd
Britain's first recognized bullycide

Bullycide
Death at playtime
by
Neil Marr and Tim Field

Contents

Tables

Thanks

This work is the product of intimate, extended, sometimes painful, talks with several hundred people who, over our years of research, threw open their darkest memories or who fearlessly spoke out from a professional standpoint, sometimes expressing views they knew would be unpopular with guarded bosses and colleagues.

They share a common wish to help end the epidemic horror Tim and I expose here for the first time.

Some are named within the pages, some helped along with guidance or considered it their duty to honestly impart what they knew and do not expect to be named. Others generously offered the results of their own private or professional research to assist. Some are old friends; some are new. All are friends.

Every one has self-edited input to assure a book without error or misinterpretation. Every one has earned the humble salute of the authors and merits the pride of knowing that his or her selfless gift to this book may save a young life this very week.

Every child and parent in the British Isles owes thanks to them.

Grateful appreciation is also extended to you, the reader, who joins the fight against this deadly, preventable disease by arming yourself with the information here.

Of course, those who gave the most are no longer able to turn the pages of any book, let alone this one. Some of their names you'll find recorded here - others only on gravestones. To them we owe the greatest, heartfelt feelings of all.

Neil Marr, Monaco
January 2001

Preface

By the end of the school year at least sixteen families in the UK will be bereaved by the loss of a son or daughter.

Claiming more lives than a Dunblane massacre every year, the secret toll has an identifiable cause: the intentional actions of a bully who gets away with murder, often aided and abetted by the wilful inaction and lack of accountability of those in positions of power and responsibility.

The pain caused by bullying doesn't end when school is over. In the UK, over 5000 people take their life annually. Suicide is now the number one cause of death for males aged 18-24. Those who survive report symptoms of trauma long after leaving school.

When unremitting gratuitous physical and psychological violence causes life to become a fate worse than death, Neil and I call the consequence ... bullycide.

Tim Field, Oxfordshire
January 2001

Authors' note

Whilst every effort has been taken in the preparation of the material in this book, the authors shall have neither liability nor responsibility to any person or entity with respect to any loss or damage caused or alleged to be caused directly or indirectly by the information contained herein.

This book contains detailed accounts of bullying behaviour and its consequences. People who have experienced bullying may wish to seek support at the time of reading due to the unpleasant memories that may be evoked.

Introduction by Jo Brand

Bullying is the human deed that makes me most angry. It is a cowardly, brutal and humiliating thing to do to another human being and, amongst children, it is particularly difficult to come to terms with. This book is about children who are so disturbed by and hopeless about being bullied that they end up taking their own lives.

It's difficult to understand how a child could become so overwhelmed by bullies that he or she feels the need to commit suicide, but if you just look around you, in this day and age, you will see that the adult world is not a very impressive provider of examples of kindness, tolerance and understanding.

Added to this we are all seemingly required to live up to such high standards and if you are different from the gang in any way, you run the risk of being isolated and picked on. Too fat, not fat enough, red-haired, too clever, not clever enough, big nose, small nose, too rich, not rich enough ... you name it, it's a reason for bullying.

I was not the target of bullies at primary school and rarely witnessed it, living as I did in a very small village in Kent, but I came across bullying on many occasions after that and always tried to do my bit.

Once when I was on my way somewhere, I came across a group of ten-year-olds stoning a child of a similar age who was in a terrible state, pleading with them to stop. What shocked me the most was the fact that I wasn't the only person around, there were many people strolling past, all completely ignoring it.

I intervened and stopped it, only temporarily I'm sure ... what a depressing thought.

At secondary school, I was bullied by a teacher who was on my back the whole time picking on my work and using me in front of the class as a verbal punchbag.

In the end I told my mother who is a formidable opponent when there is some kind of cruelty going on. She went up to the school, all guns blazing, and sorted the whole thing out.

I'm aware that a lot of kids are too scared to talk to their parents or don't feel they will get the support, but it is only by constantly bringing these bullies to account and speaking up about the excesses of bullies that bullying will ever be truly conquered.

I hope this book, on the increasing problem of the devastated children who take their own lives due to bullying, can contribute to that debate.

Chapter 1

Strawberry Fields Forever

The story of Steven Shepherd,
Britain's first recorded bullycide.

*"Let me take you down 'cos I'm going to
strawberry fields, nothing is real. Nothing to
get hung about. Strawberry fields forever."*
John Lennon

Steven Shepherd walked alone.

His longest lonely walk took him a lifetime. He never came home.

Steven lay down in the faraway strawberry fields where he had spent the only happy day of his eleven short years on earth ... and he stayed in Strawberry Fields Forever.

John Lennon had written the song a few weeks before. Then Steven died and made the words mean more than the Beatle, writing of a Salvation Army home for lost boys a few miles from the scene of Steven's death, could ever have imagined.

Steven willed himself to death and became Britain's first recorded bullycide.

Imagine that cruel January night in 1967 with rain whipping. He'd tossed away his sodden shoes. The chill nibbled like rats. And he was all but blind without the cheap wire-rimmed National Health specs he had discarded on his ten-mile trek. He'd made sure he would see no more terrible tomorrows.

He stood and shivered in the moonless black where his nightmares and dreams would finally meet. Then he lay in the lee of a drainage ditch and his nightmare faded. We can only hope his sweet dream of peace began that night;

that he did not suffer long before sleep overcame him.

It was fifty-one days before a wayward dog found what the bitter northern winter and the creeping things had left of Britain's first bullycide. No one will ever know if it took merciful hours or painful days of agony for Steven to find the solace his young heart craved.

He was an intelligent lad was Steven.

He knew that in England they laughed at a town called Wigan. It isn't by the sea but they'd tell you it had a pier. George Formby's Dad was innocently to blame for that. His famous film star son with the toothy grin and the ukulele - born a stone's throw from Steven's two-up-two-down - made it England's private joke.

Steven knew that even in Wigan folks needed a joke of their own and laughed at the huddle of scruffy terraces next door at Higher Ince where he lived. They called the stinking, smoking slag tips there The Black Alps. That was the Wiganers' giggle.

He knew that in Higher Ince there was Rose Bridge Secondary Modern School where he suffered his days. In one direction, the bus could take you to posh Hindley and Abram Grammar. The bus going the other way reached even posher Wigan Grammar School. Cost you tuppence if you had it. But Rose Bridge was where the sons of rag and bone collectors and blue-scarred pit men studied for unemployment or worse. If Rose Bridge was a joke for Incers it was a bad one because the school was better than most in poverty-stricken Lancashire.

But there was one joke left at the bottom of the pile. At Rose Bridge School they laughed at this frail eleven-year-old boy called Steven Shepherd in clinic specs and baggy Rupert Bear pants.

Steven was the fag end of jokes.

At just after four on a sweaty June day he had a right to feel he was the only one in the whole country who wasn't laughing. He was hobbling the couple of hundred yards home to Granny Nelly's in Brook Street. He wore battered football boots with some heel studs missing. His walking shoes were strung around his neck by their laces, reeking and soggy from the classmates who'd peed in them while he was on the playing field.

They'd kicked him around a bit. Par for the course for Steven at the end of a school day. But this time his left arm felt funny. It was heavy and he couldn't move his fingers.

It was numb and didn't hurt much now so he could still manage the big toothy grin Granny Nelly expected when she opened the door to say his tea was ready. Beans on toast again. She told him to wash his hands. But he couldn't. His left arm hung limp and trying to lift it with his right hand shot bolts of agony from wrist to shoulder. Granny Nelly heard his hiss of pain. Gently, she peeled off his denim jacket and yellow shirt. She ran thick, washerwoman fingers over his pale skin.

"Well. Ast go t'bottom of ower stairs! It's broke," she said. "Flippin' broke. Tha's bin fightin'."

"Playing football, Granny," Steven told her. "Tackle, like."

They didn't talk much on the two big cherry-red Wigan Corporation buses they had to take to reach the Royal Albert Edward Infirmary up Wigan Lane where the fancy people lived and where they played bowls on their manicured green. They didn't need to. Granny Nelly knew he hadn't been fighting and Steven knew the broken bone had nothing to do with a football game where he was never allowed near the ball.

It had started as it had almost daily for as long as he could remember.

First, the piss slopping in his shoes. Then the bell after games to ring the end of the school day and the start of his torment. Always it began with the same three lads. Same age as Steven. Not much bigger. Food wasn't all it might have been in Higher Ince back in 1967. Nobody was that much bigger than anyone else on a staple diet of chips and soggy meat and tater pies.

Parental separation was rare too.

So the taunts began with jibes about his parents, living in separate houses in the same little town. The fact that he had to live with old Granny Nelly and so did his Dad. Mum Theresa, who lived round the corner, and his father, Andrew, had gone their separate ways. Steven didn't know why they were apart but it would be typical for him to have guessed it was somehow his fault.

Then the bully boys would poke fun at his limp, the souvenir of an old accident when he'd been hit by a bus whilst biking over the road in terror from a stranger who'd approached him near the local park.

Uneven Steven.

They would tug at his yellow-checked pants and finger-jab his skinny chest. They'd call him "specky" and "matchstick man". His slightly buck teeth didn't help him as they'd helped Formby. Sometimes the torment would come to blows.

Steven didn't often fight. Steven was fought. It was all part of his life. Like jam butties for dinner and the cinema treat once a week.

This time was little different from the others. They'd snatched away his glasses so that the ring of faces around him became a blur like a crowd picture where everyone moved just as the shutter clicked. He couldn't tell where the punches and kicks were coming from, how many kids had joined the fun. Then something hard struck him just below his left elbow. He'd never hurt like that before.

He dropped to the gritty ground and groped for his specs with his good hand. When he found them and slipped them on he could see that he was now alone.

Soon the grubby plaster cast put on at the infirmary was covered like a toilet wall with smudged schoolboy graffiti. Even in his pain Steven was a figure of fun. Even his broken arm was a joke.

Steven's one school pal was Stanley Holland, son of a rag collector with a donkey and cart. Stan had done well for himself. He bought a big house in a smart residential area. But he didn't feel comfortable there and he brought his wife and two children back to a new home a hop, skip and a jump from where he and Steven had lived as kids.

Stan has the heart of a fine father, not only to his own children, but to the kids he coaches football free whenever he can snatch time from his busy work schedule.

"Steven didn't cry or shout. He never stood up for himself. Never complained to teachers or his family. So it was like the others thought he had no feelings. He was fair game for a ragging. Maybe if he'd just bawled or hit out occasionally? I would have. I was the same size as him. I was in loads of fights and always gave as good as I got. But ... well ... Steven wasn't me.

"We talked about it sometimes, all the insults and the thumpings, kickings, and things. He said he wasn't bothered. He said it had always been like that for him. And I used to leave it at that. You're no psychologist as a kid. I know now that Steven was bothered.

"He needed help. Ince was a tough old place in those days. You didn't go whingeing about bullies. Anyway, if you did say anything you'd only be told to stand up for yourself. Folks in Ince wouldn't have understood a lad who just couldn't do that.

"See, we were the result of two generations of world wars. We weren't supposed to do anything but fight back when our backs were against the wall. Our folks didn't understand that things had changed. It's not people you should fight, it's war itself. There wasn't a lot of help for the likes of Steven in a tough town like Ince. I wonder if there's any real help even today."

Steven's cast came off a few weeks later. He'd stuck to his football injury tale. But it was nonsense. There was no injury on the field. Everybody at school knew he'd taken another good thrashing. One of the lads had whacked him with a length of wood in the playground after school. Just for a laugh.

For Steven, the incident was soon forgotten, merging with the hundreds of other bully attacks he'd suffered for as long as he could recall. There seemed only one thing he wanted to remember.

"It was a day out picking strawberries in some fields at a little village called Newburgh ten or so miles away, near Parbold," Stanley recalls.

"A local cub mistress had invited him because there were a couple of spare seats on the coach. He made three bob for the day's work, fifteen pence. He never stopped talking about it. Said it was the only happy day he'd ever had. I remember he'd even got a bit of a suntan on his face. He used to go on and on about that day.

"Looking back, I suppose it must have been the one day in his life when he wasn't scared to death of a bully gang. Not looking over his shoulder. Just picking strawberries couldn't in itself account for how special that day was to him."

Even now Ince is in denial and Stan, like many others - in spite of police findings, his own childhood memories and the words of an investigative coroner which confirm that Steven was bullied to death - sometimes feels unsure of whether Steven was a real bullycide or the sad victim of a child murderer.

Many we've spoken with feel more comfortable with a murder theory or accidental death. Anything but bullycide.

The Cub mistress, Elsie Wilkinson, is 75 now and almost blind. But she sees the past with crystal clarity and is another who cannot forget Steven Shepherd's face: "I'd known him a long time," she says.

"He'd stand there alone at the back of the Cub hall. That day in the strawberry fields was the first time I'd ever seen him happy, ever seen his lovely smile. I wanted the clocks to stop. For his sake I didn't want the day to end. Next I heard of him he was dead in those very fields."

Steven would pay only one more visit to the strawberry fields of Newburgh and find a more permanent escape from torment. Stan would find himself playing a gruesome role ... that of Steven Shepherd himself.

Granny Nelly is long gone now. But Steven's Auntie Marjory Jolly is a lively old dear with a teenage haircut and a smile that curls and sparkles like the local River Douglas did when it was still clear and pretty and pregnant with flashing fish. She has almost psychic sensitivity and a long memory.

"He used to come to my house a lot for his tea. He'd have bruises or maybe I'd have to stitch up a rip in his clothes.

"But boys will be boys. I just put it down to scrapping. I did a lot of scrapping myself as a kid. That was Wigan. Tough. Nothing wrong with it if it doesn't go too far. Nothing wrong with it if you're sticking up for yourself like I did.

"We didn't know, you see. We didn't know Steven wasn't a scrapper. He was a victim. The signs were there all right. We just didn't read them properly. Like he'd hardly got any friends. He hated going to school even though he'd spend his nights alone in his room reading and reading and reading like a scholar. He loved to study. He hated school. Not the lessons, we know now, but the times in between.

"Tell you summat: I always felt there was going to be a tragic death close to me and mine. I'm like that. I can sense these things. I just never saw in my mind's eye that it was going to be little Steven who would leave us.

"He only went out once a week. Always to the pictures. And always on his own. I should have known. We all should have known. But, well, we didn't".

Marjory's husband, Jimmy, remembers Steven and talks fondly of the wee man who walked alone. His forceful local accent paints vividly coloured pictures of a child in torment. Weekends for Steven, he tells, were strolls along the mucky towpaths of the Leeds-Liverpool canal, lock spanning and whispering shy hellos to fishermen with as much chance of a catch as Steven had of happiness. Sometimes they were solitary climbs over the Black Alps with a dog-eared library paperback stuffed into his hip pocket. He'd carefully hide from other boys scrambling with giggles and mud-caked boots or clogs from Walter Hurst's cloggers shop up the heaps of grey industrial spoil.

But, come Monday, there was no hiding place from the terror waiting for Steven at school. Day after day he took his punishment, then grieved in silence for his life.

Until he could endure no more.

It was four in the afternoon of 25 January 1967. The usual gang was waiting as he crept out of school. The thumps, kicks and insults fell. He found Stanley Holland and, with tears streaking the grime on his cheeks, spat out the words: "I have said a prayer to God. Why do I have to live like this? If I do I must kill myself."

He limped to the home of Granny Nelly and begged his three shillings (15 pence) weekly pocket money from his father. He left behind the last book he had been reading, "Steven's Secret Trail". It's now out of print and our extensive search produced no old copies which might give a hint as to how it may have touched Steven's troubled soul at that time. Only the title suggests a clue.

At 5.15 pm he set out to walk the two miles to Wigan's Court Cinema. He sat through the early showing of, ironically, *The Agony and the Ecstasy*, the story of Michaelangelo's own suffering.

Afterwards in the pouring rain he took his long, lonely walk back to the strawberry fields. Steven's own Secret Trail. He was never seen alive again.

Old time copper Detective Chief Superintendent Harold Prescott found the missing child report on his desk less than twenty-four hours after Steven's disappearance had been reported and, with the horrific Moors Murders he'd worked on fresh in his mind, he launched the biggest murder hunt in the history of Lancashire County Police.

Steven may still have been alive when Prescott picked up the file, shivering, or mercifully unconscious in his isolated, waterlogged ditch as hundreds of police swept into action. But school bullies and strawberry fields were the last things on the minds of Prescott and his huge search team.

Ex-bobby Wally Woods - first cop on the scene when Steven was found and now retired - said soon afterwards: "There was no doubt in anyone's mind that Steven had been abducted. Probably murdered. I don't remember anyone asking much about his school life. Even if we'd known about the bullying, well, 'sticks and stones' and all that.

"No. We were sure we had another perverted child killer on our hands. We expected to find a body with marks of violence."

Granny Nelly's little house in Brook Street was crammed when Steven's disappearance was reported. His estranged parents had arrived and arranged themselves at opposite ends of a worn couch. Uniformed and plain-clothed police were sitting or standing where they could. One, a young policewoman, was fighting back tears, Neil Marr recalls. Local reporters and photographers made tea for everyone and tried not to get in the way. Press, police, and the local community were on the same team in those days. Only when the uniforms left did Steven's mother, Theresa, break down.

Only Neil was with her, a young cub reporter, stirring the sugar into her cup and shyly holding her hand. Then she wanted to talk. To talk and talk, as if by word-walking through his life she could conjure her son back into that stuffy, scruffy little room.

"He had to live 'round the corner with his Granny. It wasn't because I wanted him to. I loved him. But there's only two beds at our house and there was his sister, our Christine. Then me and his Dad had decided to separate. It was better for Steven with Granny Nelly where his father had gone to live. I saw him every day. I mean, it's just down the street isn't it?

"He was a nice little lad, you know. Fun at home. Wouldn't hurt a fly."

She gave Neil her only photograph of Steven. It hangs on his wall and is reproduced in the picture file of our book.

She used the words "loved" and "was". He'd not been missing long by this stage. But Theresa, a pretty young lass in those days, had a mother's instinct and already thought of Steven in the past tense. In a dozen later interviews she never showed any real expectation of his being found alive. She would sit, thin and pale, neatly dressed and drinking cup after cup of tea, waiting for the news she knew would one day arrive and allow her heart to finally break.

That first day of the hunt was low key in comparison to what was to come, confined to cops interviewing friends, family and neighbours. But on day two police were sure they had a major crime on their hands. Extra men were drafted in from the nearby boroughs of Widnes, Bolton, Leigh, and Chorley. A two-mile stretch of the Leeds-Liverpool Canal was drained and its foul, black bed hand-searched for clues which might have been hiding in the murk among the rusted bike frames and sacks of rotting, drowned kittens.

Sixty dog handlers scoured slag tips and wasteland as frogmen from Warrington fumbled in the filthy, chill waters of canals, lakes, and deep pit flashes. By Sunday, 200 police, joined by hundreds of local civilian volunteers, were combing Wigan inch-by-inch and coming up with nothing.

On Monday a special task force from the Regional Crime Squad visited schools in the area and interviewed teachers and children about Steven's life and habits. Nobody brought up the fact that he'd lived in terror of bullying. It didn't occur to them to mention something as workaday as schoolyard scraps and catcalling.

The search area was widened to take in surrounding towns and parklands. More than 8,000 people were interviewed. Six had seen a boy answering Steven's description at the Court Cinema the night of his disappearance. Several other supposed sightings were checked and ruled out. A single anonymous letter - postmarked Bolton - turned out to be a cruel hoax.

As the murder hunt reached huge proportions so did national media interest and the little town of Higher Ince was besieged by reporters, photographers, TV, and radio crews. For the first time in its history Ince became a familiar place name nationwide through television.

Detective Chief Superintendent Harold Prescott, who died recently, knew the value of intensive press coverage. "As long as you lads are here," he told us at one of his daily press conferences, "I've got an extra fifty million detectives in Britain looking out for this young feller."

There was always a titbit for the press. Something to keep the kettle boiling, as the late DCS Prescott used to put it. One day the titbit was Steven's pal, Stanley Holland. He was to star in the first ever reconstruction in British police history of a missing person's last steps. A stroke of police genius.

"I was only twelve," Stan said. "I didn't know what the heck was going on. I remember feeling a bit like a film star with all the attention and the cameras. But I think I knew something bloody serious was about. They told me I might be able to help them find my friend. How was I to know they really thought he was dead?"

Police kitted Stanley out as Steven's double: an identical blue denim jacket buttoned, as always, to the throat, the blue pants with their yellow check, the scuffed black shoes. His brown tousled hair was similar to the missing boy's as were his borrowed spectacles.

At precisely 5.15 pm on Wednesday, the same time Steven had left his father's house seven days before, they walked him through the streets to Wigan and the Court Cinema.

It was like the local Whitsun church parade. Only silent. And a little more holy.

People lined the curbs and in Stanley's wake followed scores of pressmen, TV cameramen, and the merely curious. It was meant to jog memories. It didn't.

No one (least of all the neighbours, who'd always said 'hope for the best' standing around the local pitheads after an underground explosion) admitted the secret feeling that Stanley was retreading footsteps to a grave.

Next, the local Wigan Observer weekly newspaper was called in to superimpose a school photograph of Steven's face onto a picture of Stanley's Steven-dressed body, a tricky technique in those days. Scissors and glue and a lot of darkroom work. It was colourised, circulated to news media and turned into posters to be plastered for miles around. Even on trains and buses.

But DCS Prescott and his massive search squad was getting no closer to the strawberry fields of Newburgh. The school bullies who had caused all of this were innocently, like most of the other local kids, lapping up what to them was a free circus.

As a rule, not much happened in the Ince of the sixties. A schoolboy joke was that they used to watch the traffic lights change at Ince Bar crossroads for a bit of excitement come Saturday night. Those were the days when "Beyond Our Ken" for half an hour on Sunday radio was looked forward to the whole week through. Broke dads used to tell their wives they were "going to the bar". They didn't mean a drinking bar. They meant Ince Bar, the local bus stop. It had a bench where they could sit and chew the fat. No money for anything better.

One of Steven's bullies was thirteen at the time. He's a man with his own family to care for now. He doesn't want to be named but told us "It was a long, long time ago. I sometimes wonder if what I think I remember is what actually happened or what I've made up in my own head since. The guilt, you know? And what folks have told me over the years.

"Don't get me wrong. I'm not trying to say I was blameless. I was part of it all. But back then, well, I was just one of the lads. Ribbing was what we did. Thumping and that. I was bullied myself lots of times. It was water off a duck's back to me. I suppose I thought it was the same with Steven. By the time I found out that wasn't the way of things it was too late to say sorry.

"Steven was a nice boy. Quiet like. But he was a bit different, what with his Mam and Dad being split up and his limp and those daft specs and Bugs Bunny teeth. Lads always pick on kids like that - different kids. We used them to make us feel bigger, like. To prove we're better. Show off to the girls maybe. Could be we were a bit frightened of people who were different. We didn't analyse it too much. Hey, I didn't even know the word analyse then. Bet my teachers didn't either!

"My own Dad used to tell me to fight back when I was bullied. But what happened to Steven changed me. I've never told my own kids to stand up and fight. I'd say to them, tell me about it. We could maybe all have a chat with the kid doing the bullying. I'd get them to try to make a friend of him. Turn the bully into a protector.

"A lot of folks around here think that way since Steven died. Ince used to be a tough town. All hard cases. Our Dads would tell us about clog fights with a couple of lads in shorts kicking shit out of each other's shins with their clog irons. Sometimes they'd sharpen them on kerbstones and there'd be blood everywhere. The winner was the one left standing. They called it `porrin'. Our Dads would laugh about it. Ince was tough. We were proud of it. Sick, eh?

"What happened to Steven made us all think again. I see the kids coming out of Rose Bridge School now, laughing and chatting. Friends like. It's like my own schooldays when I was a bit of a bully boy were from another century. Like so long ago when they hanged toddlers for pinching bread. That remote.

"Aye, we called Steven names and bashed him up sometimes. We didn't know any better.

"I'll tell you something strange. You remember Steven telling Stan Holland that he'd prayed to God to ask why his life was miserable? Well he also told him God had answered and promised that the hand that struck him would be broken and one of the gang broke his arm in a games class the day after Steven disappeared."

Another local boy, Billy Green, was the same age as Steven when he disappeared. He's in his forties now and told us: "He was different from the rest, you see, shy, timid, withdrawn, little and with those round specs and the teeth. He stood out from the gang. It made him an obvious target.

"I didn't have anything against him personally. I was one of the lads. Even I had a fight with him shortly before he went missing. That time, though, he did fight back. He might even have got the better of me. It was so long ago the memory's dim."

Theresa, Steven's mother, lives a few miles now from where Steven was born. She had a new husband in her life but has been widowed for six years. Almost from birth, the aches in her heart have been chronic.

Through another family member, she found we were writing this book and asked us to call her. She said, whispering as she might in a confessional, as though she somehow carried some blame: "I've been trying to fight it all out of my mind. But you can't do that. Those terrible days, waiting for the inevitable, are always with me. I relive them every moment of my life. They are as much a part of my being as my arms and legs.

"I would give anything for this not to have happened to my boy. But it did. Please, please ask people to give value to his life - short as it was. Tell them to do something to stop this thing happening again and again. Tell them Steven wants people to learn from what he had to do. That would be at least a little comfort. Tell them to read your book. I never will. I couldn't face reliving it all again. Tell the others ... tell them to read it."

Sister Christine was a couple of years younger than Steven when he died.

Now living in nearby Hindley with husband Frank, she says: "Back in those days nobody told us kids what was going on really. The whole episode is a kind of kaleidoscope of confusion in my memory.

"Shepherd was an unusual name in Ince. I remember them catcalling Steven 'Ba-ba' and 'go look after your sheep', 'Bo-Peep' and that kind of thing.

"But now I know most of the truth (we had sent her the results of our research - the first time she'd seen the stark truth in black and white) and it hurts me deeply. Something has got to be done to save our other Steven Shepherds. Our brothers and sisters and sons and daughters are just too precious to sweep this bullycide thing under the mat."

Like so many who have suffered a bullycide loss in the family, Christine turned to youth work as a career. Even husband Frank has become a Scoutmaster.

She said: "It's got to be more than just coincidence that I decided to dedicate my life to children and young people. I suppose I carried some guilt. You see, my training and experience now means that I believe I could have saved Steven's life if I'd known then what I know now about children like him.

"As it was, I used to see him beaten up by other lads and,

even though I was younger and a girl at that, I'd just jump on the bigger ones' backs and try to pull them off. In a way I suppose I'm still doing the same thing for others only in a more sophisticated, effective way. I've always been on the side of the underdog and I can honestly say I've effected changes which have helped save at least two children from bullycide in my time as a youth worker. Two Stevens if you like. So, in a way, his value is already showing through his little sister. His sacrifice hasn't been entirely in vain.

"Way back when Steven was missing I was going through hell. I loved him. He was always good and fun to me even if he did once turn my doll's pram into a trolley cart. Mum insisted I go to school over that awful period. She thought it would help take my mind off things. But almost every step I took on the way I'd pass posters demanding 'have you seen this boy?' and the picture was that of my own brother!

"After he was found dead I just couldn't believe it. I suppose I was in shock, denial. I kept thinking I could see him in the street. I used to pray that he would speak to me. Then, one day, it was as though he really did. It was uncanny and most probably helped me make the decision to take up youth work. It was about ten years after he died. Now I feel, when I pick up his photograph, that I can look him in the eye without that overwhelming sense of guilt.

"I was bullied myself after Steven died, not because of his death but because of ... well ... something. Maybe because I had a dyslexia problem, maybe something else. I came from a very poor family and that was good target material too. But does there have to be a reason? I used to cry every night. I couldn't understand what was happening to my life. I suppose it made me even closer to Steven subconsciously. But I got over the bullying. I became what they called 'The Cock of the School' - the best scrapper - and people started to leave me alone. But that's not the only way of dealing with the problem, of course.

"I teach my own two children and those I work with how to discover respect for each other and self-esteem, self-worth. I work on their backgrounds and make a major point of highlighting the positive things in their lives. I even teach self-counselling so that children can work out many problems for themselves.

"So often a child in danger of suicide because of bullying has many other problems, whether it be trouble at home, drug-taking, or some kind of physical difference. But bullying is the pinnacle. It's bullying that can eventually kill."

Christine added: "In my experience both in what I have been through as a child and later through my experience as a youth worker, I feel it is very important to listen to children and young people. You can listen but not really hear unless you believe in their right to be heard. When I was a child growing up in Ince, you were to be seen and not heard. Today we should believe that children and young people have a voice and a right to feel proud of themselves.

"In a way I suppose one of the differences between my brother and me was that, deep down, I liked myself. It is very hard to like yourself when bullies are constantly putting you down. Having a name like Shepherd didn't help. I was called names like 'Sheppy' and kids would call 'go mind your sheep.' 'What's wrong with that?' I would hear adults say. 'Sticks and stones.' Well, a lot is wrong with name-calling as any bully survivor will tell you. You lose self-esteem bit by bit. You lose your self.

"I remember waiting in fear as each child in class had to read out a passage from a book. It was almost unbearable. Unlike my brother, I had difficulty with reading and spelling. The ridicule I suffered from teachers and children is still with me today.

"In my work with young people now I always encourage them to write. But I always make a point of telling them that their spelling isn't important.

"A child needs to feel proud of himself and needs to like

himself. Unlike Steven, I always knew I was a strong person. There were times when I had to struggle to remember this to reach my goals and ambitions. Help sometimes comes in strange ways. I remember a teacher who could see through me - the young girl who was hurting but headstrong and acting older than her years. She took me on one side and told me I didn't need to pretend with her. She not only listened, she even heard my language as crying out for help.

"I know as a young person I needed to listen to who was around me and be prepared to help. I needed to learn to trust and to look for that special person. They were always there, I found. I was able to help myself because of love for myself - the way forward was open.

"That's why I was guilty over Steven's death. I felt for a long time that I could have saved him. I knew his qualities. He didn't. He needed to be made to recognise them. It's vital to know and to like yourself. I know this now - I didn't see it that clearly at just ten years of age."

After our conversations with Steven's remaining nearest and dearest, there was a family conference in Ince to discuss our proposed words for use here. Christine told us the family was hopeful that, at last, through this book, Steven was to be done some justice.

Steven's memorial service at the Elim Four Square Church in Wigan, just a stone's throw from where he was last seen alive, was packed. Neil was there as a reporter and invited mourner - it was his day off from the local press agency. The tiny coffin containing Steven's few remains was buried in Gidlow cemetery a few miles away in the town of Standish. Family poverty at the time precluded a gravestone.

Years later they could not even find his resting place. Neil found it for them only with help from a council worker in the huge graveyard. The grave-digger wrote the plot number on a scrap of toilet paper (no insult intended. He was a man of deep feeling but he was busy burying the 300th victim of Wigan `flu that day in March 1999 and he hadn't the time to search for a notepad).

Steven Shepherd: No: R/C 21 380.

The framed toilet paper tombstone hangs on Neil's wall.

At his burial site there was no name, no flowers, just an overturned plastic pot filled with weeds. It now sits on Neil's desk. He's growing a single strawberry plant in it.

Sister Christine, her husband Frank, and Steven's mother, Theresa, have now clubbed their savings for a headstone.

Nothing ever worked for Steven Shepherd. Nothing had been tried by those in authority who should have known his plight. He lay in his cherished strawberry field as police searched in vain for clues to a murderous pervert who never existed in the criminal sense.

It was left to chance to solve the mystery of his disappearance. An early afternoon stroll around the fields near his country home by council roadworker David Edgeley culminated in his retriever dog making a gruesome discovery.

"He was sniffing around. You know what retrievers are like. Well, he'd climbed down into a ditch at the side of the field. I knew it would be mucky and I could just see what the reaction would be if I brought him home trailing mud onto the clean lino.

"I went to the ditch and called to him to come to heel. I saw he was sniffing at something. Something like a pile of dirty old rags. I looked closer. I knew. I just knew I was looking at a decomposed body. It was the most horrible sight. I don't mind telling you I was ill right there and then.

"I was only 23. I'd never seen anything like that before. I called off the dog and ran to the Red Lion pub in Newburgh village where they had a phone. It was only half a mile or so away. I called the police."

PC Wally Woods answered the call at his station in nearby Parbold. He rushed to the scene. Looking into the ditch he could make out the checked trousers and blue jacket of the boy a whole county's police force, the second biggest in the land, had been seeking for fifty-one days.

"There wasn't much left of him. A few strands of clothing. I won't describe the rest. It's too upsetting. He'd been there a long time, you see, in that ditch. He was flat on his stomach. I didn't have to see his face," PC Woods told Neil hours after the discovery.

Minutes later, shortly after 3 pm, the sleepy stone village of Newburgh was stiff with blue uniforms.

Steven was face down in the five-foot-deep ditch, partly hidden by brambles.

Police trampled the bare strawberry fields searching for his shoes and spectacles. They were never found. Local folks think he had tossed them away, burning his bridges, determined to go through with his tragic resolve.

His remains were taken to a mortuary a few miles away at Ormskirk General Hospital where Home Office pathologist Dr Charles St Hill began a painstaking post-mortem examination. Theresa, Granny Nelly, and Steven's father did not have to suffer looking at what little was left of Steven. They identified him by scraps of his clothing.

Police set up a control centre at Woodcock Hall, the home of a local councillor, and immediately DCS Prescott held a press conference. "We are treating this as a serious crime and the Murder Squad has been called in," he announced.

Everyone in the village was quizzed that same afternoon. Scores of police combed the fields. Children were warned to stay indoors. Press arrived in noisy droves and police turned a blind eye to the long hours being kept at the local pub where reporters, police and weary search-volunteers compared notes.

The hue and cry for Steven's killer was never louder. But

the hunt, though more vigorous than any old hand had ever seen, was short. It was soon after midnight when Prescott again entered the Red Lion.

Journalists who'd being queuing impatiently for the landlord's only phone fell silent. A chair was pushed forward and Prescott slumped into it, exhausted.

The detective accepted a pint of best bitter from Jeff Barnes, the local freelance reporter and Neil's boss at the time, tossed his sopping wet green trilby hat onto a table and said softly: "It's all over."

He'd just got news from pathologist St Hill. No signs of violence on the body. Probable cause of death: exposure.

So the police file was closed and, after a standing-room-only funeral opposite the cinema where he'd watched his last film, *The Agony and the Ecstasy*, a story of suffering and suicide, Steven was borne to his final resting place. Past the hospital where his broken arm had been set, the long cortege reverently carried his coffin to an unmarked grave in Gidlow Cemetery four miles away.

Exactly one year later, Jeff Barnes and Neil Marr chanced upon each other at Steven's graveside. They each carried flowers and in their embarrassment simply nodded a greeting before leaving. Steven's tale had touched them that deeply.

Cub reporter as he was then, Neil understood that Steven's story hadn't ended in the Red Lion with the revelation that he had not been murdered.

That's when it started. That's when this book's first sentence was drafted.

It took the wisdom and nit-picking tenacity of South Lancashire Coroner Ronald A Lloyd to get to the truth and to winkle out the horror story of Steven's life. Lloyd would never have used the word "bullycide". That would not have been his style. Professionally, he was a guarded man, a bureaucrat of the Old School who permitted himself little obvious emotion in court.

Retired now, he does not want to be interviewed for this story, his son tells us. Too upsetting he said. Perhaps not even Lloyd, who faced a lifetime of needless death and horror, can forget Steven Shepherd.

But Neil was there when, after a seven-man jury in a stark Ormskirk courtroom returned their misadventure verdict, Coroner Lloyd could not hold back these words: "This was the tragedy of an unhappy child who recollected one particular place where he had spent perhaps the happiest day of his life and in his unhappiness decided to go back to that spot."

He then recorded the only verdict available to him or any other coroner: Misadventure. Cause of death: Exposure. They didn't have bullycide in those days. Coroners still don't have that option today.

Even Moors-murder-hardened Prescott, the man who predicted "bloody good killing weather" to Neil in the Liverpool Press Club the day before Yorkshire Ripper Peter Sutcliffe went on his rampage of butchery, the detective who believed to the last that Steven had been murdered, was forced to admit in open coroner's court: "Evidence has now emerged. Because of his physique, timidity and spectacles Steven was subjected to jibes and bullying. A most unhappy boy. I no longer suspect foul play."

He hung his bare head, clasping his trademark trilby in his hands out of respect, and mumbled again the words, almost as though he felt guilty himself: "I no longer suspect foul play."

He could and probably wanted to add: "not in the accepted criminal sense I have always been guided by."

The words spoken in that dusty courtroom spoke of bullycide. Steven is the first victim we can identify.

He is by no means the last.

Steven was a typical victim. Poor eyesight, thick glasses, stuck-out teeth, shy, and scrawny. Different. But look beyond the stereotype and we find a respectful, sensitive young man who loved to study but who hated school. As our subsequent survivor stories testify, many targets of bullying recover from their abusive ordeal and lead fulfilling and successful lives, often bringing about change and touching the lives of many. Every bullycide robs society of a gentle, valuable, and productive person.

Most targets of bullying like to study but are prevented from doing so by daily uninhibited violence and aggression. Bullying is a type of thuggery which even today is still ignored or dismissed by many in authority, some of whom may be the childhood bullies described in these pages. And bullying doesn't stop when school is over. The bullies interpret inaction by those in charge as approval; uninterest, denial and inaction is tantamount to condoning their violence.

As other stories in this book show, whilst Steven lived in an impoverished area, social circumstances are not a significant factor in who gets bullied. Although Steven's parents were separated, this often-identified target trait has little relevance. Many bullycides come from stable families. However, separation and divorce are periods of instability and uncertainty for children who become especially vulnerable at such times. In Steven's case, separation and divorce were less common than they are today and the subject was taboo. Whatever the circumstances, vulnerability is a major attractant to bullies.

Steven was just - different. The bullies nicknamed him "Uneven Steven" because of his limp. Derogatory names repeated ad nauseum are a favourite taunt of maladjusted aggressors.

Most targets of bullying are "different". Physically Steven was not imbued with strength which he could have used to overcome violence with violence. Targets of bullying are not like that. They know in their heart from an early age that the way to resolve conflict is not by fighting but through dialogue and negotiation. Their mature interpersonal understanding is unfortunately suffused with naivety, for they also expect the responsible adults to know and understand that too. This mistaken expectation often leads to disaster.

Targets of bullying almost always have a low propensity to violence. Bullies sense this and recognise that the child they pick on is not going to turn around and thump them. Should that happen, the cowardly side of the bully reveals itself; the bully runs straight to teacher for protection before returning to feed on easier prey.

To overcome their innate cowardice, bullies may form gangs. Some children are happy to join in and indulge their taste for violence; other children join in for justified fear of otherwise becoming a target. When subsequently challenged, justifications abound: "It [his looks] made him an obvious target". The cowardly nature is also apparent: "We used them to make us feel bigger like". Bullies and their supporters know their behaviour is wrong. Most would probably prefer not to have to act like this but the bully or bullies at the centre have no qualms.

The education culture highlights the difference between children who are aggressive and those who are not. Rewards and distinctions tend to go to the former. Like many children, Steven suffered the indignity of being forced to play school football but was never allowed near the ball because the game was not his forte. The attitude towards non-athletic pupils was one of exclusion, ridicule, and failure rather than one of inclusion, nurture, and achievement. Many adults relate stories of abuse by PE teachers who would impose indignities upon their unfortunate and vulnerable charges as a precursor for administering corporal punishment with the frequency of a compulsive abuser.

The British education system has often excluded those children who did not heap honours on their school through sporting prowess. This mindset may have waned in recent years but the change in attitudes has come about through a decline in resources for sporting activities rather than recognition of the inappropriateness of this mentality.

Violence in the pit town where Steven lived was a common occurrence. Fights were part and parcel of growing up in the harsh socioeconomic conditions at that time. Those with the strongest appetite for violence prevailed.

Eventually the bullies broke Steven's arm. If an adult is assaulted and suffers bodily injury or damage to possessions the perpetrator will be arrested and charged with a criminal offence. A child committing the same offence during school hours in Steven's day would have been overlooked. Violence towards children by other children was, and still often is, written off as "scrapping", "boisterousness", "boys will be boys", and so on. This discrepancy between society's treatment of violence towards adults and violence towards children is still apparent; corporal punishment, often an excuse for institutionalised sexual abuse, was only outlawed in the UK in 1999, over a century after parliament outlawed violence against animals. Corporal punishment is still condoned and encouraged in many countries, including some states in the allegedly civilized USA.

When Steven decided he could take no more and embarked on that fateful walk, the authorities could only think he had been murdered; there was a strong need to ascribe blame to someone evil who could be identified, arrested, vilified, and punished. That Steven had been driven to murder himself was not in the collective consciousness at that time. Many people today are still unable to grasp the depth of despair that drives people to constructively dismiss themselves from this incarnation.

Denial is ever present, from the guilty party who is directly responsible to the witnesses and bystanders who watch and observe but who take no action. Steven tried to ignore the bullying, tried not to make a fuss. What would people have done, anyway? In many cases, once parents become involved and the bullies are challenged, the bullying gets worse.

When a child dies from bullycide, the family is devastated. The cherished son or daughter on whom the family has lavished so much time, energy, and love is irreplaceably gone, denied the opportunity of a long fulfilling life. The community's investment in a valued member of society is wasted and society is denied its dividend. Parents describe a gaping hole in their lives; Steven's grandmother died of a broken heart. "I think she died a little every day" a sibling reported in another case years later having borne the memory of her mother's unending heartache.

As with all the cases featured in this book, it is the relentlessness which comes across clearly. Day after day, week after week, month after month, and year after year bullies derive their "fun" by deliberately making their victims' lives a misery. It is a challenge to convey in words the daily terror that targets face every time they leave home. Steven had nowhere to turn. With no prospect of resolution and no end in sight, desperation set in. He couldn't escape school until he was fifteen. For a child tormented daily, four more years of suffering is an eternity. His family provided him comfort but they had no power and no influence against a culture which condoned and rewarded violence, even if the reward was only to evade accountability.

However, whilst most bullying goes on for years, for some the viciousness can drive the target to bullycide in an alarmingly short few weeks.

Chapter 2

Sudden death

"Whom the gods love dies young"
Menander (c.342 - c.292 BC)

All it took was a childish squabble, a mere spark of rage in a teenage girl and just four short weeks to drive pretty young Denise Baillie to bullycide.

Her sudden but unbearable misery and senseless death was summed up in this short notice in her local paper:

> Baillie, Denise - Died April 8 2000. Denise I know that it was hard for you, for what you have been going through, but now I know that you are peaceful and safe and somewhere out there you will always be waiting. From your boyfriend, love David XXX

Denise was fifteen.

A fistful of her mother's prescription bathroom cabinet pills brought her the peace she craved and which David prays she has now found.

A tiff of rivalry over innocent sixteen-year-old David spawned an all-consuming hatred in one of her best school pals, a puppy-love jealousy which culminated in a barrage of violent threats so terrifying that Denise saw death as the only escape from daily fear. The old adage about sticks and stones didn't apply here; the worst physical violence Denise had suffered was no more than a snap on the nose. Her real pain was suffered as the result of verbal abuse. She hid its bruises where no one could see ... in her heart.

A gentle spring month in Belfast. 28 fleeting days.

Four weeks from being a happy, bubbly teenager

dreaming of a future in the art world to becoming the subject of that heartbreaking obituary from boyfriend David.

We know Denise was a bullycide because she left a final note telling the world she couldn't face another day of bully hell and felt suicide was the only way out. The bullycide note will be produced in evidence at Denise's inquest.

Unlike other cases in this book, Denise's Model School for Girls comes in for no criticism. Staff there were as shocked as everyone else by the tragedy. Their anti-bullying policy may have saved her had her terror not been so well concealed. Denise did not wish to worry anyone. Everyone now wishes she had.

Her family do not hold a passionate grudge against her tormentor.

Denise had no past history of depression or intimidation.

She was neither overwhelmingly beautiful nor in any way ugly. Not fat. Not skinny.

She wasn't too dumb or too smart. She didn't use insults but could take a bit of a fun ribbing with grace. She wasn't shy. She wasn't extrovert.

Her family was close, loving and functional.

Denise Baillie was the typical, well-loved girl-next-door.

It all happened so fast that no one realised the suffering which so quickly forced her to take her life. There was no time for even those closest to her to spot the warning signs.

The day before she died, she laughed and joked with friends and made a gay round-robin phone call to Granny and all the other relatives - her way of saying goodbye, it's believed. A successful attempt to be remembered fondly with her usual smile and giggle by those she loved.

Then she swallowed such a great overdose of pills she knew she'd never wake from her final sleep. This was, again, no cry for attention and help. Denise was bright enough to know she'd gone the whole hog - no turning back when she washed down the tablets and lay down to die.

Even in their pain - just days after her funeral was packed

with family, friends and neighbours - Denise's family made the difficult decision to ensure that her sacrifice would count and launched their own local anti-bullying campaign, even prodding the government and persuading the local press to assist in their battle against bullycide.

"If we can help save just one child, Denise will not have died in vain" is the family motto.

Denise's best friend and confidante was big sister Sarahjane. Sarahjane herself is only twenty, little older herself than Denise. They shared everything ... the only secret Denise wouldn't share was her victimisation and bullycide resolve.

Sarahjane told us a few days after her little sister's funeral: "It was purely a row over a boy they both fancied ... but the result tortured her. The bullying was just a matter of her being called names and threatened with violence. There was only one physical confrontation but the daily threats were enough."

All through this book, verbal violence is shown to be just as deadly as the physical - if not more so.

"She was scared because the other girl had a lot of friends, so Denise started to panic. It was all happening outside school so nobody in authority knew about it or could act. One day there was a fight and her nose was bitten and we had to take her to hospital for antibiotics. There'd been a lot of other girls there to watch. They didn't get involved. But just having them stand by must have been hurtful. The main problem wasn't physical but verbal, psychological torment.

"She'd told us about the bullying. But she gave us the impression after this fight incident that everything had calmed down because she didn't say much more. She came to my house regularly because we weren't only sisters but, because we were so close in age, we were also best friends - so I knew the situation was annoying her. But that was all. She gave no clue as to how much it was really hurting.

"Denise was that kind of girl - she didn't want to give us the worry. I never thought we held any secrets from each other. Never dreamed she might be keeping such a dangerous secret to herself.

"As a schoolgirl, I'd seen people being bullied at school in Belfast but it had never seriously happened to me. This kind of victimisation didn't run in the family. I thought everything was OK with Denise, that it had all blown over. I've only been out of school a couple of years myself. I've seen this kind of thing before. But who could guess it would go this far? Nobody thinks, nobody realises.

"There was no suggestion that Denise was vulnerable. She'd never been bullied before - just a minor tiff with a pal a couple of years ago. Usual stuff which blew over quickly.

"But when she took the pills she really meant to go through with it, to die. We don't know yet how many drugs she took (they were Mum's antidepressants) but she must have known they were enough to make sure she died.

"We're not unhappy with the school and we think as a family we did everything possible within the bounds of how little we knew. We don't blame anyone. But we still, ourselves, feel something I suppose you'd call guilt. Somehow we should have seen the signs.

"We wouldn't even expect the bully girl to be in touch. I am not angry against her because she's just a child too and will have to come to terms with the consequences of her actions. Her Mum came to the house the day after Denise died with cards and things. The Mum was cheeky. I couldn't believe how cold the woman was. I think I see now where the aggression was coming from.

"I know in some ways the bully girl was nasty, really nasty, but I don't believe she's evil. I think her family should have approached her about her behaviour - as it is, they seem not to think there was anything wrong with it.

"Schools and local communities should be on the lookout

for such potentially damaging environments and do something about them. There should be somebody for kids to go to to say: look, I'm having problems being bullied either in school or in the local community. Then, action should be taken.

"I was at the same school as Denise - I've only been away for two years - and I know a lot of the teachers. So when I heard Denise was having trouble I called them just to let them know what was going on. The school was very, very good. I'd asked a year head if there was anything they could do either in or around the school, you know. I said that I'd appreciate it if there was anything bad going on to get in touch straight away so I could bring her home.

"My Mammy found her. She was the one who first realised how far things had gone. It was too late. Denise wasn't going to wake up ever again. She'd gone to bed shortly after two o'clock in the afternoon and Mammy heard her snoring softly and left her to rest. Then, about five, she walked back through the bedroom door and saw her.

"The neighbours around were fantastic. They thought they could wake her up. But, after an hour, they couldn't. Everyone came to help. The ambulancemen were great. But Denise was dead. It was all over. They had injected her heart ... but her heart had given up.

"At the time I was going out for a dinner with my fiancé and I saw all the commotion outside Denise's house and I thought there was an argument or something. A neighbour told me the terrible truth.

"I think Denise was always closer to me than she was to her mother. But Denise's death has brought my Mammy and me closer together than ever we've been.

"We've neither of us any idea why she didn't pour out her problems to us. There is a feeling of guilt to be shared. I think she was deliberately hiding her fright under a bushel to save the family any more worries. If she could be here today, my first question would be *why didn't you let us know*? Yes, definitely.

"But - what would I have done? It might have crossed my mind in panic to even have thought of murdering the bully girl. Ha! Or I'd have gone to see the bully's Mum in a last desperate bid to try to solve the problem.

"Denise came to my house just the day before she died. There wasn't a hint as to what was going through her head. She sounded fine. She was laughing and joking.

"She liked boy bands and art and the boyfriend, David, a holding-hands boyfriend is all. But she was a deep thinker. We know now that she kept a lot of things inside. She didn't want to hurt us with her problems. We'd never ever seen signs of depression. I'll miss her forever.

"Poor David - for no good reason - is inclined to blame himself because he was the boy the bully girl was jealous of. He was innocently used as the excuse for all the trouble. I suppose we all do feel guilt, though. It's hard to shake, no matter how many well-intentioned people try to persuade us that we're not in any way to blame. David's family is quite close to our family. We'll always keep in touch. Denise and he were really good friends. His notice in the paper was tremendously touching.

"There's so much we don't understand yet. It's all so fresh. I spoke to some people - young mothers and friends - the other night. It's so intense. I can hardly go on ... I still can't really believe all this ever happened. I expect her to walk through the door any time.

"I've got so much support from my fiancé, Alan. It's lovely to have someone to lean on. But he's shattered too. Mum and Dad can't face speaking to anyone yet. Denise's Dad can't handle it at all. He's separated from Mammy and only saw Denise once or twice a week and that's playing on his mind. More guilt ... he's thinking if he'd just been there.

"We're Protestant and the church has been a lot of help. They've helped bring the whole community around us for support. Denise used to be a choir girl - not wildly religious. She did pray and I'm sure she made her peace with Him before the end.

"This terrible experience will change the way I deal with my own daughter - she's just one year old. Megan will always know that I'm her friend as well as her mother and that I'll always be there for her no matter what. I tried to be there for Denise too ... but in the end she felt the need to protect me from her problems.

"The memory of Denise is my souvenir ... and a few trinkets we shared. I'll always especially remember the cartoons she used to draw. Her favourite character was Tweety Pie - remember the little canary who was bullied by the cat?"

Since her sister's death, Sarahjane has appealed to the government, education authorities, police, her local newspapers, us, and anyone else she could think of in a bid to prevent another Denise Baillie tragedy.

Boyfriend David asked to speak to us to express his own feelings. He mixed bitterness, despair, hope and fear in his words: "I never ever want to see the bully girl again. I hope she's learned a lesson and won't hurt anyone else again. But I can't bring myself to tell her that. She's left the country in shame and gone to Scotland somewhere.

"I've leaned on my best friend for support. I'm in pieces. Denise's death will make kids deal with each other more kindly ... but only in the short term. We're not so heavenly-minded as to believe they're any earthly good. They'll soon forget and the bullying will start all over with some other poor kid chosen as victim.

"She'd told me about the bullying. I'd been bullied a couple of times at school - mainly physical stuff - and got over it by standing up for myself. When Denise poured out her heart to me I thought it was just a passing thing. I didn't realise how different people could be ... what might be a temporary problem to one might cause the death of another.

"You know, the last words of my death notice in the

paper, 'you'll always be waiting'? I really do believe that. Young as I am, I know there'll never be another Denise. I loved her, still do. We'll be together again some day in a place where they don't let bullies through the gates."

Like most bullycides, Denise refused to unburden herself and thus transfer the burden to her family; in doing so, she courageously, but misguidedly, sought to protect those she loved. Psychiatric injury impairs objectivity, a consequence of psychological violence that bullies cultivate. Like most targets of bullying, Denise thought she could handle it. Bullies encourage and exploit this conviction.

Unlike physical violence which leaves visible scars, psychological violence leaves few physical clues and society is not yet adept at recognising psychiatric injury.

The trauma of psychiatric injury is not limited to targets of bullying. Those bereaved by bullycide endure a rollercoaster of emotions, forever tormented with the question *Could I have done more*? Maybe, but only if you'd known, only if society recognised bullycide, only if the law specifically forbade bullying, and only if the ethos of society were wholly against bullying. Hopefully these will soon come to pass. Until then, the power and control bullies wield over their victims is usually sufficient to preclude knowledge of the assault to all but the two combatants. The bully's willingness to operate outside the bounds of society should never be underestimated.

There is little to assuage the lasting guilt of those left behind. The levels of power, control, domination, and subjugation that bullies exert over their victims ensure that even those closest to the target remain oblivious. In a society which regards victims as weaklings, the bully's engenderment of fear, shame, embarrassment, and guilt guarantee the quiescence of their quarry. This is how all abusers control their victims.

Such is the extent of emotional distress that targets won't share their secret even with those to whom they are closest. Bullies escape attention because of the secretive character of their craft. Only the bully and target know what is happening. No one else can - or sometimes wants - to see the abuse in their midst. Bullies, like most criminals, excel at evasion of accountability of which concealment is a major component.

Whilst the bully often appears to have a large circle of friends, many are likely to be hangers-on and target-types fearful of the consequences of abstaining or opposing. Despite appearances, the bully's popularity is based on friendless subjugation, although the target doesn't realise this. Witnesses and bystanders do have knowledge of the malevolence but are fearful of interceding. In the absence of adults acting responsibly, lack of support from unempowered fellow pupils is hardly surprising.

So on whose shoulders does responsibility lie? On the bully? The bully's family? The school? Or on society? As with Steven Shepherd, Denise felt she had nowhere to go and no one to turn to. Those in authority had not convinced her that they were her answer. Perhaps Denise didn't know of ChildLine or Kidscape, or perhaps she didn't feel they were appropriate avenues. Perhaps she was too embarrassed to call. Maybe as an adolescent on the verge of adulthood she felt she didn't qualify as a child or kid; almost certainly she was unaware that bullying can happen at any time of life and that being a target is nothing to be ashamed of ... certainly nothing to hide.

We shall never know what Denise thought, but it's clear that reliable, trustworthy and effective sources of help for targets of bullying are few and far between. Those that exist tend to be charitable, underfunded and overwhelmed. Given the widespread prevalence of bullying in schools it seems incongruous that there are no helplines, formal channels, or initiatives run by the UK Department for Education and Employment (DfEE) to which targets of bullying and their families can reliably turn.

Lack of leadership is a common thread in bullying cultures, a stark contrast to the strength of character of targets of bullying whose coping skills are able to withstand the most vehement of assaults, physical and psychological, in the absence of assistance from adults. The target's integrity puts to shame the bully's weak character which reveals itself through an individual who lurks in the shadows and when exposed runs straight to authority with self-serving justifications, or blames others, or in the unlikely event of these tactics being insufficient, feigns victimhood. Bullies rarely stray far from the refuge of Mummy's skirt.

This automatic process of abdication of personal responsibility is familiar to those who study the criminal mind. Socioeconomic factors provide theorists with fresh avenues of exploration in the same way they provide criminals with a wealth of new excuses. Whilst Denise's circumstances are set against a background of The Troubles, these are not implicated. The bullying was personal, kid on kid, and so similar to all bullycides.

Age is no discriminator in bullying. The younger the participants, the more likely it is that violence will be written off as childhood behaviour. Some children show a propensity for violence early on which, unlike their peers, they do not outgrow. As children become streetwise sooner, so the age of bullycide advances too.

Britain's youngest bullycide

She was pixy-faced, sad, bullied, and hanging by the neck from her own skipping rope two hours after being sent to her bedroom for refusing to go back to school.

Marie Bentham had just turned eight years old and is thought to be Britain's youngest victim of bullycide. The magic of Christmas two weeks earlier was wiped from the memories of children at the Moorfield Primary in Irlam, Manchester, on their first day back at school when headmaster John Walsh called them together to break the news of little Marie's horrific death. But the tears were not wiped from their eyes.

Some of those tears might well have been tears of guilt according to Marie's family. She had been bullied so badly, they say, that death was the only option to her young mind.

Early in 1999, Marie, whose birthday had been on Boxing Day, told her widowed mother, Debbie, she could not face a return to school after the Christmas holidays because of her infant terror of bullying classmates.

Debbie Bentham had twice complained to the school of Marie's bullying fears. Twice the complaints were investigated. No action was taken. So Marie took her own.

Her last Christmas and eighth birthday on Boxing Day had been ruined. Santa was forgotten as she spent the three-week holiday describing the nightmare of bullying to her mother and five-year-old sister, Gemma, in the neat semi-detached where a tree sparkled, cards hung on the walls, and parcels waited to be torn open.

There was a mother-daughter tiff as the terrified girl flatly refused to go back to school for the first days of the New Year and Marie was sent to her bedroom at 8 pm. After all, the school had already said she was suffering nothing out of the ordinary. Two hours later when Debbie crept in to check on Marie she found her slumped on the floor, her skipping rope around her neck and tied to the doorknob.

She cut the rope and called an ambulance. But Marie was beyond help by then. All Debbie could do was mourn the second tragedy in two years. Her husband, Philip, had died of a heart attack only 24 months earlier at the age of only forty.

ChildLine, shocked by yet another bully-related death, said Marie was probably the youngest ever to fall victim to bullycide. They also admitted she is not the first of her age or even younger to have expressed to them suicidal tendencies after abuse in the playground.

Neil Marr took his own sensitive six-year-old son out of an expensive fee-paying school after his repeated complaints of physical and verbal bullying had fallen on the deaf ears of staff and the fear of bullycide loomed.

He took advice from the late Fred Scarborough, the headmaster of a plain, pit town school called St Peter's. When Neil was there in the fifties, they still had kids in clogs who seldom wore socks on weekdays (invariably unmatched if they did). They couldn't fasten a knot in a tie even if they'd owned one, neither could they pronounce their aitches.

"When can he start?" Neil asked Fred. "How long would it take to pick him up from the other school and chuck his uniform away?" he replied. Neil told him less than an hour.

Sandy joined the school that afternoon and was never bullied again.

But Marie had no Fred Scarborough to turn to. The local Salford City Council who looked into each of her family's bullying complaints said: "These were concerns the school took very seriously and dealt with promptly. In each case the concerns were fully investigated and dealt with and the Council's anti-bullying policy was followed to the letter. Senior staff dealt with the incidents involved and they were properly logged. There was nothing to raise any serious concerns."

When these words were spoken, Marie was already dead.

But the complaints had been properly logged.

A child care worker told us afterwards: "The main environment in which the bullies act is one of secrecy. Investigations of complaints seldom do any good. There should be no complaints. Teachers should be educated to see problems before they arise and nip them in the bud."

Debbie Bentham was so devastated by the death of her

daughter that she will not now speak of it. Marie's aunt, Emma Povey, told a colleague of ours: "Marie and her Mum had a little row. It was just a minor thing when Debbie told her to get in an early night ready for school on the following Monday. Marie got upset. She didn't want to go back to school after the Christmas holiday because she was being bullied.

"Debbie just said 'go and get into bed. You've got to go to school!' Marie replied 'I hate you. I want my Dad.'" They were the last words she ever spoke.

Mrs Povey added: "The teachers knew she was being bullied. The headmaster had told the other kids to leave her alone."

Another relative said: "Marie had said she'd been bullied and didn't want to go back to school. Her mother told her not to be silly so Marie stomped off to bed. What happened next was just tragic."

A social worker not far from where the youngest ever bullycide died warned: "Never, ever disbelieve a child who complains of intimidation in the schoolyard. It's too common for complaints to be taken as a child's whingeing or an excuse to skip classes. Too often a tragedy like that which overtook Marie can result. There are three rules here: look for the signs, listen to the groans, and act."

A child's refusal to go to school is often misdiagnosed as defiance, laziness, truancy, or school phobia. These are common diagnoses by professionals unaware, some might say negligently, of the circumstances of their clients' unwillingness to attend school. Even parents, pressured and harassed by the stresses of modern living and working, may be unaware of the real causes.

Dealing with bullying at school should be the school's responsibility but all too often it is the stressed parents who find out late in the day. The parents then find themselves powerless to deal with an intransigent school which sees nothing out of the ordinary in bullying driving a pupil to suicide and a local education authority whose priority is to prosecute the parents of absent children rather than address its own failure of duty of care.

However, a policy alone is not enough; any written decree must be part of an ethos. Schools (and workplaces) still find it difficult to create an ethos free of psychological violence when beyond their premises lurks a society which prefers to turn a blind eye.

An anti-bullying policy must be more than words on paper. The presence of a policy may discharge the legal requirement but the spirit is only satisfied by the commitment to make it work. For an adult bully, the existence of a policy and thus compliance with law or regulation is sufficient; faulty thinking erroneously equates existence with effectiveness. Should an incident occur, a policy followed to the letter, or complaint duly logged, or ticked box on the prescribed procedure are sufficient to enable the weak manager to evade accountability by abdicating responsibility to procedures.

Schools may report that "complaints have been investigated" but almost always those who investigate have had neither training in bullying awareness nor in investigation techniques. To identify, apprehend, and interrogate a bully requires considerable knowledge of the disordered, dysfunctional mind that compels the bully to pursue gratification by tormenting others, sometimes to death. It is more than a matter of asking a few questions and ticking a few boxes.

Marie's story again highlights the vulnerability of a child sensitised by the loss of a parent. UK society often does not deal with grief in an appropriate manner. However, whilst death is treated with the seriousness it requires, not all deaths are treated equally.

Chapter 3

"We just don't know."
The police view

"Kids are less afraid of taking the death option. They feel they have less to lose in casting off the short and painful past than in risking an even-more painful future."
A child psychologist specialising in breaking the news of impending death to and counselling terminally ill children.

When Steven Shepherd became Britain's first bullycide, Lancashire Constabulary, the second largest force in Britain at the time, sat up and took notice. Now they have teams on permanent bullycide watch.

As a direct result of this book a circular has been sent to all coroners in the region in a bid to measure officially, for the first time, the scale of the problem.

Roger Blaxall, as a senior officer of the force's Information Unit at Preston HQ, sent out the letter after we'd spoken and corresponded several times about the number of child suicides brought about by intimidation at school. When replies reach him, he said, at least Lancashire police will have an idea of what they are up against.

"The problem is," he confessed "that nobody knows. There is no official record. Bullying isn't a crime and there is no verdict option of bullycide. Only individual coroners might be able to say how many cases they have seen where children have taken their lives because of intimidation at school. But the verdicts recorded do not reflect their inside knowledge.

"The first thing I did after speaking to you was to alert the department where they handle statistics to your findings. I found that figures for this are a great big black hole. One thing your book may do is wake up officialdom to the fact that nobody knows the full extent of this problem. There are lots of anecdotal figures but there is nobody in authority keeping a record. If you don't know the size of a problem, you can't really begin to tackle it, can you?

"Another great unknown is the number of children who try to commit bullycide but are pulled back in the nick of time by a friend or a parent and, of course, that's a statistic we can never record.

"Not only is it difficult to get a true estimate of the situation, it's also very difficult to find out why children are doing this and the ages when they're most at risk. I don't know for instance if, as a bullied child gets older and matures, whether his problems become any less or whether they never change. I don't know if there is a particular type of child who is more vulnerable. I don't know what the split is between the sexes either.

"I'd like to think - and I'm the father of three girls - that if there was any hint of a problem in our family they would approach me and my wife. I do realise that is probably the most difficult step for a child to take. It can lead to even greater retribution because a father's instinct would be to go and approach the aggressor or the school and try to tackle it that way.

"'If you tell, we'll get you back and if you don't we'll get you anyway,' seems to be the bully's motto. Bullying does thrive on secrecy. Nothing is done in front of an adult or a figure in authority. It's a terrible vicious circle and you feel sorry for anyone caught up in it.

"One of the keys to dealing with it on a family level is being open with each other, giving the child the message that he can have complete confidence that you are there to help and not to make matters worse. It's about trust and talk. Being able to plumb the depth of the problem, what form it takes, how long it's been going on for and to discuss the do's and don'ts of its management.

"We have some schools in Lancashire who have set up what they call the "Buddy System", not anti-bullying schemes as such, but a system where a child with a problem doesn't approach a teacher or any older person but one of his peers, someone who's still a schoolchild himself but in a position to offer an understanding ear and practical help without bringing in the big guns.

"There's even the approach where the bully and his victim are teamed up. They are taken out of the volatile situation and talk child-to-child and work something out for themselves without resorting to adult interference. We're all for that here."

Roger was speaking for 3,500 police in one of the toughest parts of England where schoolyard bullying has been thought of for generations as almost a form of harmless, acceptable play. But a game where the same side loses every time.

"One of the problems is that children can get picked on for a whole host of reasons - anything from the clothes you wear, the colour of your hair, being tall or short, ugly or pretty, to the money you have or haven't got, the records you buy, the company you keep, to why you don't do drugs or smoke, why you don't go to parties. There's a whole raft of reasons. Another problem is that if you, as a parent, try to make changes, let's say, in your child's dressing style you're playing into the bully's hands. He'll just switch his attention to another alleged difference and use that for an excuse to carry on his campaign.

"A bully is a bully at the end of the day. So often he's a victim himself and, although it's a strange thing to say, you feel terribly sad for some of these children who have to express their emotions in such a dreadful way."

Roger couldn't tell us how many man-hours are spent on preventing a bullycide, although man-hour figures do exist in tracking down child murderers.

"We have a two-pronged approach," Roger went on.

"First of all we have the School Community Action Teams, SCAT. They've advised secondary schools on anti-bullying schemes. Bullying isn't in itself a crime. Perhaps it should be. Meantime I do know that bully schemes have been set up; I know about plays and I do know that we support special anti-bullying projects by some schoolchildren. An animated film was made recently in Accrington and even Nick Park - you know, the award-winning animationist, the Wallace and Gromit man - has endorsed that one. It was made at the Lancashire Constabulary Video Studios and he was extremely pleased with it. It's all about bullying. It's been given backing by the Lancashire Partnership against Crime, part of the force which exists on private and corporate donations to fight crime. So we helped the children make their movie. It came to the attention of Granada TV and, hopefully, it's going to be launched county-wide to spread the story of the bully and how he learned - not his comeuppance - but to change his ways.

"The Lancashire education authority was so impressed by it and how schoolchildren reacted to it that they're giving support.

"One of our SCAT teams was looking at bullying and how they could best tackle it and they came up with the Wallace and Gromit idea ... everyone knows Wallace and Gromit. Children watch and relate. They thought it was a good way of getting the message over in a light way. There's nothing funny about bullying. But, so far, the film seems to be working."

However, all these authorities ran out of steam, time and interest and the project is now dead in the water.

Roger continued: "We have more than fifty SCAT teams based around the county for children from secondary schools from eleven to sixteen. One of the ways policing has changed in Lancashire is that we now have a much more community-focused operation in that the local beat copper won't just call at a school in an emergency, he'll be calling on a weekly basis for informal chats to get to know the kids. He isn't a strange face. He's building trust. He's someone to turn to in times of trouble.

"However, if he feels there's a deep problem in an individual, we have a Family Protection Unit where they specialise in all forms of child abuse like our Major Crime Unit and they're the specialists in all aspects of child abuse. Bullying is a serious form of child abuse. They will then step in, working closely with Social Services, with other departments of the force and if they think there is a problem at the home of the bully or at the home of the bullied they can investigate and try to sort the problem out.

SCAT only goes back to the early 1990s. Roger has been through Lancashire Police annual reports and discovered that in the early seventies, soon after Steven Shepherd's bullycide, someone somewhere had recognised the bullycide threat and set the wheels of police bureaucracy in motion by setting up specialised teams.

"I certainly couldn't say for sure 'yes' or 'no' that Steven Shepherd opened our eyes back then. But there was nothing official before his death. I'm sure there was many a police officer who was able to spot the symptoms of what was going on in a child's life and would informally speak to the school or have a word with the parents and explain 'there's something not quite right here.' But it would have been done as a caring neighbour rather than as a Bobby in a helmet and blue uniform. It was certainly not done on a formal, organised basis where notes would be written and a file opened, with intelligence taken on various people. It would be a lot more low key ... just a guy with insight doing his best for those around him.

"It would be wrong to say that officers have got used to this problem now, that it's just a sign of the times. I think there's still a lot of us who are shocked at the lengths a child will go to in order to escape the bullying.

"The last case I remember here was a little girl who hanged herself in Preston. I don't know the extent of the figures even in my own county. I'm trying to find out now, though. Officers here nowadays can see some of the pressures which can be put on young people, whereas, perhaps, older officers might just have said 'well, I could have coped with that problem by just blacking the aggressor's eye'. Officers now appreciate that the pressures on children are a lot different from ten or fifteen years ago.

"Today's cop is the offspring of peacetime parents and is probably more sympathetic to the victim who can't or won't stand up for himself.

"The problem today is that officers are so busy that they just haven't got the time they want. It's more fire brigade policing now. Rushing from job to job rather than going in, empathising, sympathising or whatever to dig a little deeper before a dangerous situation arises.

"One thing I have noticed - although this isn't official and there are no figures yet to support my statement - the bigger the town, the much bigger the bullycide problem. The increase is disproportionate. If you look at more rural areas you find that the pace of life is that little bit slower, that family life is that little bit more co-ordinated and problems of bullying might be a little diminished."

Being a policeman can be enough to bring on a campaign of bullying. Now the same age as Steven Shepherd would have been, Roger realises that the children of cops themselves can be singled out for special treatment by the bullies.

He told us: "Back in the days of Z Cars, kids were proud their Dads were police. But nowadays, I've heard of boys and girls who won't own up to what their Dad does for a living - wouldn't say 'he's a detective' or 'he's a policeman.' They feel if they say 'Daddy's a cop' he's seen as a bad guy now who picks on people and not a good guy who's there to help. Instead of being proud that Dad's a Bobby they are more circumspect and wonder why others want to know and worry that they might be intimidated if they tell the truth.

"OK, if they're four or five or six, they don't mind saying their Dad's a cop. But the older they get, the more streetwise they become, the more attuned they are to what the media is saying about their father's occupation. There's no magic formula which says because your Dad's a policeman you won't be bullied.

"I had a problem about a year ago when my eldest daughter was bullied but it was nipped in the bud because I went into the school and mentioned it. I'll give you a little bit of the history: she is quite a bright child, she was moved up to her local grammar school a year ahead of everybody else. Although we didn't want anything said about it, it soon became known that she was only ten whereas everyone else was eleven. She got good marks and that's where the problem started. Other kids singled her out as some kind of swot and the bullying started. Some parents were brought in and some children were spoken to. You'll never be able to wrap a child in cotton wool so much that it will never ever happen again. But she's out of the woods now. Because she felt able to talk to her Mum and Dad.

"I'm sure that bullying is the last straw. Where family life isn't what it should be, where life is rough, a bullied child becomes a prime target for bullycide. They're vulnerable at the outset. I feel so very, very sorry for them.

"I'd like to think that our officers are aware of everything going on around them and that they would monitor a case both on and off duty. The cops who go that far don't want to blow any trumpets. Nothing's written down. No overtime is claimed. They do it because that's the kind of people they are. I'd like to think they're in the force because of being the kind of people they are."

In spite of the strides made by Lancashire Constabulary -

which handles around two or three murders a month - the man-hours spent on bullycide are minimal compared with those spent on regular child murder. Roger now believes that bullycide forms a significant proportion of child death.

All child death is an horrific stain on a civilised society but bullycide is surely the most preventable of all. The warning signs are there. The wild card in our cities and towns, the serial murderer or spree killer who goes on the rampage, the drunk who goes too far, may always be with us. But we can spot the bully and the bullied before things reach their final, fatal conclusion. If only we had the resources and the ability to recognise the problem.

Even a compassionate police worker like Roger with powerful bosses to answer to will risk admitting publicly that Lancashire Constabulary doesn't have the data available to know how huge their bullycide problem might be. More officers are officially dedicated to preventing burglary than to saving children in danger of taking their own lives because of bullying. Only 35 out of a force of 3,500, just 1%, even have a watching brief to prevent bullycide.

PC Fred and his black and white bike

Remember Postman Pat and his black and white cat, the children's favourite postie? Let's introduce to you PC Fred and his black and white bike ... the kiddies' favourite copper. He deserves the title after six years working with children in his busy police area. He's proud that most children don't even know his second name is Barnes. He also deserves the promotion to official Youth Involvement Officer he received notice of midway through our interviews. One of his main tasks is to prevent bullycide.

Steven Shepherd, Britain's first known bullycide, died on PC Fred's patch around the area of Ormskirk (though 36-year-old Fred was only a toddler at the time). Since he became involved in community police work six years ago, seven years after joining the force, to his knowledge not one child has taken his life because of bullying on his manor.

His young charges don't seem to notice the official blue suit. They see only his smile. He's PC Fred, their playmate ... maybe a bit taller than they are, that's all. Maybe like a big brother. For some, perhaps, even a father figure. That doesn't bother PC Fred. He doesn't mind if the children see him as a friend and not a figure of police authority. He doesn't care they call him Fred.

He's not in the job to track down troublemakers. His duty is to sniff out trouble before it starts. Being PC Fred with his black and white bike is one of the ways he breaks down the intimidating fear barrier between kids and authority. He would be the last to even guess at how many bullycides have not happened on his beat simply because he's there.

He probably spends almost as much time in school these days as he did as a child himself, pals say. His colleagues tell us he's honorary member of more classrooms than he's had snatched cold butties pedalling from one job to another on the bike given to him by a grateful local trader. Wherever he props his bicycle, PC Fred is welcomed.

He said: "When I first took over the job as Community Policeman I used to go to the schools and introduce myself to the teacher and ask if I could speak to their kids. They'd say 'who do you think this bike belongs to, children?' I'd keep out of the way while they tried to guess. So they greeted me with a laugh when I suddenly appeared with my 'top hat' on. The barriers were already crumbling.

"The teachers would ask me how I would want to be addressed and I thought, well, it could be PC Barnes. But call me PC Fred, it's more approachable. And it's stuck. A lot of other Bobbies think there's not enough respect there. But I'm out in the community and it works for me. There is respect. Even more important, there's trusting contact.

"I was a policeman for years before I started community

policing and I was a tradesman before then. I didn't enter the police straight from school. I've got a lot of life experience. I know how people need to be approached. I've got two girls myself and that helps me along.

"There are computers and statistics but policing itself comes down to people. You go out on the beat and you get people shouting 'hiya Fred. Oh, it's PC Fred' and I stop and talk to them. The uniform is no longer a barrier. In fact, sometimes, when you try to enforce a little law, they know it's only Fred and that can be a little problem.

"One of the great things about the bike or actually walking is that you can stop and say hello to people, the kids especially. In a car, you've passed before you recognise a face. I only use the car when I'm on a job that's not in the community or if there's something heavy to cart around.

"Bullying's been a problem for years and years and years. It can be an horrific trauma that even leads to suicide. The first bullycide was on my patch. Murder itself is a form of bullying. Bullying can sometimes become a form of murder. The scale of the thing is massive.

"It's such a difficult problem to solve. On one occasion I was called out to a school and I adopted the approach where I just stood up in front of the assembly and talked to all the kids about behaviour and bullying. I said that bullying is wrong and that the people I'm talking about know who I'm talking to. I like to think because the kids already knew PC Fred the talk had somewhat more of a punch than if it had been a stranger speaking.

"There's something called a Values and Attitudes Package. It's a great big manual with questions in it about things like vandalism and bullying. You go to a youth club, perhaps, and you ask the kids how they would react in the place of a victim and how they would try to deal with the problem. You put them in the place of the caretaker, they're the ones who must face the problems, not cause them. It opens up a lot of young minds. You're suddenly facing twenty-two youngsters who've started to question what they're doing for the first time.

"I once gave them a list of nasty characters and asked them to put them in order of nastiness. Drug dealers were top of the list with one lass - and it was well known that her parents were drug dealers. I was working with a group who were almost grown up so most of their bullying was behind them. But still the school bully figured in the middle of the blacklist.

"I have two daughters and sometimes they come home in tears because of bullying at school - thankfully it's nothing to do with the job their Dad does. Mostly just adolescent bitchiness. Someone always wants to be top dog. There's always one who's always at the bottom, who nobody wants to talk to. They won't play with her. When it's your daughter's turn you've got to be straight. You've got to have your ears wide open to listen and they must trust you enough to speak what's on their mind.

"We've always tried to bring them up as Christian children and to think of other people first. They're going to treat people the way they want to be treated. They've always got somebody to talk to ... me and my wife, who's a nurse and has seen her own share of troubles. They will never feel isolated - and that's when bullying becomes so dangerous, when a child stands alone with no one to turn to.

"Strange, you know, I've actually had a kid turn up at my house and say 'the police came and took my Daddy away.' She was speaking to me as Fred. She didn't see me as part of that blue-uniformed force who'd taken her father. She came to me as a mate. For help.

"I certainly would never say that I'm not a policeman or that I'm divorced from the police. I like working with the police. I do a lot of regular policing, chasing after criminals and whatnot. But this is probably the most important job I've ever been privileged to do. I'm nipping problems in the bud in West Lancashire, in the three or four villages, the big towns and even the major conurbation of Skelmersdale, the Liverpool overspill new town, which has carried with it some of the big city problems.

"I remember being told of Steven Shepherd. He was the one found in the strawberry field at Newburgh. My job is to make sure there is never another like him in my manor. There is more pressure on children today than ever, designer clothes even. Once when I interviewed a young witness to a crime he could not describe the villain's face or build but he remembered every label on his shoes, jacket, and T-shirt. My job's to take that pressure off their shoulders.

"We've never had another Steven Shepherd whilst I've been on the job. There have, of course, been one or two suicides but I don't think any of them have been down to bullying.

"I'm trying to form a Canteen Culture where I can talk to the other Bobbies over an informal cuppa and alert them to the problem informally. I'm going to try to educate them, get them to keep their eyes wide open. But I've got to be very, very careful. You're dealing with people who have a ton of services to supply and who have an incredible workload.

"It's great though that I know two of the other three candidates for the job I've just been given. They were heavily committed to child problems - especially bullying and the danger of bullycide. It sends me a message that police are at last taking this syndrome seriously."

In many ways the nightmare of bullying is like the nightmare of stalking, itself only recently recognised in law as an antisocial act. Because of their intrusive and violational natures, both can be described as a long slow rape, thus placing them in the same category as sexual abuse and sexual violence. Another similarity is that stalkers and bullies announce in advance, both verbally and by exhibiting observable and predictable patterns of behaviour, their intention to commit violence. These often contain threats to kill, although few take the menace seriously.

Contrary to popular opinion, bullying isn't limited to the playground ... it doesn't stop when school is over. There's a lot of anecdotal evidence to suggest that the child who learns to bully at school and who gets away with it goes on to be the bully in the workplace, and in the family, and in the community. Bullying is a serial offence. Just as the school bully prevents pupils undertaking their studies, the workplace bully's disordered, disruptive, divisive, and dysfunctional behaviour prevents employees from fulfilling their duties. In both cases the bully seeks gratification by causing distress to others.

There's also a lot of anecdotal evidence to suggest that children who are bullied at school also go on to be the likely targets of bullying in the workplace. The compulsion to exploit the target's qualities of integrity and non-violence is as irresistible to adult bullies as it is to child bullies. Bullies transfer their aggression from playground to workplace and carry on victimising the better employees alongside whose satisfactory work record they compare unfavourably; exposed and vulnerable, the bullies' need to exercise power, exert control, and subjugate those perceived as a threat is overwhelming.

By the time a person enters adulthood their behaviour patterns are set. However, people who are likely to be bullied have a considerable learning capability and thus have a greater capacity to modify their behaviour as an adult. People who are bullies or prone to be bullies seem to have limited learning capacity or desire to learn and will often exhibit bullying behaviours throughout life. Some grow out of it but some don't.

For every child who commits bullycide, there are dozens who attempt it but who are not recorded. There must be hundreds, perhaps thousands who think about suicide but who never reveal their dark thoughts. Even undeniable acts of bullycide are described with a variety of misleading labels. The coroner's verdicts of misadventure, open and accidental death are ambiguous and allow the bully, the school, and the Local Education Authority (LEA) to evade accountability. In most cases, manslaughter or even culpable homicide would be a more befitting verdict; in some cases, given the intentional nature of the bully's choice to bully, murder might be considered.

Wilful, intentional psychological violence can kill as surely as driving a knife into someone's heart. One is quick, gruesome, and undeniable; the other may take a year or more, there may be few external signs (to the uninitiated), and denial prevails. However, in the same way everyone understands the injury that will result from the use of a weapon, any reasonable person should be able to comprehend the psychiatric injury which will result from constant bullying and harassment.

Whilst child bullies and adult bullies have much in common, there are a number of differences. Adults are selected for bullying because they are good at their job and popular with people; by contrast the bully is a weak, inadequate individual who is driven by jealousy and envy. The child who is bullied tends to be socially less popular than most children. Sometimes the child target has good interpersonal skills on a one-to-one basis but their independence and reluctance to join gangs and cliques is misinterpreted as a lack of social skills. However, in most cases it is the bully who lacks social grace and who is deeply unpopular. Association is on the basis of fear rather than friendship, with aggression compensating for lack of social ability.

Also, the education system is biased towards physical strength whilst artistic achievements are often undervalued. Children and adults who are bullied tend to be imaginative, creative, caring, respectful and responsible. Bullies, by contrast, tend to be unimaginative, uncaring, aggressive, immature, inadequate (especially in interpersonal, behavioural and communication skills), disrespectful and irresponsible.

A number of different types of bullying are identifiable. At one end of the scale are kids trying to cope with rampant hormonal changes that accompany adolescence. Moving up the scale we find children with poor social skills. Then there's the child whose family life is unstable, and beyond that the child who is being abused. None of these are excuses for bullying; many children experience these problems but do not choose to resort to bullying.

A significant difference between adult and child bullying is that many child bullies can be helped to learn more appropriate ways of interacting. With appropriate adult intervention, support, and supervision, many of these aspiring bullies can be helped to develop better ways of behaving, such as in Lancashire's buddy system.

Bringing bully and target together will work in some cases. One boy, when asked how he dealt with another pupil who kept bullying him, replied "I asked him to be my friend". Children can teach us so much.

The bully is usually friendless and their dysfunctional and aggressive behaviour does not endear them to other children (or parents). This rejection may result in further aggression.

However, the buddy system will be inappropriate for those bullies at the other end of the scale: the determinedly antisocial child and the child with the psychopathic personality. Robert Hare in his book *Without conscience: the disturbing world of the psychopaths among us* estimates the incidence of psychopathic personality at around 1% of the population.

The majority of psychopaths are not serial killers in the Hollywood mould; instead, they are aggressive, dysfunctional, disrespectful, and defiant individuals who are unwilling to accept any limits to their behaviour.

Experience with over 4,000 cases from the UK National Workplace Bullying Advice Line and website Bully OnLine suggests to Tim Field that Hare's estimate does not take account of socialised psychopaths who blend in with society and who commit non-arrestable offences rather than acts which, by the current standards of society, are antisocial or criminal. Tim estimates that serial bullies, his term for socialised psychopaths, could account for at least a further 1% of the population. All psychopaths, socialised or otherwise, have been through school.

Serial bullies have psychopathic tendencies which include an unwillingness to learn from experience (except to learn how to better evade detection and accountability) and an apparent lack of insight into their behaviour and its effect on others. However, this lack of insight can be more selective than it appears.

These types of bullies have a Jekyll and Hyde nature, are compulsive and convincing liars, and use mimicry and charm to excel at deception. Few people are able to recognise the bullying and even fewer understand the misery of feeling trapped in daily torment.

Not everyone has a PC Fred to turn to but in their despair, children can be resourceful in seeking help.

Chapter 4

Little flowers

I shall remember forever and will never forget.
Monday: my money was taken.
Tuesday: names called.
Wednesday: my uniform torn.
Thursday: my body pouring with blood.
Friday: it's ended.
Saturday: freedom.

The final diary pages of 13-year-old Vijay Singh. He was found hanging from the banister rail at his home on Sunday.

Maria McGovern whispered her secret misery in private diaries and into the ears of St Jude. She believed only the journals and the Patron Saint of Lost Causes could hear her cries of agony. Perhaps she was right. But they didn't save her and the truth of her death at the tender age of thirteen came out only after she'd gulped a fistful of fatal pills.

Maria was pretty with a smile like a cherub. But she still carried a little puppy fat. And that was enough to make her the victim of a vicious campaign of torment.

She was the blossom at Belfast's Little Flower Girls' School which drooped and faded away in the springtime of life.

Maria died at a local hospital in January 1995, the day after swallowing a bottle of her mother's blood pressure tablets. She left behind a grieving family and two diaries of despair, one of them with a prayer to St Jude hidden between its pages.

Once again - so sadly common during our investigation - teachers at her North Belfast school had investigated claims of bullying made by her concerned mother, Geraldine, and said that they had dealt with the problem. Maria's tragic death and the evidence she left behind indicates otherwise.

Geraldine is convinced the bullies are to blame and she said entries in the diaries she found in Maria's bedroom prove it. One of those neatly handwritten entries told: "She said she would be watching every move I take. The next day I didn't want to go to school and I started crying. But that wasn't the first time I'd been bullied."

Geraldine had been to the Little Flower school to advise staff of the campaign of bullying against her daughter just a few months before Maria died. But the girl's torment went on and on until she could take no more.

Mrs McGovern, so devastated that she collapsed several times during Maria's inquest, became almost obsessed with finding the truth behind her daughter's death. At one stage she even contacted lawyers with the intention of suing the school when she found the journals detailing Maria's daily terror. In their pages Maria wrote of bullies demanding her dinner money and vicious name-calling. She also noted and underlined the telephone number of the ChildLine charity, the last line of retreat of so many young people in her plight.

Geraldine related: "I was very unhappy with the way the school handled the situation. I think they were negligent.

"I went there with Maria's friend's mother. We were allocated just eight minutes with the teacher.

"After that, Maria came home crying and saying that she'd been called a baby whose mother had to fight her battles for her. She begged me not to go up to the school again.

"On the night she died, she showed no signs of distress to me. She sat and ate potato crisp sandwiches while she nursed a neighbour's baby. She wouldn't tell me if anything was wrong. She knew I'd only go back to the school and that would lead to even more taunting.

"Lisa, my other daughter, went up to see her and rushed down to say Maria had told her she'd taken an overdose. I could hardly believe it. I went straight upstairs. She threw her arms around me and said 'I love you, Mummy, but I can't take it any more.'

"She was taken straight to hospital and, there, told her sister and the nurses what had been happening to her at school. No one can ever tell me my daughter wasn't living in torment. She was being bullied at school. That's what killed her."

Teachers at the Little Flower school said later that the "secret diaries" were part of an English project on bullying. Maria's cries for help in her diaries thus became an after-the-fact rationalisation. Abdication and denial are a recurring theme.

A Key Stage 3 examination paper contains a question on bullying and as a result of Denise Baillie's bullycide, examiners marking English papers were advised in May 2000 by the Council for Curriculum Examination and Assessment to look out for tell-tale signs of bullying. The exam paper will be returned to the school to deal with, although this will be the same school which has allowed the bullying to breed in the first place.

Geraldine McGovern, understandably, doesn't buy the excuse either, and thinks it's nonsense. She was so convinced that Maria was a bullycide that, overcome by grief, she spent four months in hospital and couldn't bring herself to visit her daughter's grave.

She has not changed her mind about the bullying which pushed a sensitive thirteen-year-old over the edge.

She said: "Things can never be right for me again. I feel I can never live without her. But I must. I have another daughter to look out for.

"I know now that bullying is a problem in most schools. Teachers will deny it. Please, please, any child who is reading this and who is being bullied, *tell someone now.* Please don't let any other mother go through what I have suffered ... but, then again, my daughter did tell me, I told the school. But what did they do about it? She's still gone."

A coroner recorded a verdict of accidental death but said that, whatever the extent of Maria's suffering at school, "She was an unhappy girl. Taking an overdose was a result of that."

Geraldine puts it more bluntly: "She was petrified of the bullies. She had even underlined ChildLine's number in her diaries. She bought the St Jude prayer and wrote in her books that she prayed every single night that the two gangs who were out for her would just leave her alone."

On 10 January she came home after the first day of a new term at Little Flower after the Christmas holiday. She had wept on the bus but put on a brave face when she walked through her front door. She did her homework, a little babysitting, and went to her room at 9.45 to listen to her favourite show, Take That Song. It was 11.15 pm when big sister Lisa found her sitting on her bed admitting she had taken the deadly tablets.

Geraldine said: "While we were waiting for the ambulance and she was sitting on my knee I asked her why she had done what she had. She replied: Mummy, they are all talking about me and picking on me."

Maria became a bullycide in the local casualty unit when she died at 5.30 am the following morning.

Tittle-tattle Kelly

They buried Kelly Yeomans in her Salvation Army uniform and wished they'd listened to her tittle tattle.

That's what most thought her complaints of bullying boiled down to ... mere childish tittle tattle. The chatter fell on deaf ears and Kelly was forced to bullycide because no one understood that her whispered tittle tattle was really a scream of pain.

She was a tell-tale, they said, when she prattled on about being stabbed with sharpened pencils, her school bag being hurled into a dustbin, the hills of salt poured over her lunch, the punches, the shattered spectacles, the stones, eggs and butter hurled at the windows of her home and the cruel names she was called at school. "Smelly Kelly" was one of the mildest.

"Tittle Tattle Kelly" was the most dangerous of all and the one which ultimately led to her death. Her mother found bruises the size of old copper pennies covering her daughter's back. Kelly would limp home plastered in thrown mudballs. Youngsters would yell "fat cow" and spit - even throw eggs - at her father's car windows as he drove her to school.

So Kelly, a pleasant, chubby-faced Sally Army tambourine banger with a singing voice like an angel's, decided tittle tattle wasn't going to solve her agonising problem.

She went to bed with a handful of tablets instead.

That did the trick.

Kelly was just 13 years old.

The bullying of Kelly Yeomans was so brutal that five local teenagers were taken to court and pleaded guilty to a charge of intentional harassment, knowing they could face custodial sentences. Four of them, aged between thirteen and seventeen, got the wrist-slap of a community service order for the attack on her home.

The horror of her life was such that her father, Ivan, even contemplated suicide himself. Her mother, Julie, found sleep impossible and her grandmother died within weeks of the funeral of a broken heart, the family believes.

Shy, homely, bespectacled Kelly had suffered the torment of bullying for at least three years at school and in the streets around her home in Allerton, Derbyshire.

Her bedroom is still populated by dolls and cuddly toys. The walls are plastered with posters of her favourite pop group, Boyzone. The bed's made up. The curtains are crisp. The only thing missing is Kelly herself.

"At ten to four each day I still expect her to walk through the door from school," mother Julie told us. "Of course, she never does. She never will again. I still can't fully get it into my head that she's no longer with us.

"That's why we didn't move out of the area when she died. It's like she's still here, still in the house."

Dad, Ivan, told us: "Why Kelly? If you're different you're picked on. Kelly was different. She looked different. She was poor. She was a loner who kept herself to herself. The bullies said they did it for fun. Some fun!"

She was also overweight, wore cheap specs and a Salvation Army uniform on Sundays, and couldn't play any sport for toffee.

The Yeomans have put together a scrap-book containing cuttings about their daughter's death.

They've also pasted in records of her achievements including certificates for written work and her beautiful singing. One from her primary school praises her for "being very mature about handling difficult situations in class."

But these "difficult situations" got out of hand when she reached secondary school and she developed a terror of her classmates. Walking home was torture. She would make any excuse to dilly-dally behind the herd or even make detours to relatives' homes to avoid her contemporaries.

She said very little at home about her ordeal but her astute and loving parents read the signs: the missing glasses and shoes, smashed or trashed by the tougher kids. Kelly didn't cry. She merely withdrew.

The Yeomans tackled Kelly's teachers over and over again about the bullying. They even sent solicitors' letters demanding an end to the campaign of torture against her. As is common in the stories in this book, nothing (or at least not enough) was done.

Kelly's sister, Sarah, says: "They didn't do a thing. They always said 'we'll sort it out' but they never did. The teachers would just say 'sit down, Kelly. Don't be a tittle-tattle.'

Mother Julie said: "You can't blame the teachers all the

time. When I tried to talk to the father of one of the bullies he told me to get off his premises and slammed the door in my face. If I tried to approach the bullies themselves they'd just tell me to F... off and give me a mouthful of abuse."

"It's so quiet here now," says Ivan. "The bullies have gone. Now that Kelly's no longer here there's no fun around our house for them. Her sacrificed life hasn't altered anything at school. It's still a hotbed of bullying."

Even after she'd been hounded into bullycide, bullies couldn't leave Kelly in peace. Her small coffin in the local chapel of rest was filled with teddy bears and posters and in her death-cold hand lay a packet of her favourite spearmint chewing gum.

Her body, dressed in the smart Salvation Army uniform after her parents had discarded the hated school uniform which symbolised her torture, was disturbed.

Her chewing gum was stolen.

A local appeal was launched to pay for a headstone but police discovered bogus collectors claiming to be Yeomans' relatives, cashing in by keeping for themselves the donations they collected.

The bullies always like to have the last laugh, sometimes even after they've driven their victim to the grave.

Neil's covered so many tough assignments he should be hardened to it but his talk with Ivan and Julie and the others in this book have been some of his most upsetting experiences. Friendly, gentle, deep thinking, cooperative people are the Yeomans but their story as they told it in simple, honest Derby accents was a heartbreaker for him.

"We've always hoped that Kelly's sacrifice would change things and that the bullies would realise what they were doing", continued Julie. "We were wrong to hope for that. Nothing's changed. The school's not really bothered. They try to say there is no bullying but how can they say that? Kelly's dead.

"After her bullycide we made the decision not to move

house. There's too much of Kelly in every room. We must pass her bullies in the street. It's worth that pain not to abandon her by changing address.

"But I'm not the timid little woman I used to be. If I see someone being bullied these days I march straight over and sort it out. You see, Kelly used to come home with bruises and with lead in her body where she'd been stabbed with pencils. But when I asked her if she was being bullied she'd say 'No Mum, I haven't.' She was trying to protect us from the worry.

"We did worry, of course, and I went up to the school. We got no help. They just told us there wasn't a problem and Kelly was just a tittle-tattle.

"None of her bullies has ever come to us to apologise. They're not bothered. They still live around us and they're still heartless bullies and when I see them I just leave them alone but always think - hey, if you hadn't been so nasty, Kelly would still be with us.

"It hurts me that they haven't changed. When we went to the police and they rounded up the gang, one of them said that he wanted to go to the Yeomans' and say that he was sorry. But I said 'no'. I wouldn't accept any apology. They'd taken my daughter away from me and left her for dead. I wanted to say 'You've done it. You've done the damage and that's it!'

"Before the bullying, Kelly was a very happy little girl. It was only in the later stages of her life that she had to live in misery.

"I think she just got fed up with living. She did have some friends at school but I think they were being bullied as well. It could be that she took her life to make a statement ... to try to help these friends. It could be.

"She said to us on the Friday night that she wanted to die and we thought we'd talked her out of it. But she was bullied again at the weekend. On Sunday I found her dead in her bedroom. There was no question about it.

"She'd come down and taken my tablets.

"People used to spit at our car when my husband drove Kelly to school. They even threw eggs. But there has been a change of attitude towards us since Kelly's death. Maybe the bullies are bored now because they don't have a target.

"But, bullies or not, we can never leave here. The house is too full of so many memories of Kelly. It's like she's still here in some way. We've not left her bedroom exactly as it was. She's still got everything in there but it's not exactly a shrine. We're not being silly about it."

Ivan offered us his thoughts: "It's altered our lives. When we had Kelly it was all very happy and we felt very lucky. You know what I mean? Although I've got our other daughter, Sarah, and I love her as well, the house is so different without Kelly being here.

"We'll never ever leave even though we see the bullies almost every day. It's a matter of 'up yours!'. You know what I mean? She's made us fighters.

"Julie never wore a Salvation Army uniform but Kelly and Sarah went the whole hog. The Sally Anny has been supportive. She was buried in her uniform. Maybe there was an unconscious point being made there.

"Her school uniform represented her nightmare and the Army uniform represented her dream. She really did think there was a better life out there somewhere where she could enjoy playing her tambourine and singing in her beautiful voice.

"No. We couldn't leave here and her. Strange thing, a lot of the neighbours whose kids were responsible for this have up and gone. They've left, not us.

"Even now we don't know what went wrong or what made her a bully target. The bullies just decided to have a good time and they beat her up in the playground for fun.

"One time her new glasses were smashed. She told us she'd dropped them. She was trying to protect us from worry. Sarah, our other daughter who's a couple of years older than Kelly, was also being bullied and she didn't tell us either. I'm still not sure whether it was for our protection or whether they felt some kind of shame for having become underdogs.

"To me, people don't know what it's like. You can pretend to cope with it. But only pretend. It's always there. I dream about her and then have to wake up thinking Kelly's still here and realise that, golly, it was only a dream. That's how it is.

"I hope talking to you will mean there are a few kids alive next year who might have taken Kelly's route otherwise.

"You know, when Kelly was in her open coffin we put a tube of her favourite chewing gum in her hand and it was stolen. It made me really sick that somebody could do that.

"You'd think the bullies would have been satisfied with killing her. But it carried on even after her death. Both boys and girls still tried to intimidate her.

"Why? There was an old woman who played the piano and Kelly - she could read music - always used to turn her pages over for her. Any time any of the old folks around had got trouble they'd phone Kelly. That's how good she was.

"It's very weird. How could anyone attack a girl with a heart and a face like hers?

"One thing is that we don't feel guilty whatsoever. There was no little signal that we might have missed. She knew we were here for her but she was just too kind-hearted to lumber us with her private pain.

"I still go to her grave and talk to her out loud when I'm there. There's no recrimination, only love from the voice I hear in my head. On her headstone there's a picture of Kelly and on the other side's a picture of her favourite band, Boyzone. The same picture is still hanging on her bedroom wall.

"That's all we have. She didn't leave us a suicide note. She wanted to keep the hurt to herself, I think. We've thought about this and whether she really meant to kill herself or if the overdose was more than she meant. We now honestly believe she really meant to go the whole hog. To never wake up to another day. Life had become too much of a burden for her to bear. She'd had enough.

"Me, I hate the bullies but blame the school. They were there in place, so-called professionals, and knew what was going on but just wrote Kelly's problems off as tittle-tattle.

"The headmaster wrote a letter saying there was no bullying in his school. Only two teachers came to Kelly's funeral. Purely as friends, not as official school representatives.

"In my mind the school is to blame and there's still horrible bullying going on there even today, even after Kelly showed them how lethal it can be."

Kelly's sister Sarah is 18, two years older than Kelly would be now. She's engaged to be married soon and Kelly's death turned her life around.

Sarah told us: "I used to be shy and timid and bullied. Since Kelly died, I fight back. I don't take any nonsense from anybody. I've become a protector - I've got a pal a few years younger and a six-year-old I help look after and they're both being bullied. So I go out to bat for them. Kelly's death has given me this strength.

"My Dad's not rich but he'd bought me and Kelly some new white trainers one day. The bullies poured tomato sauce all over them and ruined the shoes. We did nothing about it. If the same thing happened today they'd be in deep trouble with me. Kelly's death has given me, well, anger, the power to fight things that just aren't fair.

"I was shy and couldn't even fight my own battles before. Kelly's made me so strong I can now fight other people's.

"But I'm not all that tough and nasty. I still lock myself in her old bedroom at night and talk and, sometimes, cry with her."

Kelly's uncle Ken Yeomans told us: "I went round to the house the morning they'd found Kelly dead. It's a pebbledashed little place. The walls were splattered with rotten eggs, butter and cruel graffiti. It was only then - seeing this - that I realised what they'd all been going through.

"The house was so scarred with sorrow that I will never understand how my brother, Ivan, and his wife, Julie, found the strength to stay there. But they did. The bullies left the area instead.

"We can only hope and pray that they're not still playing their deadly games in some other part of the country."

The compulsive nature of bullying means this wish is unlikely to be satisfied. Bullies, as with many criminals, are adept at selectively switching off the emotions of guilt and remorse which stop normal people from hurting others.

Kelly's case is reminiscent of Steven Shepherd. She was artistic, thoughtful, considerate, and with mature interpersonal skills for her age. Someone who cared, whilst those at school couldn't and wouldn't. Like most targets, Kelly didn't fight; she wasn't equipped physically or mentally to resort to violence. Instead, in the absence of the responsible adults fulfilling their responsibilities, she withdrew.

All the bullycides featured so far have involved non-athletic children. However, despite the preconceptions, bullycide is no respecter of looks or physique or athletic ability.

The day the music died

His fine dark hair and a dusting of childish freckles made handsome David Tuck look like a young Disney movie star.

With a wealthy father, a luxurious home, and a fine mind, he had all the chances life could offer. He could have chosen sport. Dad was vice-chairman of Gloucester Football Club. David could have chosen to become a local tycoon. His family owned a successful business. He could have chosen music. He was a gifted instrumentalist.

Instead, the desperate twelve-year-old schoolboy chose

bullycide.

On the day after he'd begun another term of torment at school he sobbed to his father, Michael: "I just can't take it Dad." He refused to leave the house and face the bullies for another day and when Dad came home David was hanging from a banister by his dressing gown cord. He was dead.

The school was no Rose Hill at Ince near Wigan. It was the exclusive Sir Thomas Rich's Grammar School in Gloucester. But class didn't save him from the schoolyard thugs. His father, the owner of a firm of successful estate agents in one of England's richest counties, said his sensitive son had been the victim of playground torment.

"Ever since he started at the school," Mr Tuck said, "he was exposed to bullying. Mainly verbal abuse."

After just one day back at school it was obvious to Mr Tuck that his son was in serious distress. The boy was weeping as he described his misery.

Mr Tuck called the school but was assured there was no problem. Just hours before his death on 7 January 1997 David joined a family conference with his father, brother Richard and sister Michelle to talk things over.

"We talked in turn about bullying and he seemed calmer," Mr Tuck said. The following morning David was in a sloppy track suit instead of his school uniform, refusing to attend the second day of term.

An inquest heard later how Mr Tuck was so worried he even telephoned his estranged wife for help. During the fatal day he was constantly on the telephone to his home to speak to David. At 2.30 pm there was no reply. He rushed back from his office and found David swinging by the neck from the staircase banister. He fought frantically to revive him and called in rescue services. But it was too late.

David had become a bullycide.

Even cautious coroner David Gibbons said bullying could have lead to his death. Recording an open verdict - the only one available to him - he said: "I really cannot explain or even comprehend what happened to David. We will have to accept that we will never understand what was going on in his mind. He will have found in his own mind his own solutions. I suspect that this was a cry for help."

Margaret Duckworth, an experienced ex-teacher linked with groups tackling the bully problem, told us: "If a school tells you they have no bully problem, then that school is where you are most likely to find that very problem."

Perhaps, then, it is not too surprising that the head of Sir Thomas Rich's Grammar had this to tell the inquest into young David's death: "I could find no evidence of bullying." In fact he said he could find no evidence of David or anyone else being bullied there. The school, he said, prided itself on having a group of sixth-form children ready to counsel their younger school pals with problems.

Headmaster Ian Kellie went on: "I think if it had been a wider problem, as a school we would have picked it up. We have no evidence that David had any wider problems at school. I do believe we are a caring school. We are constantly on the lookout for bullying."

David is dead. And he told his father why.

A retired grammar school teacher, sister of one of the UK's former highest ranking policemen, told us: "When a school says there's no bullying going on, they've not been looking hard enough."

David had faced the break-up of his parents' marriage. His father emphasised to the coroner's court that he did not feel the separation had unduly upset his son.

All Mr Tuck could suggest was the syndrome he had never heard identified in one word: bullycide.

Maria's, Kelly's and David's cases demonstrate vividly the difficulties that parents face when dealing with school authorities. All too often complaints of bullying put forward by pupils and parents are dismissed; assertions of looking out, investigation and action are rarely supported by evidence.

All too often both the pupil and parents are regarded as troublemakers, even sometimes as bullies themselves for having dared to raise the issue. Powerless and impotent, the parents do the right thing but the school fails them. In contrast to parents' concern for the welfare of their children, and that of other children, the school's lack of understanding is often perceived as callous insensitivity and indifference.

Sometimes teachers protest they have investigated claims and say they've "dealt with the problem". Anyone who understands bullying knows that you can't deal with the problem overnight. It doesn't go away until the chief bully is dealt with, and even then, other bullies appear.

In those cases where the school acts, the solution is often expulsion, but that only passes the problem on to someone else. The question of how to deal effectively with violent pupils has yet to be answered.

Children who suffer bullying are often terrified of their parents intervening. Once the bully finds out, and in the absence of effective action by the school, the bullying gets worse. Much worse. The target is now labelled a baby or a wimp.

Giving a target of assault a crash helmet is never going to solve the problem. Modern society seems to have forgotten that problems are solved not by treating the effects but by identifying and dealing with the causes. However, in today's cash-strapped schools, cost and expediency prevail.

Kelly's bullies were, uncharacteristically, called to account through the process of law. However the seriousness of the offence was not reflected in the verdict and, apart from a minor admonishment of a community service order, the perpetrators were effectively let off. Compare this to the case of Josh Belluardo in Cherokee County, Georgia, USA, who died as a result of being punched on the back of the head by his tormentor, Jonathon Miller.

Miller, who had a history of antisocial behaviour, was found guilty of murder and sentenced to life imprisonment. He will be eligible for parole in around fifteen years' time. Those bereaved by bullycides are never released from their sentence of suffering.

Bullies often harbour deep ingrained prejudices which serve as the vehicle for blaming others for the bully's own failings. Those who are the target of such prejudices also suffer throughout their lives.

Chapter 5

Racial violence
The embattled identities

*"Few people can be happy unless they hate
some other person, nation or creed."*
Bertrand Russell

A phone-in survey by one of Britain's biggest child care organisations found that only 2% of racial minority groups complained of bullying whereas 37% of white children claimed that Asians and blacks were the bully's favourite target.

These figures did not surprise John Pitts, Professor of Social and Legal Studies at Luton University and Director of the Vauxhall Centre for the Study of Crime. A respected expert on interracial violence, Prof Pitts is the author of an official Home Office report based on a study in two Merseyside and two London schools entitled *"Preventing School Bullying."*

The report includes a large appendix of guidelines for teachers in schools where racial bullying is a threat. Prof Pitts told us: "Bullying takes various forms according to age and whereas younger Asian kids, for instance, are called names a lot and have arguments with kids in class, the real violence is for older kids, thirteen, fourteen or fifteen. By real violence I mean assaults on individuals by bullies armed with knives, with bits of wood, people being beaten up, that kind of thing. And normally taking place outside the school."

Other studies described later in this book point out that the older the child, the less likely he is, through embarrassment or fear, to make an official complaint.

"One of the things that we have become aware of in schools is that you go there any day and you'll hear people say 'Paki bastard.' It's just routine. When we talk to the Asian kids about that, they say 'Oh well, that's custom. That's just what people do.' They don't see racist taunting of that sort as anything untoward. It's part of the backdrop.

"When you get to the more serious forms of violence, I think there's a sort of masculinity thing there. Older boys are far more reluctant to talk about their victimisation. They're much more likely to go and sort it out on their own.

"If a school has between a third and 38% of Bangladeshi kids in it, then the victimisation will be very high. Once it's over 40%, the victimisation figures will fall to a similar level as those of white kids. I base this on the surveys of four schools in Merseyside and London. Levels of victimisation of Asian kids in a school is determined by their level of representation there.

"In one school we encountered there was an 80% Asian student body. There was a very low level of anti-Bangladeshi victimisation there but quite a high level of white kids who wanted to transfer out saying they were being victimised. But, on balance, victimisation tends to go white to Bangladeshi and not the other way around.

"Some kids victimise, others get victimised. We must look at the psychodynamics of victimisation and the victim. I had a discussion recently with Kidscape's director, Michele Elliott, who told me that children could become a target for any number of reasons, colour of hair, stature, psychological makeup. I agreed. But one of the problems with Asian or African kids is that they do get identified as different very easily by people who want a scapegoat. On a broader scale, one has to see the overrepresentation of Bangladeshi kids in some areas as a functional conflict existing out there in the neighbourhood.

"I've never been aware of any minority member who has been driven to suicide as a result of bullying. Perhaps, if you see yourself as part of a group of people, all sharing the same characteristics which attract bullies, it is very different from feeling yourself isolated and taking it all upon yourself and taking the blame upon yourself. Even though there may be white kids kicking you in, tomorrow you can file it away under 'racism'. It isn't because of me as the kind of person I am. It's racism and I can get some support for that. A white child might feel himself utterly alone with no recourse to anything or anyone, feeling there is no help at all.

"If you want the issue to come to the surface you have to create all manner of informal opportunities for that to happen. Confidential opportunities perhaps, where a child could speak to any teacher privately and it wouldn't go any further if they didn't want that, and peer mentoring where they could speak with an older student about the problems they're having. In the schools where we were working, we instituted an informal time where teachers could talk to students and introduce questions of bullying and victimisation.

"Some schools in the UK are taking this problem seriously. Others aren't. There are a lot of tensions in schools. They are under a lot of pressure to achieve. We're doing work on school exclusion (expulsion) at the moment where parents have signed petitions to get rid of particularly violent pupils because they're beating up their kids. So that's the tension in schools; time and resources at the moment are going into anti-exclusion work. They're focused on problematic kids who are making a nuisance of themselves very publicly as opposed to all those kids who are being battered into oblivion. I think teachers would say that they want to be more available.

"I think another thing is that they just feel hidebound by all their legal responsibilities because now, if somebody says they're being bullied, they've got to devote a couple of hours to go through some kind of quiz or legalistic process with witnesses and everything. They have a busy week, so there's pressure to ignore it. There are a lot of pressures in a school which work against an active, preventative anti-bullying strategy. The schools I've worked in I've been very impressed by. One of the things needed in school is pastoral care. But it's a specialised task. You have home/school liaison specialists, you have child care officers, you have unattached education welfare officers. Of course, when the squeeze goes on, those are the only people to go to.

"Black Afro-Caribbean kids don't come in as much for bullying. Often they pass as honorary whites. But many of the new, rising generation of Bangladeshi kids are serious. They're serious on the one hand with their parents because they're fed up of this kind of crap, they offer them no role model. And they're angry that schools and the police don't take their plight more seriously. There's a lot of anger.

"In London, where we've done most of our research, the Bangladeshis are the people who are victimised most. The image of them used to be that they are a people who won't stand up and fight back. Until the mid-eighties, that may have been true. White youths would rampage through, say, Brixton picking people out. Then there was a big backlash, led by some Bangladeshi guys in their twenties and thirties, and they tried to secure their area and generate safety.

"I think the reason I have never come across what you call bullycide is a social thing. The minorities are not made up of people in isolation. There's a kind of unified force. I think for a kid to end up killing himself he must feel incredibly isolated from everyone around him. That's the major factor. The Bangladeshis down here have strong families behind them. It's hierarchical.

"The experience of migration has made quite a dent in some kids. For example, a number of single-parent Bangladeshi kids have their problems. The migration change takes its toll. The research we're doing on school exclusion, for instance, shows up a number of Asian kids from Afghanistan and, increasingly, Eastern European youngsters, unaccompanied minors. There's a big flow, for example, between Kashmir and Luton and sometimes parents are away for a long time. Their Daddy's around but he's on the move.

"Another thing, of course, is drugs. Youngsters are being put away, ironically, because they're in trouble for drugs. In Kashmir drugs are incredibly cheap. They're coming over with a suitcase full. Our traditional view of the Asian family as a solid bulwark against bigots isn't the way it always is.

"It is the case that, in spite of your character or size, if you're a Bangladeshi young man or woman you have a heightened vulnerability to attack which is much more likely to come from white youngsters than anybody else."

Professor Pitts and his team have spent five years studying 2,000 children. His conclusion: "I call it The Embattled Identities. Victimisation tends to come from groups who think they own and have a right to their own neighbourhood. They feel social structures are unravelling. It's no accident that in the East End of London you find a high concentration of minorities. This goes beyond having a very high Bangladeshi population that moved in quite fast. You also have a working class community that at one point was prosperous, integrated, close, which has now fallen apart. Their local schools seem to have been taken over, they feel the quality of housing has started to cramp and they don't want their children to live there.

"It is the case that the racial minorities which become victims are fairly poor, they move into areas that are poor, they move to live alongside many poor white people, normally in a neighbourhood which is on its way down. So the minorities become the empirical evidence that the neighbourhood has declined. They draw cause and relationship from the fact that there is a growing population of minority incomers. Some of them act accordingly. What the kids do is to sustain the parental attitude."

Over the last quarter of a century the UK government has strengthened existing laws and introduced new laws to deal with harassment and discrimination. The passing of a law is a signal that society has rejected a type of behaviour that was previously acceptable.

Because there is no law on bullying, many people are inclined to not take the issue seriously. Bullies take absence of law as justification of their behaviour. To make significant inroads into bullycide and near-bullycide, bullying needs to be criminalised.

Open door policy

Schoolteacher Richard Riley is a tough guy with a tough job in a tough comprehensive school in one of Birmingham's toughest and poorest inner city areas. Ninety-eight percent of the kids there - between 11 and 19 years of age - are non-whites, from all ethnic backgrounds.

Bullying is a problem. So is the threat of bullycide. But the school's new and unique open-door policy has saved at least two children from death in the last year alone.

We've chosen to use his closing words to our interview to open his tale: "Of course bullycide has reached epidemic proportions. When a child commits suicide through intimidation at school, it means we're not dealing with the problem."

As in Prof Pitt's studied experience, Richard's school has found that being in a small minority is not a problem. White children and kids of mixed race who make up such tiny groups don't come in for victimisation. It's where racial groups reach near-equal numbers that difference sparks war in the playground.

"I've not had a single white kid come to me and say he was being bullied by another pupil. All the bullying seems to be between the Asian majority groups.

"I've probably saved two lives among that group in the last twelve months. No need, though, to go into the details of overdoses and rushes to hospital, the counselling.

"Our feeling at school now is that we know there are bullies out there in the schoolyard. They know we know who they are and that they and their victims are being monitored. We work on it subtly.

"We've put our anti-bullying policy together ourselves because our school is so uniquely formed through the massive Asian representation that the measures in place at other schools wouldn't necessarily apply here. It's based on previous knowledge and the experience of other institutions. Even if it isn't exclusive and we've borrowed ideas from the experience of others - we've never had a bullycide here. Some kids have seriously tried - and we've spotted it and saved them. Things are getting better."

Richard and the staff don't police the playground. Theirs is an open-door policy which provides sanctuary and a caring ear before victims reach the bullycide extreme.

"Some kids have been insulted and campaigned against here to the extent that they've tried to take their own lives," Richard told us. "But our policy seems to be effective to the extent that we've been able to make sure we haven't lost one yet.

"For instance, I work from seven thirty in the morning to six at night and my office door is always open to any pupil who wants to come in and talk over his bully problems. Kids will just wander in and say 'are you busy? Can you spare a minute?' Then they pour out their troubles. Just talking it all over is so much a part of winning the battle. Suffering in silence can be deadly.

"Using the same technique some years ago I was able to change the attitude of a bully who came through that door to tell me his own story. It's a matter of reconstructing the self-esteem of the victim and, in some cases the victimisers.

"Lots of my colleagues feel the same. We've got strict policies in place here to deal with bullying. There are those teachers who live in Cloud Cuckoo Land and still sit there and do nothing. They just don't seem to believe that bullying is not a Billy Bunter joke - it can be lethal. Many teachers are naïve. They never left school themselves.

"I've been a professional footballer, I've driven lorries, worked on building sites, I took up as a hobby being a balloon pilot. So I can speak to kids with some experience of life and with a little authority. And there is no anti-bullying literature unread and gathering dust on my bookshelves.

"It's all about team work. If you have a problem you must have somebody to pass the ball to, a friend, a teacher (who's hopefully also a friend). It doesn't matter who - just somebody in the right position at the right time. I'm putting this message across every day and so are loads of my colleagues.

"It's difficult to say how effective the idea is. You can only count casualties in this area, not survivors. But we've had no casualties. In the past twelve months or so there doesn't seem to be the same level of physical or verbal violence.

"Teachers really should stand up like drunks at an Alcoholics Anonymous meeting and admit: 'Hi, My name's Joe and I've got it all wrong.' They've got to face the fact that there's a massive problem and work with everyone around them to try to solve it. But this bullycide thing is being kept carefully under wraps - folks who should be dealing with it are either so unaware, so uncaring or so damned blind that they're doing nothing to battle it. They just won't admit it's there.

"You find that different racial groups from the Asian subcontinent will move to different parts of the UK when they arrive here, which is why Prof Pitts has emphasised the Bangladeshi community so much - he just happened to choose the schools for his study where that group was predominant. I suppose the feeling is that there's safety in numbers from the point of view that they have other people - friends and family - from their own original base to relate to.

"Here in our school, though, there's a mixed bag for some reason. Only 2% white. Including a very few of mixed blood, the other 98% are Asian and it's in this biggest group where all the bullying takes place. They are all trilingual English, Urdu, formal local dialects or whatever but the verbal abuse can be in any language. Mainly English because it's shared by all. The worst insult is 'Your Mum' which carries all the dirty, hurtful connotations it suggests in the well-known American insult.

"The bullying is based on difference of Asian home region, religion and other more obscure factors known only to the children. There's a dramatic imbalance between the teaching staff and the kids. Most of the teachers are white - about proportionally opposite to that of the students - and don't understand the languages and dialects they use to subtly hurt each other. I know a little Urdu but what I've mainly picked up is the swear-words.

"Funny that the call-name 'Paki' is considered one of the most horrible, as though just coming from that country makes you third class. You never hear kids calling 'Beni!' or 'Afghani!' You don't even have to be from Pakistan to be hurt when that word's hurled at you. It just means 'up-yours, you're a bum!' It seems to be a universal term of abuse.

"It's strange that the various groups don't keep themselves to themselves and form cliques apart, isn't it? There seems to be something in each of them which makes them want to identify an enemy and join a fight. Often it could be something not racial, just having a vicious go at the way a kid does his hair or something. It's not healthy competition like in sport when you try to put one over on the other guy. It's nasty and dangerous.

"It's a puzzle to me that people from the same subcontinent with so much in common can be so bitter toward each other to make bullying a major, potentially deadly problem here. Some bullies are held in high esteem at home. A bully can sometimes be thought a hero in the family, a victim nothing more than a shameful wimp. Many parents are villagers in their country of origin and remote from the modern ideas of cities, clinging to the values of their grandfathers; they leave it to the teachers, the bosses as they think of us, to sort out problems. Open as our doors are and as much as we try we can't be with every kid every minute. The parents must take some effective responsibility too.

"Teaching's more than just instilling knowledge of a particular subject. It should also be about providing protection. Growing up is traumatic and we must help the youngsters cope with the kicks life is giving them."

Sometimes Richard's love of the world and its people forces his mind to wander to times when he flew in balloons shaped as strawberries or bunches of bananas as he tries to formulate dreams of future high-flying tomorrows for the promising kids filling his class.

During one of these daydreams he was interrupted by a fourteen-year-old girl pupil: "Hey, Mr Riley. Are you OK?" she asked.

Richard replied: "Sure, why?"

"Because you're being very silly."

To be concerned with and that openly familiar with your teacher shows that Richard Riley and the school he enjoys and is proud to work in are anything but silly. He didn't take the comment as an insult. He laughed along with the class. Better the kids can joke with him like a pal than hide their smiles and tears as we of earlier generations had to.

Unfortunately, many people mistake such informal

interactions as a decline in standards of behaviour or a lack of respect. In fact the opposite is true. Schools in which bullying is minimal or absent tend to be environments where there is equality of respect and interpersonal skills are taught not by curriculum but by example. Conversely, in schools where bullying is rife, interpersonal skills by senior staff are poor and respect for staff by pupils and for pupils by staff is low or non-existent. In such schools the head often does not have control of discipline. Deprived of his cane he, nevertheless, continues to cultivate a culture of fear whilst floundering amid unconvincing claims of "there's no bullying here".

Bullies are driven by jealousy and envy. Jealousy of other people's relationships and a false perception of exclusion therefrom (which tends to be self-perpetuating), and envy of other people's possessions, abilities or talents. Closely related to jealousy and envy is prejudice. Most bullies hold deep prejudices. The more intelligent the bully, the less likely he or she is to reveal those prejudices. But they are there, fanning the flames of anger and hatred like a bellows.

As their objectives bullies seek power, control, domination and subjugation. These objectives are most likely to be met if the target has a vulnerability. Racial differences provide plentiful opportunity. Anyone with a coloured skin is easily identified as "different".

Bullies are obsessed with "difference" which forms the focus of their prejudice. Racial abuse is so appallingly common that many non-Caucasian kids accept it as part of life. Children who are recent immigrants find themselves vulnerable, separated from social support systems provided by the extended family and community, and with their command of English and that of their parents often limited.

Refugees are especially vulnerable, a fact confirmed by a study published in November 2000 called *I didn't come here for fun*. Compiled by Save the Children Scotland and the Scottish Refugee Council, the study revealed that almost all refugee children who had arrived in Scotland had experienced racist abuse and hostility.

Coming from a variety of backgrounds, refugee families may have had to flee without warning and without preparation. Landing in an alien culture, regardless of background they are easy meat for bullies. Having perhaps lost everything in their flight to escape persecution, their hopes for safety and security are dashed by now finding themselves the targets of a different (or not so different) form of persecution.

Whilst racism is a common expression of bullies' dysfunctional behaviour, bullying is the common denominator of most violent behaviours including harassment, discrimination, racism, prejudice, abuse, conflict and violence. The bully has an irresistible need to displace his or her anger onto someone else; prejudice serves as the selection process.

To reduce the visibility of their crime, bullies claim that their torment is "only a game", "a bit of horseplay", or "just a laugh". Only bullies and harassers use these self-serving justifications, therefore their use is tantamount to an admission.

The bully sees his target as an object, as a non-human being. With a poorly-defined conscience, the emotions of empathy, remorse and guilt are selectively suppressed in order for the torment to be effected. Perpetual lack of empathy results in the development of a callous insensitivity and indifference to the needs of others.

Chapter 6

Just a Laugh

"Thou cam'st on earth to make the earth my hell...
What comfortable hour canst thou name
That ever graced me in thy company?"
William Shakespeare (1564-1616)

There's an horrific scene at the end of animator Richard Fearn's anti-bullying film when the villain and his gang throw their victim into a canal ... just for a laugh.

They stride off not knowing or caring if he survives. The audience, too, is left to wonder if poor Dickie lives or becomes another bullycide statistic.

What Richard didn't know when he and his school friends invented Dickie and dreamed up the distressing closing to his film was that the scene had already been acted out in real life. Ten years before, a bully gang in Winson Green, Birmingham had hurled six-year-old Allan Jones into the icy waters of a local canal and strutted away without a backward glance.

We do know the end to the real life drama. Regardless of his own safety, Allan's nine-year-old play pal Adrian Watts dived in and manhandled him to the bank. He had saved his life. Because, Allan's mother Karen said later, her son couldn't swim. The bullies had left him to die.

Richard also didn't know when he entitled his film *Just a Laugh* that the bullies who drove Kelly Yeomans to her bullycide had tormented her to death "just for a laugh".

"It just goes to show," a senior Manchester police officer told us, "just how close to real life Richard's fictional animated film really is."

Richard was still a schoolboy when he made the movie, a

seventeen-year-old A-level student who, with help from a team of friends, produced *Just a Laugh* to highlight the horror of playground torment.

The Lancashire Constabulary was so impressed with the script and Richard's skill with plasticine modelling that they gave him the use of their own video studios to complete the movie. Wallace and Gromit creator Nick Park wrote a letter of encouragement to Richard giving his full endorsement to *Just a Laugh*.

A spokeswoman at his Bristol base said: "The film is quite amazing and it sends a vital message that hits you like a punch."

Richard and his team, all former pupils at the St Christopher's High School in Accrington, Lancashire, started on the project three years ago when English teacher, Carol Whittam, set her class the task of writing a play script on a subject connected with crime. For most children the job was soon over and done with. For Richard and his team it became a labour of love which lasted through their mid-teens.

Richard told us: "It started as a play. The team met as a group with the teacher and decided on bullying as a theme. Six months after the script was finished, I was in the house one night when Mum and Dad were out, thinking about things and I decided to animate the whole thing using models like Nick Park does in his work. I started by using my Dad's video camera, making the figures out of plasticine and building the sets with cardboard. The original only took me about a week. I took it to school and they really liked it and showed it to the Schools Police Liaison Officer who, in turn, showed it to Lancashire Constabulary. They gave me the use of their Video Unit to remake the film professionally with them.

"We were working with the Liaison Officer who goes around schools to try to stop bullying. We'd had a bit of bullying at school - mainly name calling and being nasty, being pushed over, not heavy duty violence - and we were setting up an anti-bullying scheme. I was lucky because I could laugh it all off. I know some of the people in my group had become quite upset by it. The play competition at school was about general crime issues but my team saw bullying as a crime and focused on that for our work. We managed to avoid shaping characters on the bullies and victims we knew. We moulded our characters on stereotypes. The bully was always dressed in black and had a skull and crossbones on his T-shirt, big, heavy eyebrows. The victim was small, timid and thin.

"Because the film was aimed at primary school children, those who might first encounter bullying, we wanted to make it obvious. The big and butch against the weaker. We've had feedback from younger children who have already seen it and done follow-up work on the problem.

"When we stereotyped the big, macho, cigarette-smoking bully and the shy little bullied boy, I think we probably subconsciously were trying to make them both (bully and bullied) learn from what we had to say. We wanted children to identify with one or the other and do something about themselves. They both suffer in their own ways, the aggressor and the victim. That thought has only become clear in my mind lately.

"When we put the original story line and play together there was a small team of us involved (James Riley, Hayley Berry, Kate Mayers and Natalie Ingham) all about the same age, in my year. We had a meeting with Mrs Whittam. We casted and I took on the part of the victim - his name, Dickie, was a diminutive of my own. We got a lad called Scott to play the bully and Kate to play the bully's girlfriend. At the start of the film Dickie is happy and cheery, looking forward to his new school adventure. He doesn't know what he's in for."

Richard's problem was an ending. In his heart he knew bullycide was a natural conclusion but he chose to allow his viewers to discover that on their way home.

Richard presented a question as Dickie struggled: "What's the difference, isn't it bullying itself that kills?"

"As young people we're aware that bullying can go that far. I'll never forget the tragic case of the Salvation Army girl, Kelly Yeomans. Why did Kelly die? The front-page headline on one of the papers said 'Just for a laugh.' It was eerie. Two years before Kelly's death we had chosen that title and here were our thoughts mirrored in real life. It was horrifying when we read the headline in the Daily Express. We suddenly realised that we were telling a true story.

The last line in the film comes from Scott, the bully, who says to the grieving mother: 'Well, I'm sorry Mrs Chesworth. It was just a laugh.'"

So often in the cases investigated in this book, children have been terrified of speaking out. James Riley found it difficult to talk about his torment. But at the height of the bullying campaign against him he became narrator of the *Just a laugh* film to tell the world about the misery he was suffering.

"I was going through day by day, perpetual verbal assault. I just didn't seem to fit into the group. I didn't drink and I didn't swear. I didn't do the kind of things the others expected of each other. It was just a matter of them singling the odd man out ... that was me. But it was constant. That's what made it so bad. Every day was a bad day for me. I remember crying sometimes when I'd been put upon really seriously. I never got to the stage where I felt suicidal because I had a father and a mother I could talk to.

"The funny thing is that half the kids who were doing it were friends. When you think of a bully you think of the dregs of society. In my school the situation was different. They started off as my friends and then exercised power on a psychological level. Most of them are at college now.

They weren't the stereotype like the big toughie we used in the film. Didn't make it any easier on me, though. They were clever. They would find out what annoyed me and what wound me up and they'd exploit that. Like one time when I hadn't done very well in an exam and I came in for so much stick over the bad marks - not from the teachers, from the kids. They knew I was ashamed of the mark so they used it to make me feel bad.

"I didn't like football and other sports. So that set me apart, too. I just wasn't part of the crowd. It reached a peak around the third year when I was about thirteen or fourteen. It got to the point where I had to have a physical confrontation with the main bully and asked him why he was doing it. He couldn't explain. He thought it was some kind of big joke and everything carried on as normal.

"These days I have no problems. Actually, I feel stronger because I went through all of that and came out undamaged at the other end. I worked through it with help from my parents. I even feel proud to be who I am today. Really the bully was the one in fear and not me.

"My intention was to make some sense of my own problems. While I was doing the job I tried to distance myself from what I was suffering personally. I knew there were parallels that others - the bullies themselves - would see.

"The people in the project group knew that I was troubled by bullies. They knew I was being made fun of too. But I don't think they knew the full extent of it. How miserable I was being made to feel.

"My work wasn't really a way of fighting back. But I was in a position to know how badly a victim could feel and knew that it could become even more extreme. Looking back on it now, I realise I just wanted to do something definite ... to be confident, to be bold. I wanted to make a difference and I threw myself into that no matter what the consequences might have been. I knew speaking out can make the problem worse. The retributions coming from just speaking to a teacher about your problem, for instance, could be horrendous.

"There was some negative comeback. Bullies tend to come from a group which doesn't like anyone else taking part in extra-curricular activities at school. You're not supposed to do something you don't actually have to. So then you also become 'teacher's pet'. At high school level many of the pupils try to get away with as little as possible. They couldn't understand my going ahead with something I chose to do for the school. So I did get extra abuse because I was involved in something I wasn't forced to do. Sorry, but I think they were too dense to realise why and what I was doing.

"When I have kids myself one day, my advice to them would be: 'be yourself'. Don't think that you're in any way inferior. Self-confidence is everything. If a bully, especially a verbal bully, realises that he can destroy self-esteem, it becomes part of his armoury. Sadly some kids actually begin to believe the terrible things the bullies are saying about them. They take it to heart and they are damaged for life ... or even worse.

James's father, Ron, told us: "Verbal bullying gets to those children who are more susceptible to bullycide. The more sensitive and intelligent the child, the more vulnerable to the bully. I'm proud that my son's helping do something about that."

Carol Whittam was the English teacher who started Richard and his team's ball rolling.

"Their idea was appropriate to the problems of today. Richard decided to adapt it and animate it. It was a natural progression ... from talking-point, to play, to competition and eventually to animation."

There are 900 children at Carol's school. But through a close class-tutor relationship with intimate groups she has earned the confidence of her charges.

"We have non-uniform days and I remember one child suffering because his everyday clothes weren't really trendy. Just for that he suffered. Bullying can take so many different forms.

"The bottom line of teaching is that we impart knowledge of a particular subject. I feel a lot of responsibility as a kind of temporary parent when I'm working. Some people have got into the job through their subject. I'm a teacher because I love children. So, for me, it's not a problem to offer help and guidance as part of my classroom routine. I have to say there are some teachers who are not as perceptive towards their children as they might be.

"The main thing to me is to let them know that you're approachable. The way I do that is to use anecdotal information from things that I've experienced. Some teachers are too private. I remember being ostracised when I was twelve-and-a-half and I've recounted that story on many occasions because I remember going outside and crying because nobody would talk to me. If you make children aware that you, yourself, have had problems they're more likely to see that their own worries aren't unique and can be coped with. They can take strength from that and deal with it.

"I can imagine Richard and the team's scenario happening in my area. In fact, I live near the canal. Someone was pushed in a matter of a few weeks ago - not a school situation. It was older people. A young man had been pushed into the water. Still bullying, though. The aggressors didn't care if he could swim or might have had a heart problem. They just walked off laughing. He was saved by a passer-by.

"The problem today is the fear of stepping out of line and worrying too much about what other people think.

"Let's keep communications channels open. Parents must be there and aware. I've heard parents at primary school tell their kids 'I'm gonna smash your bloody face in!'

I heard one woman the other day. She looked all right. She was walking along with a three-year-old and she called him 'pillock'. That's how they talk to them in the streets. What are they saying behind closed doors? How can you expect a child to hear something like that and speak well to other people ... not react by becoming a bully? There are more guilty adults than there are guilty children."

Britain's best-loved teacher

William Roache, as Coronation Street's Ken Barlow, is remembered as Britain's best-loved schoolteacher, even though he's never taught a class in his life.

William's an actor, in fact the only original cast member left in the UK's longest-running soap show. His job, almost a lifetime's work, was to portray what he and the Granada scriptwriters believed a teacher should be ... not what they actually are.

Though William has never been a teacher in the official sense of the word, he knows plenty who have been. Part of his acting work while he played the caring teacher at the fictional local school was to know about bullying. Part of his life has been to recognise the danger of bullycide.

He told us: "The only defence is openness. But so often speaking to a teacher or a parent or any other adult results in even greater abuse, being labelled a tell-tale and a Mummy's boy."

William didn't do his own research to become a TV teacher. A team of top writers did that for him, sitting in on classes, speaking to children and their teachers.

"However," he says, "it just so happens that two of my best friends at school became teachers. So I had a kind of natural feel and maybe that's why I thought I'd be OK in the part of a teacher in The Street. People don't realise this about actors: you may go somewhere if you need to pick up a certain attitude and things like that. I already knew through my friends what it was like to take a class and relate to children. I had enough in me and then the writers did the deep research.

"But there is in me a concern and a consideration in this area. I think that bullying is something that if I can do anything about I want to do something about."

Already William has encouraged children at one local school who have made their own anti-bullying video, and the police brought him in to plug a campaign.

"It appealed to me. I thought it important and so I fronted it. The police thing was about truancy where children try to escape school and leave themselves open to all kinds of violence and abuse. I think that relates to some extent to bullying, doesn't it? If a boy's bullied at school, of course he will try to stay away. Bullying has so many offshoots all over the place. Sexual harassment, even murder is a form of bullying.

"There is no such thing as an insensitive actor or an insensitive bully victim. I was not bullied myself at school. I was lucky. I was good at sports, I was a prefect, I was fairly successful. Though I wasn't exactly brilliant academically, I was OK and I was very popular. Life was OK to me.

"I was at a boarding school from the age of seven and I think that, certainly the junior school where we had matrons and people like that, they're always aware when a child is unhappy. All of us, the children, we wouldn't tolerate it. If one was known to be bullying, the rest would not like that. He would be ostracised. It was not sporting, bullying was not the thing to do. But, I'm talking about a different generation. I was at school in the 1950s. Now, I think things are very different. There's no respect for anything. There's no respect for law, parents, teachers, anything. It's tough on children.

"I'm interested in the spiritual aspect of life. I'm trying to get a programme on television which is to do with helping people who want to be spiritual, who believe in a God, understand the spiritual nature of a human being and know where to turn to. Cults, of course - the leader of a religious cult can be a sort of bully. If they're good, a true guru, a true teacher who can lead you up to where he can help you, fine. If he's a bad man and a bully he'll for his own satisfaction and gratification lead you down the wrong avenue.

"How many hundreds of cult members have been bullied into mass suicide by charismatic crank leaders over recent years? Whole communities of bullycides have stained the pages of the international press.

"Bullying does extend into pretty well everything. True spiritual teachers, and there are many coming in now not necessarily belonging to any particular religion, all say the same sort of thing: there has to be love, compassion, kindness for all and we should recognise that in every other person no matter what or who they are.

"If that was there, there would be no bullycide. Kindness is love in action. That's all it is. True love which is giving all and asking nothing in return just doesn't seem to apply any more.

"The bully has suppressed his own spiritual nature to the extent that he doesn't give a damn about or consider the other person. If he for a moment put himself in the position of his victim and had some sensitivity he simply wouldn't do it.

"You know, people in my position have to be careful. Just because we in acting do a job which makes us famous we don't necessarily know any more or any less than anybody else. We are heard more. This is why Princess Di was heard. Trouble was nobody was listening. I now only allow myself to become involved in a worthy story if I'm in harmony with it.

"I have two children at boarding school but they've never had bully problems because of who I am. We have a very open family relationship where they can say anything they want to. They can come to us with any problem. At the school they're both in we look for that sort of compassion.

Kindness, to me, is the greatest thing in the world. If you've got kindness, everything else will fall into place.

"A bully could have suffered a lack of this. It could be one of two things, sometimes a child will do something bad because his parents are like that, sometimes he'll do something bad as a reaction against his parents not being like that. But we all have free choice. Because you were bullied as a child you have the free will to make sure nobody else suffers as you did. You don't have to pass on the misery. If your spirituality is awake, that is how you would respond. If your spirituality is covered and buried then you'd tend to feel: 'well, I've had this I'm going to make others suffer too.' That's bad. It's not a good person who does that.

"You can't blame the generations as such. You could say that the times we are in are different, communications are rapid, and the period is absolutely mad. The spiritual side of life has virtually gone except for those who take the trouble to seek and find it for themselves. I think to some extent the bullies are to be pitied because they must be so incredibly insensitive and unaware.

"They have a lack of awareness which makes you feel sorry for them. Because sometime, I believe, you pay the price for everything you do. You reap your reward. They don't know what they're doing because if they did they simply wouldn't be doing it.

"I think the bullies should be pitied and that would begin to break down the awful confrontational thing between the bullied and the bully. If you look at it from the bully's point of view you begin to break down the problem. The victim can't do anything about it but the bully can if we open up the compassion in him. They can learn from their bullying. There are always two sides to everything. You can understand the victim and feel sorry for him but if you start to understand the bully, maybe some results will come. Rather than condemning them and punishing them, give them responsibilities toward those weaker than they are. Lack of understanding is the cause of most of the problems in the world."

Strangely for a programme famous for taking on controversial issues, Coronation Street has never focused on playground bullying as a Street issue although Emmerdale did.

"Very early on we had a character, Rita, who came into The Street and my character, Ken the teacher, was parenting because the father was abusing Rita's child. That's the only time we've focused on any kind of bullying but it was in the home rather than in the school. It's up to our fine team of writers to choose the story lines used - I just act."

A colleague on the scriptwriting team of Emmerdale told us: "We did focus on schoolyard bullying and even considered bullycide as the conclusion to the story line. We decided to steer clear of it; people don't want to face it".

Chapter 7

Life on the line

*"I should have been bloody hanged. Didn't
even get a slap on the wrist from a teacher."*
A former bully who now admits to having
contributed to the bullycide of a classmate.

One encouraging statistic ChildLine can pin down is that
over 100 children phone in every week just to say:
"Thanks. You've sorted out my life for me."

"It's so exciting," said Patricia, a counsellor at ChildLine.
"One of our problems here is that you get so involved in
people's lives and you seldom find out what's happened to
them, whether your advice was helpful over the forty or
fifty minutes we normally spend with a child on the phone."

Before she joined ChildLine, Patricia was once
residential manager for a home for children who had been
sexually abused. One of the things she realised in her new
job was the importance of a child being put into the
powerful position for the first time in their lives.

"They're in control," she said. "They can ring up and don't
even have to tell us their real name or even the town they
live in. They can be anybody and they can say whatever
they want. They're boss. If they want to call me an old bag,
then they can, and it's not often you can say that to an
adult without having a great deal of problems. It's
important for these children that, for once in their lives,
they are in the power position. They have control of the
call.

"I've taken calls from children who are speaking from bed
under the duvet. At no other time could we do that. They
don't want to go to a counselling room and meet adults face

to face. On the telephone, they can do it in their time and in their way.

Anatomy of a bullycide

As a child, Marilyn Price was bullied almost to the end of her tether. The one friend she loved and trusted had turned against her. There was name-calling, violence, stealing from schoolbags, as well as jealousy and resentment.

It was family support which gave Marilyn the strength to forge a renewed friendship with her tormentor. Now Services Manager of Child Protection in one of Britain's biggest southern counties, Marilyn has counselled thousands of children in her thirty years on the job.

She takes what she calls "The Holistic Approach". Bullying alone, she believes, cannot push a child to bullycide. There are many factors involved in driving a child to the final solution. Bullying she agrees, though, can often be the fatal last straw.

These are the predisposing factors in child suicide, according to Marilyn Price:

- parents who have such problems that they are not child-centred and become over-preoccupied with their own private concerns.
- critical parenting when a father, a mother or both are too quick to judge their child negatively; quick to chide and slow to bless
- middle-born children who are neither the dominant force nor the mollycoddled baby of the group
- low achievers in intellectual or physical pursuits
- onerous responsibility on a child such as too much babysitting or other household responsibilities
- different appearance like height, weight or hair colour, spectacles or race, being too attractive or gifted
- unusual impact of adolescence
- unrequited parental, peer, or romantic love

She says the effects on a child can be:
- low self-esteem
- depression (reactive or clinical)
- morbid thoughts involving death, knives, guns and ropes
- no sense of future when a child can see no escape from his misery
- social isolation, standing apart from the peer group
- inability to verbalise feelings when he can't speak to teachers, parents or relatives about the horror he is experiencing; an inability to contextualise a feeling saying: "I don't know what's wrong ... but there's something up"
- irrational guilt when the child blames himself for his father's drunkenness, his parents' separation, his brother's wheelchair. He may turn to booze, glue-sniffing, drugs, or anorexia to punish himself.

"I don't know if I have ever prevented a bullycide at any of my schools. Let the fact that I have never experienced one stand for itself.

"To sum up my own feelings: no, bullycide is not *solely* the result of schoolyard bullying. A victim is prepared by other social and family conditions. The bully might be the killing factor. But the victim is already in danger because of his or her life profile."

Children can survive bullying - although the damage can be lifelong and they should never be placed in that position to start with - but ongoing practical support is crucial.

When a person is tormented, bullied, and abused every day and repeatedly and aggressively advised of their worthlessness, eventually they start to believe it. Once that threshold is crossed, a fatal avenue has been entered.

Human hyenas
In September 1994 twelve-year-old Lynette McLaughlin had been found dead, hanging in her bedroom after being

set upon by schoolyard bullies. Terry, a newspaper colleague, was assigned part of the story. Cynical hacks never realised bullycide was so close to home. It didn't only happen to "other people." A fellow reporter shared the agony. His own son had become a bullycide not long before.

"We know how Lynette's family must feel," Terry wrote. "Our son, Adam, was bullied too. Ten days before his death last July from solvent abuse he had taken an overdose. An inquest recorded a verdict of accidental death.

"Adam was good looking and popular. He was athletic and won medals and cups for springboard diving and played water polo. Everyone seemed to like him.

"He had been at school in Essex for just over a year when it started to change. In the Spring of 1993 when he was just thirteen we noticed that he was looking ill and had lost weight. We were worried because he had always been so happy and we took him to our GP who diagnosed clinical depression. After six months on antidepressants, he improved. But he was never again the boy he used to be. It was as though he had walked into a black cloud. He never talked to us about how he was feeling.

"I think he was too proud to admit he was being bullied. We didn't suspect a thing, not even in June 1993 when he got into a fight with a boy three years older. When my wife picked him up that day, he was so badly hurt he had to be taken to hospital. It hadn't been a one-on-one thing. He'd been beaten up by a whole gang. He didn't say so at the time. They were like a pack of hyenas. When Adam tried to tackle one of them, the others would move in.

"Then one night he came home apparently drunk. Then he did it again and I thought 'hang on, he's not drunk.' He'd taken tranquillisers and he admitted he'd been bullied. One of the bullies had wanted to go out with Adam's girlfriend and that's how we think it all started. They picked on him because he was too popular. They were all jealous.

"We discovered the bullying had been horrific. He had been taunted in the street and spat upon both in and out of school. We complained to the school and the physical bullying stopped. But the threats didn't. We learned that he'd been threatened in town by a boy with a knife.

"By March he was quite frail and his character had completely changed. Although the school had stopped the physical bullying, the boys told Adam that they would get him when they left school in the May. I even received a death threat telephone call and we had to get the police involved. They could never trace the caller.

"Adam's teachers said he had become disruptive in class, never nasty to other pupils, just confused. They couldn't understand him and neither could we. In April Adam was referred to a psychiatrist and we discovered he had been taking tranquillisers and smoking cannabis as a relief from the stress. Then, ten days before he died, he took an overdose of tablets. We took him to hospital and had his stomach pumped out. We were devastated.

"The following week he seemed the brightest he had been in months. Ten days later - the day he died - he'd been awarded a school certificate for coming second in the triple jump. He said he was going off to get fish and chips for lunch and I gave him a couple of quid. He said it was youth club night and I said 'I suppose you want some more money then?' He grinned and I slipped him another couple of pounds and went off to work.

"The police broke the news to my wife and me while we were working. Adam had died on the common at 2.30 pm after inhaling butane gas. He'd been in a car with four other lads. None of them had been sniffing. We believe he'd been driven to it by bullying.

"The way forward must be through education and openness and the schools themselves must play the key part. It's hard for parents to help. Most bully victims are terrified of their parents intervening because of repercussions. Instead of denying they have bully problems, schools should set up teams of older pupils who the younger ones can turn to.

"Adam was the last person you'd expect to have fallen victim to the bullies. But he did. And it cost him his life."

Anyone can be bullied. And anyone who is bullied will suffer psychiatric injury which can take years to heal. Tim reports that some callers to his Advice Line are still traumatised from bullying one, two, even three decades on. Having talked to so many survivors he says he can recognise the signs in a person's voice almost straight away. The wound is still open and raw, their life is blighted, their contribution to society impaired, and their potential impeded. They're still bewildered, confused, embittered, and angry. They've survived, but they exist rather than live.

As a frequently-sought source of counsel in the absence of professional understanding, Tim feels that targets of bullying are often traumatised threefold: first, there's the psychiatric injury from the bullying and harassment itself, second, this is compounded by the unshakeable denial of those in authority and the consequent inability to make progress and, third, if the bullying is recognised and a formal case started, the target has to recount and relive the entire nightmare yet again, often in the presence of the bully's legal defender whose behaviour can be more bullying than his or her client's ever was. Victims of rape, abuse and other harassment crimes will be familiar with this scenario.

Relentless insults such as those which characterise bullying have disproportionate impact compared to the kindness of a compliment. Over time, and in the absence of support, the target of bullying becomes sensitised, and ultimately hypersensitised, to the daily violation of their being. As sensitisation increases, the resulting harm intensifies sensitivity in a vicious circle. The cumulative effects result in trauma.

People who are born with high levels of empathy - and who often go on to make a difference in the world - may have higher-than-average levels of sensitivity, thus making them more vulnerable to the harmful effects of personal violation. Children and adults traumatised through accident, disaster, violence, childhood abuse, grief and loss will also exhibit above-average levels of sensitivity.

Whatever a person's initial degree of sensitivity, daily abuse and rejection by peers and adults leads to a growing sense of betrayal - which is what breach of duty of care amounts to - that can be especially injurious and long-lived.

Unresolved trauma may be one of the reasons why suicide has become the major cause of death for 18-24-year-old males, at least two of whom choose to end their life every day in the UK. From having dealt with so many suicidal and potentially suicidal adults, Tim has identified the sequence of events that starts with bullying and ends with bullycide. That only intervention and support prevent the traumatised target attaining the next step should be self-evident.

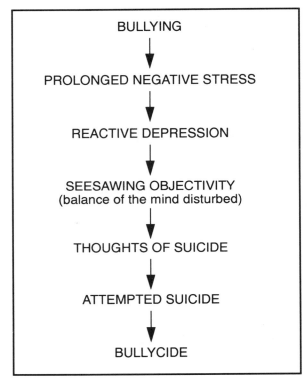

Table 1: How bullying leads to bullycide

Chapter 8

The bitches from hell

*"I'm so, so sorry that the bullies have got me down so
much. Nothing has changed at school and I can't take a
day more of those horrible girls. Tell them I forgive them.
Tell the teachers they should have looked after me. Now
it's all over. No bully can touch me again. I'll still be your
little angel. But now I will love you from heaven. Forgive
me for not being strong enough any more."*
Words penned by a schoolgirl artist just minutes before
she swallowed a drug cocktail to end her misery.

The press called the heartless bullies who made Katherine
Jane Morrison's life unbearable "The Bitches From Hell." A
Sheriff said that KJ's bullies were "contemptible and
cowardly" before jailing them.

A policeman on the Scottish Isle of Lewis described them
to us as "down and out bastards who should be removed
from society for the rest of their lives. We're still trying to
find the other sods that did this to her."

The bullies were accused by the judge of being liars. A
Scottish reporter put it more simply: scum.

In her suicide note, KJ (as she was known) didn't call them
bitches or scum, not even contemptible or cowardly. She
simply and with typical gentleness merely referred to them
as "Those messed up girls that are making my life hell."

The story of KJ

KJ had a lot going for her. But her special pride and joy
was her luxurious raven hair and her academic
achievement. The jealous bullies threatened both. Pass
any more exams and we'll shave your head, they told her
hours before she committed bullycide. She had good

reason to believe the telephone message. She'd recently been beaten to a pulp by a bully gang - one of the ringleaders had been her lifelong friend - and had to be rushed to hospital.

Ten girls battered her outside the Woolworth store in Stornoway, whilst at least twenty-five other guilty bystanders lapped up the show. One of the bullies cried out "Anybody want a free punch?" At least four onlookers took up the offer.

KJ's story starts with her birth in the small town on the windswept island off the west coast of Scotland. She shared her first day at school with best friend, Michelle McBratney, born the same year and who lived next door to KJ's grandparents.

They held hands as they walked into class for the first time, folks say. They were inseparable. Almost like twin sisters.

But things went sour. So sour that pretty, bright KJ took her own life through bullycide at the age of sixteen, oppressed by Michelle (who likes to be called Shelly) and a platoon of wolf-like tormentors.

KJ had a bubbly personality, brilliance, pretty face, gorgeous hair and a burning ambition to become a journalist or business executive in America. She'd already gained five As and two Bs in Standard Grade exams and was tipped to pass all her Highers with ease.

But her smile masked a sinister secret; she was being bullied to her death.

The Morrison family is still so devastated by KJ's bullycide that they will not open up to new interviewers. Journalist colleague Iain Maciver - a fellow Lewisman and friend of the Morrison family who lives in the same town of Stornoway - and other newspaper contacts who spoke to the Morrisons and those around them after KJ's death have all helped us to understand KJ's problems and the backlash which her bullycide caused.

Maciver wrote: "Two teenaged Scots girls were found guilty yesterday of their part in a savage gang attack on a schoolmate who later killed herself. A chilling phone call was made warning Katherine Jane Morrison, 16, about yet another plan to beat her up five weeks later. The terrified teenager from Stornoway was found dead the following day.

"She had committed suicide by swallowing a bottle of prescription pills. The nature of the tragedy unfolded to her parents in a tear-stained note found in the bedroom where her body was found. The bright teenager wrote how she was unable to face the girl thugs of the local school, the Nicolson Institute.

"They had made her young life hell. Death was the only and final way out for the clever, university-bound teenager.

"At a Stornoway court, classmates Michelle McBratney, 17, and Lee-Ann Murray ... etc."

The bullies were sentenced to three months' youth custody, the maximum allowable in Scottish law for assault. There were appeals, of course, but they didn't wash. Convicted bully McBratney tried to persuade the court that there had been a reconciliation after she helped lead the gang attack which landed KJ in hospital. But Procurator Fiscal Frank Redman told her straight: "You know KJ can't put her side. There was no reconciliation. It is just a callous lie to save yourself. You took part in a cowardly gang attack."

KJ was a giggly baby, a fun-loving kid who grew into a pop music-blaring teenager, seldom seen without her beautiful grin. Then, suddenly, things became quiet - no radio blasting out, no laughing or singing. It was the silence that made her father, Iain Morrison, realise something was wrong. It was time for KJ to leave for school that Monday morning, 5 February 1996. He couldn't get an answer when he called so he broke down KJ's bedroom door.

It was too late. The two suicide notes which lay at her

side explained why she had taken her own life.

Mum Millie Morrison said: "I can only think of happy times when I think about Katherine Jane, even after going through that terrible morning, the good memories blot out the bad. She was my daughter, she was my friend and she chose to keep her bully problem from me.

"Her hair had become her pride and joy. The night before she died she was warned these girls would shave it off if she passed another exam. Can you imagine what that meant to her?

"We'd never had a clue until the beating what had been going on. We've only found out now that it's too late. Talk to school friends if your own children don't talk to you. But find out if you have the slightest feeling that your child is being bullied."

The attack was savage. It lasted fifteen minutes. At least ten girls were involved and, after they'd run out of steam, a pop bottle was smashed over KJ's head. Twenty-five others stood by and watched or even joined in. Police still can't identify them or the others in the thug gang they say. In fact we have evidence that five girls were initially reported but the teenage code of silence made it impossible to make the attack charge stick with three of them.

Sheriff Ian Cameron said: "I am satisfied from the evidence that others were involved."

Her father said: "There are other girls out there who bear responsibility for my daughter's death. Some of them are hiding, others are laughing. I want them to realise how much anguish they have caused this family. I want to say this to them 'just because you haven't been caught doesn't mean you are innocent. You all pushed Katherine Jane to the precipice, then shoved her over the edge'."

Iain Morrison also slammed his daughter's headmaster at what the locals call "The Nick" school. He claims he'd telephoned Donald Macdonald after the Woolworth attack but that the message had not been passed on to teachers. "I was appalled to learn that nothing had been done," he said after KJ's bullycide. "He ignored the problem."

The Procurator Fiscal also complained that his office hadn't been able to obtain a copy of the Nicolson Institute's policy on bullying after several requests.

Frank Redman said: "We did not receive anything, but we got a copy of the school's anti-bullying policy from the local council's education department months after I had marked the case for prosecution."

The Nick's policy states: "Bullying is any activity designed to cause needless distress to others. This is generally characterised as being provocative, repetitive and one-sided."

So what went wrong? What prevented KJ making it to her New York newspaper office or Wall Street banking house, or to her university? Inspectors were sent to the 1,000-student school by Scottish Education Minister Brian Wilson on a special probe mission under section 66 of the Education (Scotland) Act 1980. They reported "serious weaknesses" in the way its staff handled matters of bullying and called for urgent action.

A report by government inspectors disclosed "a climate of mistrust and suspicion." The report added that teachers' files on bullying were incomplete and did not provide a good record of key steps taken "in many cases." Scottish Office inspectors also found that some Nick teachers were unfamiliar with the anti-bullying policy.

School boss Macdonald was criticised because he was found lacking in childcare policies. Macdonald maintained there was no bullying crisis at his school in spite of revelations by other pupils. He was condemned publicly and two local councillors criticised him for complacency. Education chiefs later disciplined him for responding to that criticism by secretly crawling down a fire-escape after one disciplinary meeting to avoid waiting press.

The row continues but nothing can bring back KJ.

The Deputy General Secretary of the Educational Institute of Scotland, the country's largest teaching union, said: "Bullying has been swept under the carpet for too long. There was a tradition that it was not reported."

Not long after KJ's death, the little town of Keith in Scotland was shattered by the news that three fourteen-year-old girls had attempted bullycide.

It brought back sad memories for Dorothy Morgan, whose ten-year-old son, Keith, was hounded to death by bullies at the Keith Primary School sometime before. Her shy, only son had cowered in the school cloakroom knowing the fate that awaited him for the third time that week at the hands of a bully gang who lay in ambush.

He was caught and thrashed, punched and kicked. He fled across a nearby field in a desperate bid to escape his tormentors. His heart, tightly gripped by fear, gave out and he died, still clutching his school satchel.

Cardiologist Professor Alex Campbell blamed his death on "Persistent persecution, the fear of bullying and the severe physical exercise of being chased by a pack of five, six or seven boys at a time."

One of Keith's victimisers (unnamed at the Fatal Accident Inquiry) said: "We did it because he was the weakest in our class and he wasn't a pal of ours."

Goldsmith's College, London discovered after six years of extensive studies that bullying decreases as boys get older but increases as girls do. Kidscape says that girl-on-girl bullying leapt by 50% in just two years and that there's been a tenfold increase in helpline calls about bullying over the last decade.

Anne Campbell, a senior lecturer in psychology at Durham University, has studied girl bullies in both the UK and the USA. She said: "By behaving aggressively, girl gangs feel they are gaining equality with men, gaining respect in their peer group."

Perversely, equality is taken by some as the right to emulate the worst in their peers or former persecutors.

Bright and gentle as she was, KJ Morrison wouldn't have put it in quite those terms as she was being battered over the head with a bottle.

The Welsh paradox

During research on this book, we found the bullycide syndrome running like a plague through the UK. But in Wales we could discover only two cases. And they were borderline bullycides. Coroners and police were never convinced that these deaths were a direct result of schoolyard intimidation.

Just why bullying rates of children in Wales are lower than in the rest of the British Isles has intrigued us. Theories range from the high number of rural areas with their strong traditional rural ties and smaller schools, to higher rates of church and chapel attendance, and even the bonding effect of the Welsh language.

Apart from the industrial belt of Newport/Cardiff/Swansea along the M4 motorway, most of the population of 2.8 million live in rural areas dominated and united by the close-knit farming community. Families in these villages grow up together, share common interests, problems, and hardships; they also work and harvest together.

Such communities are extended families and extensive social networking makes bullying easier to identify and tackle at an early stage.

Where communities, particularly in North, Mid and West Wales, are Welsh speaking, families easily trace ancestors back four centuries or more. It can take decades - even generations - for "new" families to be accepted.

According to Dr Lance Workman, a psychologist at the University of Glamorgan, this community bond, which involves the bulk of the Welsh population, is the caring tradition which has kept Wales a nation within a nation.

He said: "In rural areas like the South Wales valleys you will find several generations of families living in the same communities - sometimes even in the same street - and supporting each other, aware of every single thing going on around them. Sensitive to every hint of danger among the kids. They support one another and they talk to each other day by day.

"If there is a problem it's not bottled up. It's out in the open, free for family debate. Fathers know each other through working, singing or playing together. If there is a bullying problem it will be spotted, talked about and sorted. In many cases the first approach will be by the women with the men left in reserve as the big guns."

Half a million people live in the South Wales valleys and, despite urban development, folks in areas like the Rhondda are still closely tied. Migration rates are low, even among young people and, in spite of rising unemployment, commuting is rare. Smaller school sizes are also thought to be a factor in the lower bullying rates and near-absence of bullycide.

Many of the primary and some secondary schools in rural areas are dramatically smaller than the UK national average, with some primaries having fewer than twenty pupils. Some of these schools, particularly those with fewer than ten children, have been closed. But several still remain scattered around the country.

Education historian Peter Williams says smaller schools make bullying easier to spot and bullycide a near-impossibility. "When there are only a few pupils in the school the bullying would soon become apparent and more easily dealt with. All children perform better in these schools and become more confident by being part of a close team."

Another reason for this Welsh anomaly of minimal bullying rates is that many areas of Welsh life is still structured around a sense of uniqueness, of belonging to a country and culture set apart. Many clubs and some libraries are run by local committees. Wales has its own Welsh language radio and TV.

Religion too might play a part. Some communities are still dominated by the Chapel minister and the structure surrounding the local ministry.

"Although attendances have declined, in many communities there's still a strong tradition where the minister will take a lead in local issues and offer advice to local people. A bully is likely to be pointed out and chastised during service with the whole community looking on.

"The head of the local school, the minister, and the GP are a powerful trinity to combat social issues like bullying. That approach isn't available in more populous urban areas."

There is some belief that the growing use of the ancient Welsh language among young people forms a bond of belonging. In some parts of North Wales 94% of children aged 3-15 are members of this exclusive language club. Others believe that language could, in some situations, give rise to situations where bullying could thrive. Where Welsh speakers are in the majority or minority, it's argued, there will always be groups of children different from the others and, therefore, targets for the bullies.

However, the valleys may not be as tranquil as they appear. Prompted by Sir Ronald Waterhouse's report into child abuse in children's homes in north Wales, the National Assembly in Cardiff is in the process of appointing an independent Children's Commissioner to report on children's services in the principality. During 1999, 22,000 Welsh children - almost one in ten - called ChildLine, many to report bullying. And a survey by the NSPCC published on UN Children's Rights Day (20 November 2000) suggests that the reason for official figures being so low is silence. Forty-three percent of 18-24-year-olds from across the UK said they had experienced bullying at some time during their childhood.

Suicide has always been regarded as a "mental health problem" with the inference that the person had something (always unspecified) wrong with them. The coroner's verdict of 'balance of the mind disturbed' tends to foster rather than allay this perception. However, "balance of the mind disturbed" is a euphemism for impaired objectivity, a symptom of psychiatric injury, not a confirmation of mental illness.

Taboos relating to bullying and bullycide are compounded by society's "blame the victim" mentality. If a person is unable to comprehend or deal with another's suffering it can be easier to conclude that the sufferer must somehow be responsible for their distressed state.

If a person commits suicide, they're regarded as having had "a mental health problem". Or perhaps there was a "problem in the family". Whilst some (but not all) bullycides have "problems" within the family, they are no more than the kinds of problems faced by most families. Parental separation in the UK is now at an all-time high with more than one family in four affected.

The pool of bullied children is so vast that almost every circumstance will occur. Bullies are adept at promoting any opinion or prejudice which diverts attention away from themselves and their behaviour.

The psychiatric injury caused by bullying, as with bullying itself, reveals itself through a pattern of events, rather than through any one symptom or incident. The analogy with a jigsaw puzzle is apt, and although with practice one can identify single pieces of the puzzle, it's not until pieces are joined together that the full picture emerges.

The symptoms of psychiatric injury are sometimes misdiagnosed, and frequently diagnosed in isolation. When taken individually and out of context the cause becomes obscured. Western medicine tends to focus on prescribing pills to mask the effects of illness and injury rather than identifying and dealing with the cause.

Psychiatric injury is an injury, so when the *cause* is identified and dealt with, the injury starts to heal.

However, targets of bullying excel at coping with and masking the symptoms of psychiatric injury. Children bear the suffering and pain in silence and isolation. Often, when they do speak out, the responsible adults aren't listening or don't want to listen. Even when the cries are heard, many adults don't know how to handle bullying, find authorities difficult and sometimes obstructive, and can find no official channels or agencies with responsibility or clout. Better recognition of the injury to health caused by bullying (and its relatives, harassment, victimisation and abuse) could result in doctors and mental health professionals playing a more prominent role in preventing bullycide.

At present there is no legal remedy that can be used specifically to deal with bullying. The laws of assault and harassment have been used and are often recommended but fashioning a crime to fit laws designed for other purposes is unsatisfactory. Forcing a target to commit bullycide sits between manslaughter and murder and while it may not have been intentional to kill, the *pattern* of behaviour reveals premeditation, planning, execution, and evasion of accountability over a long period of time, often years. With bullying it's the patterns that reveal intent.

Bullied children, as with bullied adults, are of the unshakeable opinion that "I can handle it". However, targets of bullying rarely realise they are dealing with violent sociopathic behaviour that is beyond even the ability of mature professional adults to deal with. Targets are encouraged in their belief that they can handle it, being strongly dissuaded from "telling" or "grassing" for fear of consequential violence. Society's stereotypes of "wimp" also come into play, with the view that those who can't stand up for themselves must be defective. Sometimes the issue is clouded with obfuscations about "blame".

However, bullying is not about blame but about accountability.

Conscious of the legal liability from any admission of responsibility, however small, the instinct of most schools and LEAs is to deny everything. "We've investigated and found no evidence" or "The children responsible have been talked to and the matter is resolved". Bullying is rarely resolved. It is a serial offence.

The world was stunned when Thomas Hamilton walked into the school in Dunblane in March 1996 and shot dead sixteen children and a teacher. Words could not express the magnitude and horror of such a senseless act.

Tragedies with multiple deaths are guaranteed front-page headlines whilst single deaths often do not attract attention, nor do they generate the same sense of shock. Our research reveals that each year in the UK *at least* sixteen children commit bullycide and around eighty children attempt bullycide. The number of children who think about bullycide is unknown.

Bullycide claims a Dunblane of children every year. Between the school massacre which shocked the world and the completion of this book, bullies have secretly, out of the headlines, been responsible for much more than a Dunblane-scale slaughter of innocent lives.

Chapter 9

Is it news?

"The school didn't give a tuppenny toss"
A parent who lost his daughter to bullycide.

Bullycide: death at Playtime is the result of Neil Marr's investigative reporting of thirty-five years and Tim Field's decade of research and personal experience. The authors are surprised that no one has investigated bullycide before. Although no official figures for bullycide exist, our researches have convinced us that an annual toll of sixteen is a conservative estimate.

Drawing on data collected from agencies including coroners, their assistants, hospitals, ambulance controllers, social workers, doctors, court journalists, academics, police and child-care charities we have compiled a case load which paints a terrifying picture. What is chilling is their similarity.

A coroner's clerk will tell the authors that a verdict of accidental death has been returned on a thirteen-year-old drowning victim. Privately, the local police reveal to us that there has been a history of bullying complaints, a school or education authority unofficially confirms this, a family doctor tells us of fading bruises to the jaw which couldn't have been caused by walking into an open door, a social worker speaks to us off the record of her unrecorded interviews with the victim, and a child contemporary admits the playground hell his friend had suffered. A thug says 'We pulled his plonker.' Mum says school was a nightmare for her child.

No official agency is in place to collate this information. Newspapers no longer cover coroners' courts as a matter of course so that few unusual deaths command a public lobby for thorough investigation, reporting and exposure.

We have concentrated on what can be backed up with a minimum bullycide toll of five to seven hundred lives lost since Steven Shepherd.

In 1988 seven cases of bullycide became high-profile stories in the national press. For every bullycide reported in the papers, we estimate that as many as three others were not.

We asked national newspaper news editors, regional newspaper editors and major freelance press agencies what percentage of bullycides hit the headlines. The answer? No more than one in four.

James Grylls, former News Editor of the Scottish Daily Mail and now their education correspondent, explained: "Many years ago, when coroners' officers still trusted the press, we were told about inquests (we call them Fatal Accident Inquiries in Scotland) which were likely to be of major media interest. So we covered them. Now there isn't the same cooperation between officialdom and the press.

"Long ago when reporters were paid a pittance, we could afford to take pot luck and cover everything. But now they're paid proper wages and we have to be selective as to what they cover. A lot of what you call bullycide slips through our fingers, simply because we weren't aware that it was going to make an FAI newsworthy enough to justify a reporter's expensive time.

"What you tend to see in the national press is the result of an inquest being staffed because we have prior knowledge that bullying may have been involved. We'd had a very rare tip-off. Maybe one in four cases."

Even local freelance reporters can no longer speculate valuable time covering a coroner's court which might produce no publishable results. Chasing a Spice Girl and her new boyfriend pays the bills, dozing in a dreary courtroom might leave you with nothing but a headache, a blank notepad and an empty pocket.

"So the result is," said James, "that a lot goes unreported. Even when it is, we're finding on news desks these days that bullycide is becoming so common it's almost like a car crash or a domestic murder ... it's just not newsy enough. We're more likely to pick on the angle that the kid who killed himself had lost his pet dog than that he had been bullied at school. The bully issue is fogged or dropped. Sad. But there it is. I have spiked stories - thrown them away - when the bully angle isn't dramatic enough, even though it seems only we in the media know it's become an epidemic. You have to have a heavy-duty bully suicide to make it worth a paragraph or two otherwise the papers would be crammed with little else.

"Don't think that makes me a hard guy. I was bullied at school because I was little. I know how dangerous it can be. Most reporters are frustrated writers, creative types, not hard-bitten, cynical bastards, like we're portrayed. Most of us went through bullying at school. We look out for and identify with the problem.

"I've covered these stories myself in Scotland, England and Ireland and I really feel for the kids. But as a news editor I had to decide what was news and what wasn't. Sometimes what you call bullycide just wasn't newsworthy enough. Yes, multiply the number of cases reported in last year's national press by three and you've got just about the bullycide stories even submitted. There are many, many more simply missed by the reporters in the field or covered up in one way or another."

Mercury Press in Liverpool, one of Britain's biggest and most prestigious news agencies, employs ten journalists to cover news on the ground. Editor Chris Johnson told us that, because of work pressure, less than 40% of all inquests in the city are covered by press. In other towns in his area like Birkenhead, Southport, Formby, Ormskirk, even fewer. The agency does make a policy of sitting in on enquiries into the deaths of children - perhaps 80% are covered in the city if reporters are free.

Of the cases covered, 20% are worth writing up for submission to newspapers. Of those, 20% make a few lines in the papers.

Chris told us: "Whereas we would once be given a hint by a coroner's officer that a case was worth looking at because of the bullying angle, for instance, we no longer get that cooperation. Also, where we know there is bullying involved in a child's death through solicitors, police or general contacts and we put a man into court, nothing comes out. The bullying is swept under the carpet and never mentioned. Other reasons are given for the death of a young child. Coroners are reluctant to record verdicts of suicide, they much prefer misadventure or accidental death. It helps ease the heartache of the parents, but it also lets the bullies off the hook.

"Also, there are very few one-man freelancers now, the grass roots guys who used to cover everything and find stories like this in the remotest corners."

Raymonds of Derby freelance press agency said: "We've had some high profile deaths put down to bullying in our area, but they in no way represent the full picture. Just the tip of an iceberg. We have two coroners' courts in Leicester, for instance, one will give us details so that we can prepare coverage. The other sends us a fax the day before court with nothing more than name, address, age. We can't cover everything. It's only viable if there's a chance of something so interesting it will cover the reporter's expensive time.

"I would say that your figure of a minimum sixteen bullycides a year is very conservative."

David Wooding, News Editor of the Sunday People, told us: "Coroners' courts are held during the week and reported in daily newspapers, not Sundays. This kind of situation needs in-depth Sunday paper coverage. So it goes unreported.

"We used to pick up on the big cases - the high profile stuff - for features. That kind of story lends itself to Sunday reading. But there's more on our plate now. I don't remember having to consider the value of what you call a bullycide story. We just don't get them through to the desk any more. It suggests the syndrome is so commonplace to newsmen that it is no longer automatically considered newsworthy. Pity nobody in authority has realised that."

Dave Calderbank is now head of the Barnes News Agency in Wigan, founded by the late Jeff Barnes who broke the Steven Shepherd story in 1967.

There used to be two press agencies in Wigan representing the national press, radio and television. The town was covered by an active weekly newspaper, The Wigan Observer, and four evening newspapers, the Liverpool Echo, the Lancashire Evening Post and Chronicle, the Manchester Evening News and the Bolton Evening News.

Inquest courts were stiff with journalists and, when the workload became too heavy and cases were heard in different courtrooms, reporters would clandestinely share the courtrooms and swap notes later. The local coroners' officer, DS Green, got a visit from a team of journalists every morning before nine and he would freely give all the details (much off the record) he had of the previous 24 hours' sudden or suspicious deaths in his area. That was part of his job. Death never went unnoticed or unreported.

Things have changed, according to Dave. "These days, cooperation with the press has reached an all-time low with the authorities. We are just not kept informed. The economics of the situation are that I can't afford to send my operatives to an inquest just on the off-chance that they might be able to cover their wages. We probably cover half our local inquests these days. In the rural areas, the percentage is much lower.

"When there's a child death, especially where suicide might be suggested, of course we follow it through. I can remember at least two cases where we had been told only unofficially by police contacts, parents, solicitors, teachers or whoever that bullying had driven a child to take his own life and, when we attended the inquest, that side of things wasn't even mentioned in court. Coroners are reluctant to put an accused child on the stand; if they do, child protection officers and the rest become involved. Bullying is swept under the carpet when it reaches this lethal peak. It's too hot a potato.

"You're right. Only seven bullycides made the national press last year. It seemed in vogue, if you like, and journalists were keeping a keen eye open for it. But even so, from experience, I would suggest that probably three times that many were missed. The kids would go down in the records as having taken their own lives through misadventure or accident without bullying ever being brought into the open. Many other cases are never even monitored by the press because no one had given us a clue that something dire was afoot in a particular death. We just can't cover everything any more.

"You say your bottom line figure is sixteen a year. I feel it should be higher. Much higher. I feel, and there's some expert support opinion, that it might be as high as thirty."

The sweep-it-under-the-carpet approach

Peanut's Charlie Brown once asked in his bedtime prayers: "why me?" A voice replied in the darkness: "Nothing personal. Your name just happened to come up."

Almost in defence of the bully, bluff pundits might cite dysfunctional families, clinical depression, poverty, physical difference, timidity and a whole host of contributory factors. Sometimes there is some evidence of this in cases we have investigated. More often there is not. A majority of bullycides come from warm, two-parent homes or, at least, settled situations ... their names just happened to come up.

One child-care worker told us: "People can live with all these awkward hitches and still have self-esteem and happy lives. It's random victimisation. Bullies can target anyone. We can't go on making excuses about broken marriages and T-shirts with no designer labels and sticky-out ears to explain away bullycide."

Whilst all UK schools are now legally obliged to have an anti-bullying policy in place, it's only as effective as the commitment behind it. Bullycide cases show that sometimes the will is wilfully absent.

One which does work is ambiguously called the Lame Duck scheme. It was described to us by junior school deputy head teacher Carol Close who has thirty years' experience dealing with children in a tough Northern working town. Carol now teaches in a new greenfield school five minutes' car drive from where Steven Shepherd set off on his last walk.

She said: "It's simple. The bully wants attention and to feel important. So he belittles the weaker child. We just redirect him. We team him up with his victim and make him the protector. He still can command importance, but for a much better reason. He becomes a hero instead of a villain. The original title, Lame Duck, was about children in need of help ... you know when a migrating duck falls from the sky, two others fly down to help him? We found the bully himself could be a lame duck and tried to provide a crutch for him too. Here, we've renamed the scheme Buddy Grouping. And it has worked in every case.

"Mind you, you must know the children you team up. You must know what's behind the bullying. Sometimes children just perceive themselves as a victim which is just as serious as if they actually are. If a child thinks he's being bullied, he is.

"A lot of bullies have, in fact, been bullied. This is a way of pointing their resulting aggression in a positive direction. I believe in my area things are being brought out into the open more. We even had an acting group with us one time, who brought in the children and had them act through bullying scenes. Here it isn't the dark secret it might once have been. We have now got a climate where we feel children don't suffer in silence.

"Within our school we have teachers who will admit to having been bullied as children. We're aware and approachable as people who've been there, done that.

"Every teacher in the school is trained in Circle Time which is running a kind of open forum where any child can say anything openly and without fear of criticism or retribution. We can tease out these issues. When I say 'tease' I mean winkle, encourage, get the children to speak their own minds because of well thought out, gentle questioning by the teacher. Facing the problem is half way to solving it."

One problem, Carol admits, is that schools are insular. Although she meets colleagues from other schools in her immediate area, she rarely learns what is being done to combat bullying in other parts of the country.

"We don't seem to cross borders," she says. "The actors from London I spoke about gave us anecdotal information. But there are no official national figures to study. All I can say with certainty is this: we have a small school of just 240 children but we have never had to exclude a child because of bullying. The day I say it's solved, though, is the day I'll start having problems and question myself. You've always got to be aware that even if it isn't obvious, bullying is still lying there under the surface and it could rear. You've got to be ready to solve it at any time. If a school says it has no bullying, that's where you've got the problem."

Every other child

One child in two becomes a victim of school bullying, according to a report to the British Psychological Society by education psychologist Sonia Sharp. Her study involved 700 children between the ages of thirteen and sixteen in Sheffield. On its conclusion, she warned of playground taunting which ends in tragedy. During her research in the Sheffield area, she discovered that thirteen youngsters had died or been seriously injured because of bullying in a two-year period. She found that 43% of children interviewed had been physically attacked and injured, called vicious names, had possessions wrecked, had been subjected to evil rumours, or had been intimidated into handing over protection money.

Victims reacted mainly by playing truant, becoming ill or deliberately inflicting self-harm to avoid the fearsome threat of bullying. Twenty-seven percent of bullies, Sharp found, had been bully victims themselves before they chose to go on the attack.

Boys found name-calling the most distressing form of bullying whereas girls were more afraid of physical abuse.

Her research prompted a DfEE move to establish guidelines for schools which involve identifying persistent bullies and handing out punishments. In this book you will find many experts who insist that punishment is not an answer.

A survey by the Children's Society in 1999 revealed that each year in the UK at least 100,000 children run away from home or care for at least one night. Almost a quarter of those questioned cited bullying at school and parental pressure as primary reasons.

The Suzy Lamplugh Trust, a pioneer in personal safety, is concerned about bullying at school as well as suicides of young people. Their helpline *Get connected* provides advice and referral to young people who need help with any issue of personal safety. "Calls on this helpline demonstrate the vital need to take this problem very seriously", reports Diana Lamplugh OBE.

The University of Strathclyde runs a teacher training centre on its campus in Glasgow. They have two separate courses for 700 potential teachers and each has a professional studies module to make teachers aware of the bullying problem.

Donald Christie, senior lecturer in Professional Studies at the college, does not believe punishment or exclusion helps. He said: "Exclusion can't solve the problem. It isn't fair on the bully that he should miss out on education. Of course the victim should never be blamed but we should look at the real reasons why someone becomes a bully: are they insecure about themselves and feel that if they become a bully then no one will bully them, are there problems at home? We explore both sides of the divide, both the pro-social and anti-social behaviour.

"The forms of bullying are complex, we try to emphasise that it must not be trivialised by saying that every piece of unpleasantness that takes place between children is a form of bullying because that doesn't capture the essential elements of it. What's important is the elements which deal with repetition and an imbalance of power. The bully is perceived a real power and the victim powerless in the relationship. When they go into the playground, one day it might not happen. But it could. It's the repetition that matters."

Bobby McKay, a training and outreach officer for ChildLine in Scotland, responded: "It is all about empowering young people to take a more active part, to do things for themselves. Pupils will define how issues will be tackled."

University graduate Jan Kemal who wrote his thesis on bullying and featured the people mentioned above, points out that, because some bullying takes place outside school premises, teachers too often pass the buck to the police, who often pass it back again. "In the end," he found during his study, "no one gets involved because of the muddling of boundaries."

One headmaster Kemal spoke to told him, in spite of the recent and nearby tragedy of a high-profile bullycide: "I don't know everything that goes on in my school. I'd be very surprised if a sustained campaign was being waged here. Most adolescents would get quickly bored."

It's surprising that some of those entrusted with the welfare of children have so little insight or interest in patterns of behaviour which are so destructive.

Bullying is a compulsive behaviour. Whilst bullies get bored with school and with authority, they don't get bored with the gratification they derive from exercising power, control, domination and subjugation. For the inadequate individual with low self-esteem and a propensity for aggression, these are highly addictive.

Government packs giving anti-bullying advice are regularly sent out to schools. One child-care worker told Kemal: "There's hardly ever time to discuss it. Most teachers don't even get around to reading the material. Teachers even now - even after the suicides - still don't see bullying as a potentially lethal problem. They refuse to take the issue on board. They're more concerned about scoring in exam results. I believe it's fair comment to say teachers don't have a clue as to what to do. Punishing a bully isn't any help. Punishment isn't the way to tackle this syndrome."

Chapter 10

A call away

*We have had to deal with about 100 child
suicides because of bullying in the 15 years
Kidscape has been running."*
Michele Elliott, founder of Kidscape

Kidscape is a nationwide child protection charity founded
in Britain in 1984 by Michele Elliott. Michele started her
organisation after having worked for several years as a
psychologist with children and families.

"I got fed up picking up the pieces of all this abuse and
bullying", recalls Michele. "I thought there must be a better
way and that had to be prevention. That had to be getting
some sort of message to kids and teachers and parents
that this didn't have to go on. All the other major charities
are in place to pick up the pieces after events have
happened. We do prevention work.

"The higher figure of eighty or more children committing
suicide each year because of bullying might be right. We
do not have a complete picture of what happens to
children because it is often covered up. In fact the idea
that so many children would attempt or succeed at suicide
because of bullying seems so horrifying that many people
would not want to believe it. Even more disturbing are the
lengths that some education authorities will go to to
distance themselves and the bullies from the suicide of the
child.

"But it all seems so sensational that people wouldn't
believe it. It's just too much to take on board. And nobody
can prove it. You have a verdict, perhaps, saying this is a
suicide. But sometimes when everyone knows what led up

to the suicide, the school authorities come screaming to the defence of the children who are named in the note saying 'this could be malicious. The deceased child was having other problems anyway'. Personally, I have never found this to be the case. The constant bullying is usually the key to the torment that led the child to take his own life.

"It's very, very hurtful to the parents to hear that their child has committed suicide and it was his or her own fault when you know yourselves that somebody else has driven them over the top. We know that often bullying is the whole cause.

"We even have a parents' helpline specifically because of this and we hear so often that parents have taken their children out of the school they were in, put them in another school situation or educated them at home, and the kids are fine. In other words they were removed from an untenable situation. It wasn't their kids who were at fault but the prevailing bully situation. It's the bully who's the problem - not the victim. Also it's the wider school situation which allows that bullying to go on unchecked. And they're doing the bully no favours either.

"I've spoken to many parents who've suffered a suicide after bullying in their family. But coroners and others are reluctant to lay more guilt on the children who were bullying the victims, perhaps because they don't want them to have a life-long trauma, perhaps because they feel they can't prove it. I don't know if that is the right or the wrong approach. I do know that there is a great deal of anger from the parents of children who have taken their lives because of intimidation at school. It's bad enough a child has died without the shock of finding out, after the fact, that bullying had been going on for months and maybe years. Coroners tend to be kind, compassionate people. They don't want parents to feel any more guilt."

In 1985/86 Kidscape undertook the first ever survey on school bullying in the UK including the input of 4,000

children and found that it was a "tremendous problem."
Just over two-thirds of children interviewed complained
that they had been bullied.

"When we released our findings," said Michele, "there
was a hue and cry saying 'this is ridiculous. There is not a
problem with bullying. You are sensationalising and
looking for an issue.' A spokesman for the National Union
of Teachers said that on a BBC news programme. We
found that schools didn't take bullying seriously at all then.

"But they are taking it more seriously since we started
putting out books and pamphlets and started schools
programmes against bullying. We found back in the
eighties that schools had become interested in doing
something but they didn't know what to do. So we started
training programmes with the teachers. Then, when there
was media interest, we were able to point them to schools
which had good anti-bullying practices.

"Good anti-bullying practice is when a child comes into a
school and the first thing he is told is that this is a school
which will not tolerate bullying at all, assemblies are held,
contracts are drawn up which children and parents sign,
boxes are put on the walls so that children can make all
kinds of suggestions anonymously - they're called bully
boxes. Schools like that which go on to have anti-bullying
themes through the year such as poster contests,
kindness weeks and drama productions are making sure
the message is reinforced."

Michele told us: 'We started ZAP assertiveness courses
for children who suffer bullying so we do have a database
of names of real people and details of their cases. Of
course, in the cases of children committing suicide, there
is nothing more for the parents to lose by speaking to us
and telling us the names of their children. We have had to
deal with about 100 child suicides because of bullying. We
met with the parents. The children had already died by the
time we were approached.

"Parents' response to a suicide after bullying is normally one of intense anger. A woman, Ruth, rang me about her fourteen-year-old daughter, Lucy. Everything had been fine until a year ago last January. Then one of the girls in the school class decided she could destroy Lucy and turned all the girls against her. Ruth tried desperately to talk to the daughter about what was going on but she said it was OK, she could handle it, as these kids quite often do. Mother rang about four weeks after her daughter had died. Hadn't rung us before. She felt very badly that she had no idea her daughter would go to these lengths.

"One of the girls had rung Lucy the night she took her life and said 'you will die. We have decided that you will die.' When the other girls had said they were going to kill her, she took a massive overdose and was found the next morning with a note she had left. Her brother broke his hand, hitting the wall in anger and frustration.

"The mother had gone to the school a week before this and talked to the school nurse and said 'my daughter's in trouble, we need some help.' She thought the school had been wholly unresponsive.

"I was in contact with her, as I am with many of these parents, on and off for four, five or six months.

"The adults want to be back in touch with us. They want to have some kind of continuity in help. They want to have a named person that they can talk to.

"I've thought about whether the problem is growing or whether we're just becoming more aware of it. Kidscape did the first ever retrospective survey of 1,000 adults who had been bullied as children. The adults in that survey - published by Kidscape in the book *Bully Free* in 1999 - included respondents, some as old as 82 years with very, very bad memories of bullying. The difference we find in bullying today, I think, is that it does appear to have become more serious, more violent and nasty and insidious. We did find in the survey, which included an extensive five-page questionnaire that people voluntarily filled out, that older women were not reporting the kind of physical violence against them that the younger women were reporting. As the women became younger in the survey we noticed a definite trend towards broken bones and weapons being used. Nasty violence which we had previously associated only with boys.

"Now, on our helpline, we hear about incredible pain and sadness. Many of the parents that we talk to had themselves been bullied in childhood. They're horrified that it's happened to their own children. I've found amongst the people who have been bullied a strong - and I don't mean strong in terms of physical strength and I also have nothing to base this on statistically - link between kids who come from sensitive, gentle, articulate, caring families where even 'teasing' is not a way of life. They are so vulnerable to what might well roll off someone else's back that, because of this sensitivity, they react.

"Quite often the victims are blamed but I thoroughly blame the bullies and I thoroughly blame the people who don't stop the bullies. There's nothing the matter with those sensitive kids being that kind, indeed many of them grow up to be some of our finest citizens who have a lot to contribute."

Many years after Michele started Kidscape, one of her sons was, himself, bullied. "He told us straight away," said Michele, "and I called up the other boy's mother and said we should have a meeting with us all - the boys too - at the school. And she came. We sorted it.

"In the cases we deal with at Kidscape where children are either much older or from a different school, there is very little chance of creating empathy by bringing them together, nor is it fair to the victim. Imagine, some of these bullies have attacked or assaulted their victims. This must be taken extremely seriously and, in some cases, the police need to be involved. The idea that a) you don't blame anyone and

b) you bring those completely different people together, feeling that somehow there is justice and that is going to help the situation is incredibly naive.

"We have been keeping records since about 1990 and we have counselled on average about 15-17,000 children, parents and many school teachers a year. It's impossible to say how many children we have saved from suicide. We can only count the casualties. We have saved children, that's certain. For instance, one mother phoned Kidscape and subsequently sent a letter. She'd found pills and a suicide note from her daughter who had then read a Kidscape article and changed her mind.

"Given the fact that we have schools programmes that have reached about three million children and given the fact that we offer our helpline and send out three or four hundred free leaflets a week to kids and parents on bullying and how to prevent it, we have to be saving sixty, seventy, maybe even a hundred kids from bullycide. The trouble is, how do you measure what didn't happen?

"I think that anyone who works in this field would say that your bottom line of sixteen suicides a year is conservative. The trouble is that if we publish greater, and probably more realistic figures, people will think you're trying to grab headlines.

"Suicide after bullying does exist, it must be seen to exist, and it must be ended."

Even when a bullycide attempt is unsuccessful, lives can be wrecked. Kidscape's *Long-term Effects of Bullying* study published in *Bully Free* in 1999 reads:

"Forty-six percent of the respondents (bully victims involved in the survey) had contemplated suicide. Twenty percent attempted suicide, some more than once. Compared to the non-bullied group, this is an incredibly high rate. A mere 0.07% of the non-bullied had contemplated suicide and 0.03% had attempted it."

With Kidscape's permission we quote widely from the

report which Gaby Shenton co-authored with Michele Elliott. *Long-term Effects of Bullying* involved the participation of over a thousand adults who had been bullied during their schooldays. The report states:

Kidscape has conducted the first ever retrospective survey of adults to discover if bullying at school affects people in later life. The survey, funded by the National Lottery, shows that being badly bullied as a child has a dramatic, negative, knock-on effect throughout life.

The extensive survey of over 1,000 adults shows that bullying affects not only your self-esteem as an adult but your ability to make friends, succeed in education and in work and social relationships.

Most received no help at the time to stop the bullying and telling either made matters worse or had no effect.

Of the respondents who were bullied, the overwhelming majority left school at or before the age of sixteen, many citing bullying as the reason they left.

A 37-year-old woman wrote: "I knew I would die at the hands of the bullies or by my own hand. I left school as soon as I could, aged sixteen, although I was bright, I left with no qualifications and ended up in a series of dead-end jobs."

Forty percent of the bullied respondents said that the bullying had affected their plans for further education.

For the overwhelming majority, bullying started between the ages of seven and thirteen. The highest peaks seemed to correspond with the ages of children entering secondary school, ages of eleven or twelve. A significant minority related bullying starting at a very young age of five or six, as soon as they entered primary school.

Most adults thought they were bullied as children because they were:

- shy, didn't answer back
- too short or too tall
- too good or bad looking

- not interested in or bad at sports
- too sensitive or cried easily
- parents divorced, deceased, or in prison
- too intelligent or too stupid
- of a minority race or religion
- skinny or fat
- talented in music, art or poetry
- too poor or too rich
- had a posh or a lower-class accent
- wore the wrong type of clothes

On average the bullying went on for between two and six years. Several respondents were bullied throughout their entire school careers (for nine to eleven years).

About 18% of respondents were bullied by gangs, 59% were bullied by more than one person. The respondents felt powerless.

Two percent said they'd been bullied by teachers. One 70-year-old woman said that her maths teacher bullied her so badly that she only has to see a column of numbers to break into a cold sweat.

Among males, 61% were bullied by children of the same sex, 34% by both sexes and only a small number by members of the opposite sex. Seventy-five percent were physically bullied, 85% were verbally bullied, 30% of males were excluded or ostracised. Many suffered all three forms of intimidation.

The types of bullying reported were nauseating to read and listen to: broken bones, internal injuries, scarring, operations to remove damaged testicles and kidneys, stabbings, being blinded in one eye, severe beatings, being strung up upside down in toilets and almost drowning, being thrown from cliffs, pushed into water or in front of oncoming traffic, having objects inserted into various orifices, and more.

Sixty-two percent of female respondents were physically bullied, 93% were bullied verbally and 60% were excluded or ostracised. Examining the figures more closely, Kidscape finds that the reported patterns of bullying by girls appear to have changed over the past five to fifteen years.

Women between the ages of thirty and fifty who were reporting bullying that had taken place twenty years or more in the past describe physical attacks as hair-pulling and being tripped over and pushed as the most common form of attack. Bruises, broken bones, black eyes, stabbing were not mentioned.

Many women between the ages of eighteen and thirty reported horrendous bullying in the last five to fifteen years. This included severe physical attacks, stabbings, being kicked in the head, stoned, slapped, having bones broken and other injuries requiring hospitalisation.

What this survey highlights is that the increase in violence by girls seems to have been happening over the past five to fifteen years.

Based on the data of kinds of bullying in the past, the key factors seem to be:

- there has been a changing pattern of physical bullying by girls since the mid-1980s
- severe physical bullying by girls was rare before this time
- verbal bullying by girls was and still seems to be the most common form of girl-on-girl intimidation
- boys are still more likely to be violently physically bullied in spite of changing patterns

Men and women report a wide variety of feelings about how school bullying has affected their subsequent lives. Women feel they cannot trust people and are afraid of new situations. They also feel they are easily victimised and are afraid to succeed. Men report similar feelings but are more likely than women to feel uncommunicative, shy and be loners.

When the adults who were bullied as children are compared to those who were not bullied, the differences are dramatic. Adults who were not bullied are unafraid of new situations and do not become uncommunicative or loners. They feel now they are better people than when they left school.

Difficulty in making friends was one of the outcomes of bullying. Nearly three-quarters (73%) of victims reported problems in comparison with only 11% of the non-bullied.

The Kidscape report concludes: "This is the first time adults have been questioned about their experiences of being bullied as children and how this might have affected their lives. The oldest respondent was 81 but, as with the rest, time had not dimmed the memories.

"Contrary to popular opinion, being bullied at school does not help children to cope better with adult life. In fact it has the opposite effect. Adults who were bullied as children tend to have problems with self-esteem, feelings of anger and bitterness, suicidal thoughts and attempts, and difficulty relating to people.

"The lessons for us today are clear: if we allow bullying to go on, we are condemning another generation.

"It should be borne in mind that the results of the survey reveal only the tip of the iceberg. Many have suffered worse treatment than those who took part ... they have succeeded in their suicide attempts."

Just in case anyone should still believe the myth that bullies are tough and successful, former victims who know of the fate of their tormentors report that the bullies have led lives full of failure and lacking in fulfilment, often continuing to damage the lives of those with whom they come into contact.

ChildLine

ChildLine was set up fourteen years ago as a phone counselling service for children in distress. Its number has been found in diaries and scribbled on scraps of notepaper by several children who took their own lives. Eight hundred volunteers handle over 3,000 calls a day in centres all over the UK. Thousands more children try to make contact but can't because the lines are so permanently busy.

A special study, entitled *"Why Me?"* by ChildLine researchers Mary MacLeod and Sally Morris focused on one of their young clients' major menaces ... bullying. The message in their report is clear: "Bullying's a massive schoolyard problem and it does kill."

So great is the problem highlighted by their in-depth research that senior ChildLine official Natasha Finlayson did not raise an eyebrow when we gave her our bottom-line figure of sixteen bullycides a year in the UK.

"Very probable that it's more than that," she said.

In a ten-year period, ChildLine counselled more than 60,000 children with bullying problems. They even set up a special experimental Bullying Line for a seven-month period. Five thousand children called in to talk out their fears - almost five times more girls than boys. Only one in a hundred calls came from a self-confessed bully. Whilst the line was in operation there was at least one bullycide who'd underlined the helpline's number in her diary. All calls are treated anonymously so no one knows if the girl ever did make contact before taking her life.

The case echoed the words of many youngsters ChildLine has talked to: "I don't think I can go on any more." "I wish I could go to sleep and never wake up." "I would like to end it all. I can't take any more of this. Suicide would be better than going to school again."

In a research sample of 1,500 child callers to the Bullying Line, more than sixty had contemplated or attempted bullycide. Seven hundred parents also picked up the phone, most of whom had made serious but unsuccessful attempts to get schools to end their children's torment. In fact the study found that a great deal of bullying takes place inside the classroom. Secondary school children describe it as the one place they are most likely to be bullied, suggesting a disquieting and unacceptable level of teacher tolerance or lack of training and support.

The report says of its young callers: "They bitterly complained about adults who advised them to ignore bullying and it would stop. They cannot ignore it and adults should stop telling them to do so. We heard from both children and parents who were in despair because they felt they had done everything they could and the bullying continued.

"The overwhelming majority (97%) of children calling the Bullying Line and who had told teachers or staff were phoning because the bullying was still going on. They reported being met with various responses when they told: 31% said telling had resulted in no action; 13% were advised to ignore it; 6% were not believed; 3% were told 'there's no bullying here'; but 39% reported action being taken and 8% that the bullies had been excluded (expelled)."

In all, more than half the complaints were ignored and even in the 40% where some action was taken, the bullying went on and on. "Our study shows little evidence that the enormous range and richness of guidance for teachers and schools is being routinely used to reduce bullying."

The report adds, as have so many adults who have contributed their thoughts to this book: "Promoting a culture of 'decency' within a school seems to be the bedrock on which real success depends. The role of the head teacher in this process appears to be pivotal."

Sheila called the Bullying Line about her daughter who was being subjected to what she called 'daily verbal torture' by two girls who used to be friendly with her. She had reported the matter to the head teacher who had put Julie in front of the school during assembly and asked the bullies to stand up.

Not surprisingly no one rose to the occasion and Julie's torment intensified because of the almost unbelievable insensitivity of the school's head.

The ChildLine report agrees with the government Elton Inquiry's view that schools which rely too heavily on punishment to deter bad behaviour are "likely to be disappointed."

"In our view," say MacLeod and Morris, "school complaints procedures should exist with a clear remit to address issues of bullying so that parents and children can know they have a right to complain about inaction or inadequate action to protect children."

Intimidated children find it hard to speak of their private agony, what they often feel as their shame. Whilst the Bullying Line was open for seven months, it received a total of 58,530 calls. Only 4,494 kids and 691 adults felt brave enough to open their mouths. The others simply couldn't bring themselves to describe their agony and hung up. This suggests that more than 90% of tormented children are so fearful and confused that they can't even speak anonymously over a phone line about their secret misery.

This concurs with Tim's Workplace Bullying Advice Line which reveals that many adults are so traumatised by bullying and harassment at work that they are similarly unable to articulate their experience, thus precluding grievance and legal action.

Those who did speak out were reluctant to give their location, so ChildLine isn't able to pinpoint regional areas of specific concern. But kids did give their ages and sexes quite willingly. Four times more girls than boys used the Line. The largest group of users was girls aged eleven-fourteen. Fifty-six percent of all callers fell into the eleven-thirteen age group. There were only half a dozen calls from seventeen- and eighteen-year-olds.

The disproportionate number of girl callers, the report says, does not reflect a larger scale of female bullying, merely a male reluctance to talk things over (other studies reach the same conclusion). The study also found that bullying was the main problem complained of by children in residential care, accounting for 35% of runaways, and that it was also the most common problem troubling boarding-school children.

Surprisingly, when we remember claims earlier in this book that shattered, dysfunctional homes make children more vulnerable to bullying, 70% of bully victims belonged to two-parent families. Two percent of children seeking help from ChildLine said they were from a minority ethnic group or had a physical disability. Almost all of these few callers complained that these factors were the major reason for them being targeted by the bully gangs.

MacLeod and Morris drew up a simple table to describe the type of bullying being suffered: 54% complained of physical bullying or the threat of it, 37% of name-calling, teasing and purely psychological attack. The rest called to explain the problems "friends" were experiencing.

Some schools are still reluctant to answer the simple questions on a ChildLine questionnaire which include: level and frequency of bullying, nature and effect of anti-bullying policies and strategies for dealing with it, and most appropriate form of help for victims. The schools were afraid, the report hints, that involving themselves in a study might stir up a problem they do not want to believe exists.

"Their response illustrated the resistance to the subject of bullying persisting in some schools."

ChildLine's questionnaire was answered by 63% percent of children, 28% of parents, but only 12% of teachers.

MacLeod and Morris tried to define bullying. It was a tough job and one they couldn't handle themselves. Instead, they quoted children and experts:

The children: "It's pushing and calling you names, saying they're going to hit you."

"Being nasty to people and making their lives a misery."

"Picking on a person, taking the Mick out of them, taking advantage, like if they want something they're just going to get it, otherwise they'll hurt you or something."

"Punching, biting, spreading rumours about people, name-calling, blackmail."

"People getting picked on - either name-calling or whatever. It's bullying if the person who's getting called names is disturbed by it."

The experts: "Long-standing violence against people who cannot defend themselves."

"A student is being bullied or victimised when he or she is exposed, repeatedly and over time, to negative actions on the part of one or more students."

"Bullying is a wilful and conscious abuse of power."

Same difference, really.

The transcripts of calls to ChildLine are chilling: "If it's physical, it'll be like a cut then go away; if you're being called names it stays with you, you can't put it out of your mind." The caller was ten. A fifteen-year-old said: "I was made a fool of in class today, called a spastic and a Mongol and the teacher laughed. I felt very humiliated. I'm very angry with the teacher for letting these boys get away with it." "The things they say to me feel like a dagger in my back," a ten-year-old said.

"My Dad says I have to fight my own battles," said another ten-year-old target of physical bullying.

"I am at the stage of wanting to die instead of going to school", said an eleven-year-old boy who'd been physically attacked.

Twice as many boys as girls complain of physical abuse although girls are more frightened by the possibility of it. And, as is shown in the case histories in this book, many bullies were former friends. Eighteen percent of victims, according to ChildLine, have been turned on by their pals.

Juvenile racism plays its part as suggested by these sample calls: "I am the only Asian in the class. They have started calling me 'Paki' all the time ... maybe it's because I do well in my exams. I don't want to tell Mum and Dad and upset them."

Claudette is 14. She is bullied because her father is black and her mother is white. She is called names but recently a group of children attacked her outside school and broke her nose. Police were called and warned the gang off. But Claudette is terrified of the next assault.

Dean is 13 and black. After police were called as a threatening gang of white boys gathered outside his home, he was warned by the bully leader that there would be reprisals for calling in the law.

The problem of racial bullying could be more widespread than the ChildLine study suggests. Nearly a third of children responding to survey questions admitted that black children and those from other minority groups were most at risk. A white eight-year-old said: "It's 'cos they don't like them, their skin colour, they come from another country and speak a different language."

Only two disabled children were in the study. Both had been bullied because of their physical difference from others. Seventeen other disabled children who called the helpline said their disability was the sole reason for them being singled out as targets of bullying.

Over three-quarters of bullying goes on in or around school and, even where anti-bullying schemes are in place, 64% percent of primary and 45% percent of secondary school pupils fall victim to it at some time during their schooldays, half of them several times a week over long periods and mostly in the playground, classroom, school corridors and toilets or dining areas. Others suffer after school-time on the bus or the walk home in their local areas.

The survey also discovered that, although 99% of girl bullies chose other girls as victims, 41% of boys chose girls to bully too. Thirty-seven percent of bullying follows the Richard Fearn *Just a Laugh* stereotype of older children bullying the smaller and weaker. But most bullying goes on among peers.

There are many theories as to why children bully; insecurity, machismo, passing the buck after falling victim themselves, violent home background, jealousy or sheer bloody-mindedness. Bullies who called ChildLine confided: "I want to stop but I'm scared the ringleaders will turn on me."

"I started so I'd seem 'hard,' so no one would pick on me. Now it's a habit and I can't stop but I really want to."

"My family deal with arguments by being violent. I need to find other ways to settle arguments."

"Probably because I was angry about something and I was taking it out on someone else, I think."

"I've had to push to protect myself from bullying sometimes."

"Children who bully," say MacLeod and Morris, "talk about opportunity, habit, pleasure, followed by remorse. Many ascribed their bullying to their feelings of anger or jealousy. Bullying for entertainment was next on the list. Interestingly none of those surveyed singled out their own or the victim's characteristics as an explanation."

One child calling ChildLine said: "I cry every day. I feel so bad. The teacher said I set it off myself."

A world-respected psychologist has published the view that victims are often themselves to blame for the agony they suffer. He published a paper in which he claimed to have identified "provocative victims", children who get up other kids' noses to the extent that they almost deserve this so-called "provocative response."

Specious defences of premeditated physical and sexual violence are still prevalent; barristers who defend rapists portray the victim as a loose woman. Paedophiles use beguiling pretexts to justify their vile acts. Misperceptions and misguided blame-the-victim views are still propagated by those without experience and by those who seek attention for themselves on the back of others' suffering.

No child we've spoken to has ever invited torture. None

of our young bullycides welcomed the torment that drove them to the grave.

ChildLine also makes little of this oddball theory. They concentrate on the fact that 70% of bullying is carried on by groups and say far too little attention is being paid to understanding gang mentality and group dynamics. "It's clear", they say, "that strategies for dealing with bullying have to focus on group behaviour - staff understanding the dynamics of children's groups and learning how to deploy group skills."

"Recently I've started thinking about suicide. I feel too scared to have a social life. I spend my days in fear both in and out of school." This was how a thirteen-year-old girl called Jill cried her pain down the phone to ChildLine after a brutal months'-long hate campaign of name-calling and threats of physical violence.

ChildLine said: "Jill's friend from infant school who now went to school elsewhere had been provoking children at Jill's school to gang up against her. Her parents had been to the school several times to try to resolve the problems, but they had not been able to see the head teacher. The school liaison officer had told her mother that she should keep Jill off school for a time."

Jill was part of the small but frightening group of 4% in the MacLeod-Morris study, representing 62 children, who discussed suicidal feelings or suicide attempts with counsellors. That makes her one of those many children who consider bullycide a better alternative than life.

During the study another seven children were reported by friends to be on the brink of bullycide and two parents called who had arrived in the nick of time to find their sons hanging and near to death. Suicidal thoughts and attempts are almost twice as common among boys, 7% of all boys calling the Bullying Line compared with 4% of all girls wishing to take their own lives.

Words don't have to come to blows. The survey points

out: "It is important to note that these cases were not confined to particularly brutal or physical bullying actions. In fact over half (52%) of the children were experiencing exclusively verbal forms of abuse, mostly common name-calling. Rejection, humiliation and vilification are experienced as a child's sense of self. It is extremely difficult to go on believing you are loveable and worthwhile under a barrage of this kind of harassment.

"The effects and consequences of bullying can devastate a child's life and in some cases lead to suicide. Several child suicides each year have been linked to bullying and reported cases are not confined to children experiencing physical attacks but, also, children suffering verbal bullying. The cases of children who reported feeling suicidal or attempting suicide suggest that it is dangerous to label some forms of bullying as 'mild.' Instances of bullying dismissed by adults as trivial can fundamentally undermine a child's sense of well-being and self-esteem.

"Since there is no sure way of identifying children who may react in a self-destructive way to different types of bullying, the onus must be on adults to listen to and be guided by the child's expressed thoughts and feelings, rather than by any preconceived ideas about the relative severity of different types of bullying."

Recent research in Tower Hamlets, London showed that most bullied children do talk about their problem. ChildLine reckons only about 17% bottle it up. But fear of speaking out and the possible repercussions from bullies grows as the child ages, with teenagers keeping especially tight-lipped. Seventy-two percent of children whose parents or care workers approach their school to tackle the problem find that the bullying continues or gets worse.

ChildLine says: "Staff in schools were commonly described as having denied there was a problem, either by blaming the bullied child, saying they provoked the other children or were oversensitive to comments made by

1. *Steven Shepherd*

3. *Stanley Holland today*

2. *Steven Shepherd's Uncle and Aunt, Jimmy and Marjorie Jolly*

4. *Steven Shepherd's school pal Stanley Holland in a police reconstruction*

5. *Denise Baillie*

6. *Marie Bentham*

7. *Maria McGovern*

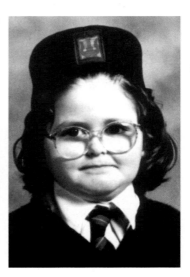

8. *Kelly Yeomans*

9. *David Tuck*

10. *Neil Marr pauses by Steven Shepherd's grave*

11. *Targets are excluded and isolated*

12. *Katherine Jane Morrison*

13. Peter McQueen with his Mum and Dad

14. Nicky Hudson

15. PC Fred and pals

16. *Prince Naz before his fight with Wayne McCulloch*

18. *William Roache from Coronation Street*

17. *Elliott Stephens with Prince Naz*

19. *Brian Jones, round-the-world balloonist*

*20. Richard Fearn and his team (L-R) James Riley, Natalie Ingham, teacher
Carol Whittam, Richard Fearn, Hayley Berry, Keith Gorton and Kate Myers*

21. The final scene of 'Just a Laugh'

22. Why me?

23. *Dani Goss*

"24 Caroline Worth's art"

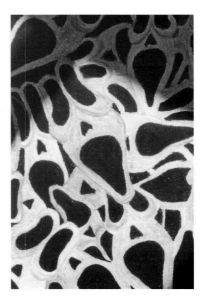

25-26. *Caroline Worth expresses her pain and anguish through her art*

27. *Lucy Forrester*

28. *Lucy's parents, Richard and Elizabeth Forrester*

29. *Salli Ward*

30. *Congleton railway station, scene of Lucy's bullycide*

them, or that parents were being overprotective and refusing to let their child come to terms with everyday interactions with other children. If a child or parent kept on complaining, *they* would begin to be dealt with as the problem, much to their distress."

Fewer than 1% of bullies are removed from school for their brutality, the study found. And bullied children often find themselves cut off from the decision-making process after they have alerted staff to their problem.

The MacLeod-Morris Report concludes: "The very term 'bullying' is a euphemism for assaults which adults would describe as harassment, verbal abuse, actual or grievous bodily harm, theft, intimidation, extortion, blackmail, sexual or racial harassment, sexual assault and, occasionally, attempted murder ... all criminal offences in the adult world.

"The study showed disappointingly little evidence that the wealth of guidance on anti-bullying strategies is bearing fruit in schools. It is hard to escape the conclusion that most books and packs are gathering dust on school shelves.

"It is time to view bullying as a disease in schools and on the streets and to adopt a nationwide strategy to tackle it."

The 124-page ChildLine report ends with advice which is incorporated in the final chapter of this book.

Valerie Howarth is Executive Director of ChildLine. She, too, agrees that our figures for death at playtime may be conservative in the extreme.

"The worst end of it is when children take their own lives. Often they do it mostly under psychological bullying. Therefore people say 'Oh, children have to grow out of it' or 'it's just one of those things.' They're not treating it seriously enough.

"What we've done is to put ourselves in a position to hear about bullying from the children's point of view. They tell us how it is. They've got nothing to lose calling ChildLine, we don't know who they are or where they are, they can accept or not what we suggest and they can find their own solutions through our examples.

"Our first piece of research really changed the status of bullying in the way people thought about it. Previously it was only, externally, about the way adults saw it - you know, being bashed up in the playground. Children tell us a different story about this emotional hurt. But also much more about the scale of the violence which I don't think had come out before.

"The other thing that children told us was that adults could make it worse in the way they handled it, and that young people could help young people better than anyone else, which is why we've developed peer counselling and peer support services through our schools.

"But, at the end of the day, they expected adults to understand it and stop it. I think the great difficulty is that many adults - parents and teachers - don't know how to.

"There must be programmes in place to tackle it. That's much better than schools who say 'there's no bullying here'. I say that children grow up by knocking the edges off each other, it's part of interaction, but adults have to control it and manage it."

Valerie continued: "Children are socialising, are learning how to negotiate, they're learning about interaction, they're learning the power relationships between themselves and that's part of the reality. You can't eradicate bullying because out of all that interaction bullying will rear its head. Adults have got to recognise that and deal with it.

"What happens, though, is that, when the thing goes underground and the child suffers terrible verbal abuse or perpetual physical attacks or both, is that it's not noticed. If the child isn't heard when he tries to talk, if the thing persists, then it has a desperate effect on the child's self-esteem and, in the broad term, their mental health. At the bottom of that they decide it's not worth going on, that there's no way out of it except to kill themselves. When you look into the circumstances you often find that, certainly, people knew about it, there was an inkling there was something wrong either in the school or at home and people just didn't take it seriously. You don't have to be too intense just to occasionally ask your child if everything's OK.

"At ChildLine we tend to say about ten [bullycides] a year. The figure's not accurate. We know there are far more because authorities want to spare family pain or it's unclear or the facts never come to the surface. Your figure of sixteen bullycides a year does not surprise me. And, apart from the children who end up taking their own lives, there are the ones who seriously attempt it. They are the children we go for who are failing to achieve at school and whose lives are blighted. They give up on the academic side. They don't want to go to class. We get children who are terrified all the time they are sitting in their classroom.

"A lot of children would get through the peripheral problems of family dysfunction, stature, physical difference and the rest were it not for the bullying, when their self-esteem was ruined. It's how children feel about themselves that leads to bullycide. How you view yourself in the future and how you view yourself in relation to other people. If you'd not got bullied and you had problems at home or whatever, you might stand a chance of coping with it. If you really feel that people are getting at you, picking at your self-image, pulling at you and making you feel anxious, then, psychologically, people start to lose a grip."

ChildLine's message is simple: for many kids, life is a fate worse than death.

Chapter 11

What the education authorities say

"Years of bullying made me think I was stupid, ugly and would never amount to much. If someone tells you that often enough, you end up believing it."
Survivor of bullying, now adult

Enquiries of government organisations, the Department for Education and Employment (DfEE) and local education authorities (LEAs) have elicited only the data in the tables below.

The DfEE's anti-bullying pack *Don't Suffer in Silence* was issued in September 1994 but there appears to be no statutory requirement for schools to read it or to implement it. The School Standards and Framework Act 1998 includes a specific duty on head teachers to determine measures to prevent all forms of bullying among pupils. In September 1999 it became a legal requirement for all UK schools to have an anti-bullying policy. Rather than distribute a model policy for local implementation, it appears every school in the country has had to devote scarce resources to reinvent the wheel.

The common thread throughout this book is that education authorities do not take the problem seriously. A year after her daughter's brush with bullycide, one mother, a teacher herself, could still not prod the local education authority into action.

Her latest letter to authority bosses read: "I cannot begin to tell you how upsetting it is to see such a raft of excuses for the dreadful way my daughter has been made to suffer during all of her school years. At no point in the whole process have we received anything like an apology, an

Table 2: DfEE figures 1997
• £20.5 billion annual budget • 8,260,000 pupils of which... • 4,460,646 primary school children • 3,072,822 secondary school children • 500,000 approx at independent schools • 214,558 primary school teachers • 206,556 secondary school teachers • 63,495 teachers in independent establishments • no data on bullycide

Table 3: Home Office figures for 1997
• 18 suicides or "unclear deaths" of children between 5-14 years of age • 480 males and 110 females between the ages of 15-24 had their unexplained deaths investigated • 292 accidental deaths between 5-14 years of age • 4,500 child deaths over the age of 14 • no data on bullycide

admission of ineptitude, an explanation of unprofessional behaviour or an acknowledgement of the damage that was caused by systematic and uncaring management.

"Your letter [to us] comes across as just another justification suggesting relief that you feel there is nothing for you or the county to worry about. Your response seems cerebral, detached, defensive and devoid of any feeling and understanding of our daughter as a sensitive and bullied individual. Indeed your fervour seems to have been expended in protecting your employees. We are very, very disheartened indeed.

"The LEA's excuses, rationalisations, whitewash and all

manner of other justifications have been offered in the face of failure to take appropriate and effective measures. The bullying episode is the final, dreadful chapter and you gave scant attention to it.

"We must not forget that, after all, schools fundamentally exist to help parents in the education of their children"

The writer of this letter was still struggling to help her daughter over the trauma (Post Traumatic Stress Disorder, PTSD) of her horrendous experience at school and latterly in a hospital intensive care unit after a suicide attempt.

UK society, with most democratic countries, demands deference to authority. When that dependence is betrayed, deference can turn out to be deadly. Long-term bullying and bullycide are consequences of the failure of those in authority; expectations of resolution by those who have already failed in their duty of care are, as in the cases featured in this book, unlikely to be realised.

Since its inception in 1996, teachers have consistently formed the largest group of callers to the UK National Workplace Bullying Advice Line. They report being bullied by colleagues, heads of department, deputy heads, but most often by head teachers. There is anecdotal evidence to suggest that if bullying is rife in the staff room, then bullying is also rife in the playground. Children learn most by example. The behaviour style of the person at the top determines the standard of behaviour throughout the school.

Ever-increasing workloads, the ogre of OFSTED (the UK Office for Standards in Education), constant interference and criticism and blame by government and an obsession with tests mean that teachers now experience one of the highest levels of on-the-job stress and lowest levels of recognition of any profession. Needless to say, teacher recruitment is in crisis to such an extent that LEA bosses in South London have resorted to flying in temporary teachers at undisclosed cost from Australia.

In September 2000, Lord Puttnam, chairman of the General Teaching Council, a new professional body for teachers, echoed the need to recognise "that teachers are the key to high standards and achievement in our schools". One of the GTC's first actions was to publish a survey revealing a contradiction in the public's negative perception of the education sector. In contrast to OFSTED and DfEE officials' constant blame-the-teachers mentality, over 80% of parents are happy with the work of teachers whilst over 90% of adults believe teaching to be a highly-skilled job.

A TV advert by the Child and Juvenile Delegation Department in socially-progressive Sweden states that six out of ten bullies will grow up to become criminals. Given that bullied children often turn out to be high achievers and contributors to society and that bullies live lives of failure, the wisdom of giving children the best possible start in life should be self-evident. Pupils form the next generation of employees and entrepreneurs as well as the pension-payers of tomorrow.

It's not only kids who are driven to bullycide. Teachers are also turning to suicide as an escape from bullying.

Teacher's torment that led to bullycide

Teachers themselves are not immune to intimidation, many suffering stress breakdown or quitting their careers because of bullying. At least one teacher took her own life rather than face another day of classroom torment and the lack of understanding of her boss.

English and social and religious studies teacher Jean Evans was one of those sensitive staff members most at risk from the very children they are dedicated to helping. She was just 43 when she hanged herself in the garage of her home in the West Midlands, leaving behind three young children and a grieving husband.

Husband Peter, himself a teacher but now retired, placed

the blame firmly on the shoulders of classroom bullies and school authorities who would not take Jean's plight seriously enough to allow her to break her two-term contract and escape her terror.

Jean was in her first term at a secondary school when the campaign against her began. It went on and on until the day she could stand no more and took what she saw as the only way out. "Suicide" according to the inquest into her death; "bullycide" according to those who knew her best.

Jean had been a teacher for nineteen years, often struggling hard to help youngsters who were themselves targeted by bullies. But in her final weeks, she herself fell prey to the Blackboard Jungle predators. Husband Peter agreed that bullying was the major factor in his wife's fatal misery. But he is also furious with a head teacher who refused to allow her to leave her job when she was under deadly pressure. A deputy headmaster of the same school committed suicide shortly after Jean's death. Tellingly, a recent child bullycide attempt featured in these pages involved a child from the same school.

Peter told us: You cannot say that bullying was unconnected. But there also were various factors in my wife's life including the behaviour of the head teacher when made aware of my wife's problem in class."

He said: "She went to an upper school nearby which I didn't like because I thought she was better suited as a teacher of younger children, particularly because of the sort of job it was. It was a temporary job and the job was available, it seemed fairly obvious to me, because the teacher she was superseding had not been able to cope with the situation there.

"There were two or three tough classes, but one particular class where there were what she called 'mouthy girls' and, in particular, one boy. She had been in youth work before she went to schools, she was well aware of how difficult kids - I mean teenagers of 15, 16, 17 - can be.

So there was no problem like that. She was a good teacher, she had good class control. But by this new bullying she felt, unusually, physically threatened and in a dangerous situation. She had not been attacked physically but the situation was that she was afraid that could happen at any moment.

"But the real problem was that it was supposed to be a two-term contract and the crunch moment came before the end of the first term and she got into a very depressed condition over it, literally a depressive illness is how the doctor described it. I tried to persuade her that she'd got to leave school right then regardless of career prospects because it was really upsetting her and, through her, upsetting the family which included three young children.

"In order to do that, to resign early, she was going to have to see the head teacher. So she went to see him and he was very unsympathetic indeed. Other people on the staff who had a fair idea of what was going on, including the head of department and the deputy head, were very supportive. But the head was not. She had an interview with him on the Friday before she took her life and she told me it had been 'grim'. In other words, he'd been very unsympathetic. I think this was the crunch feature.

"We went to a local theatre on the Saturday and she was doing preparatory work on Sunday for the coming school lessons. I went to school on the Monday leaving her here at home and, of course, she committed suicide while I was out.

"The crucial feature was that because the head teacher was so unsympathetic, it sparked off an underlying insecurity in her. That was really what triggered the suicide. You see, she'd been a child sexual abuse victim as well. Indeed she didn't need any more troubles in her life.

"Until the point when the problems started, she'd been at a local middle school as a one-to-one tutor of extremely difficult children with severe behavioural difficulties which requires a special teacher to be in the classroom with the child. So she was used to dealing with children with problems. She was used to dealing with youngsters in the youth club. She'd already been a teacher when we met at the upper school where I was teaching. There was no lack of experience.

"It was a particularly difficult situation with a particularly difficult class with these 'mouthy girls' and this one very threatening boy which produced the situation which prompted me to say she couldn't carry on there because it was just too upsetting.

"If she'd got into the situation where she'd begun to think of herself as being worthless, which is a common feature of victims of child abuse, that's dangerous. If a teacher can't control a class - I've some experience of that situation but not as bad as she had obviously - it really gets to you. It's right on your mind. It strikes at the very basis of our profession. In her case she was particularly vulnerable because there was this sense of worthlessness lingering from childhood which we'd overcome to a very large degree during the course of our marriage.

"The reason she went to the headmaster was because she was going to tell him that she couldn't carry on, that she wanted to resign as of the end of the first term which would have been in a few days' time. One might think he ought to have picked up on the problem earlier and done something about it as opposed to adopting a quite different attitude.

"She had spoken informally with many children who may have faced bully problems during her career. If you haven't been a teacher, I think you don't appreciate what this sort of situation can do to you. You very often do find good teachers who just can't cope with particular classes and they're always ill on those particular days when they must face them. They may be genuinely ill, psychologically ill or in some psychosomatic way. Whatever, it's all brought on by the thought of going in and facing this bully situation once again. I've come across this myself. It's pretty common.

"There was certainly support from other teachers at the same sort of rank level and from the head of department and from the deputy head who also later committed suicide. But the head himself is a person of some power in a school whom people look up to and if the head's opinion of you is low that is a significant thing. That hits your self-esteem and, as on this occasion, the head really knocked her down when she came to see him and this was the crunch thing really. I have no doubt that had the head been more understanding she would still be alive today. I have no doubt about that at all.

"I carried on teaching after her death. Not for all that long. Just for a couple of years. I took early retirement but carried on for three or four years after that as a supply (temporary stand-in) teacher. Jean's death had given me a severe psychological jolt and made me ... shall we say ... not quite the character I had been. I'm quite sure that I was less effective from a discipline point of view than I had been before.

"I think I'd always been a tough character as a teacher before. I'm not saying that because it makes me look good, that's what people told me. I don't think I was as tough after Jean's suicide as I had been before.

"As individual teachers we had always been aware that bullying existed between peer groups. But it wasn't the problem it has now become. I noticed instances of it after my wife died and I had retired and was doing supply work in a middle school, in fact the same school where Jean had taught children on the one-to-one basis. It was very noticeable that there was a lot more bullying - and obvious bullying - there than I'd ever noticed at the school where I'd been teaching.

"I think that women teachers are more susceptible to

obscenities from boys, sexual innuendo, that type of thing. I really don't know if women teachers in general are more vulnerable than their male colleagues.

"We had so brief a time to sort this out for Jean. She went to this school in the January and it was fairly obvious why the other teacher had gone. It was a rather unfair timetable in the sense that there was no levelling of bright classes to compare with the rather not-so-bright classes, only middling at best. That there was nothing to look forward to might be an exaggeration, but there were no brilliant classes you could do something with.

"She was one of those people," says Peter, "who was everyone's auntie, who people did talk to in that way, to whom people go for a friendly ear. I would add that she would naturally be the first resort of children who were her particular concern as form tutor or youth leader. But I've never spoken to the children responsible for bullying my wife. I'm afraid that if I had I might have been very badly tempted ... I'm sorry. Early retirement suited me."

After her bullycide, Jean's own three children experienced bullying as a consequence of her death. Peter told us: "My son had just started at middle school and it so happened that, although he was a big boy at that time and he's pretty huge now, probably because he was one of the youngest of his year, the bully type picked on him ... particularly because of the hassle with his mother. This wasn't just teasing. We're talking real nastiness. Verbal bullying is so much more dangerous than the physical.

"The bottom line is that the bullying and lack of sympathy of one headmaster who would not appreciate her plight and led to the resurgence of the sense of worthlessness which was a result of the child abuse pushed her over the edge. If it hadn't been for the bullying, she would not have had to go to the head, he wouldn't have been seen as unsympathetic.

"When you think of what she did to end her life ... imagine

how terrible the alternative of facing another day at that school must have been."

The local education authority in a statement after Jean's death, as is so common in bullycide cases, said only: "The authority, governors and headmaster are satisfied that discipline at the school is good and there have been no complaints from parents."

They put it their way ... Jean put it hers. Discipline is good but a teacher and a deputy head teacher both commit suicide? When it becomes law, it will be interesting to see how the Corporate Homicide Bill can be used to hold those responsible accountable.

That Jean's children became targets of bullying because of their mother's suicide is not unique. Bullies sense vulnerability, none more so than that caused by bereavement. Sensing their victim's susceptibility at a time of shock and acute distress, bullies zero in on their prey.

The most common scenario in around 800 cases from the education sector logged by Tim's Advice Line involves a competent and popular teacher who has control of discipline. By contrast, the bully, be they a fellow teacher, a manager or a head teacher, does *not* have control of discipline, despite protestations to the contrary. To hide this shortcoming, the bully makes unsubstantiated but superficially convincing allegations of underperformance (and occasionally of fraud or abuse) as a pretext for imposing a competency procedure leading to dismissal.

The bully then goes out of his or her way to make life difficult for the targeted teacher, for example allocating the most disruptive pupils, the worst classes, the most difficult timetable, the most inconvenient locations and so on. Faults are found in everything the teacher says and does, although the criticisms cannot be authenticated. Requests for substantiation are met with charges of insubordination. After months of being set up to fail, and with health severely damaged, a mistake inevitably occurs and the bully immediately activates dismissal proceedings.

In the same way they fail to deal with child bullying, education authorities are not alert to bullying by employees and almost always back the wrong horse, as in the case of *Pepper* v. *Reading Borough Council* (who inherited the problem from the reorganised and defunct Berkshire County Council). The taxpayers of Berkshire funded the council's flawed defence which resulted in compensation of £120,000 to Mrs Cherryll Pepper for damaged health and a career ruined by a head teacher's false allegations. Even these large sums of money, which are based on what the employee would have earned had they remained in employment until normal retirement age, fail to compensate for the detriment to health, career and professionalism. Neither do they compensate for damage to the family who are the unseen victims of bullying.

Whilst adults have some legal redress through employment law, discrimination law, and health and safety law, children who are the targets of bullying and families bereaved by bullycide have few options for legal redress and no union to fight for their rights. This is not the only circumstance where the life of a child is valued in monetary terms at considerably less than that of an adult.

However, some cases have fired a warning shot across the bows of negligent education authorities.

In *Carnell* v. *North Yorkshire County Council*, the first legal victory since it became mandatory for schools to have bullying policies, former Harrogate Grammar School pupil John Carnell accepted a settlement of £6,000 in respect of a year of bullying at Harrogate Grammar School.

John's mother, Mrs Liz Carnell, said the county council chose not to back the school. She continued, "this should send a clear message to all school governors, and those at Harrogate Grammar School in particular, that they have a responsibility to know when complaints of bullying are made and that they should sort them out.

"In 1998 Harrogate Grammar School applied for but failed to achieve Investors in People accreditation. The report of the IiP assessor said that staff made comments about "bullying" and "autocratic" top management, adding: 'There appears to be a degree of fear in voicing concerns, making objective observations and suggestions'."

If that's what the teachers have to endure, what chance do the kids have?

In October 2000, a former pupil of Sale Grammar School was awarded compensation of £1,500 by a judge at Manchester County Court who ruled that the school had breached its duty of care having failed to protect the pupil from eighteen months of verbal abuse and name-calling.

Meanwhile, in November 2000, Leah Bradford-Smart took High Court action claiming damages for having suffered personal injury through alleged "persistent and prolonged bullying" whilst a pupil at Ifield Middle School, Crawley, between 1990 and 1993. Whilst the judge accepted much of her argument, the LEA successfully claimed that bullying outside school premises was beyond their duty of care. Ms Bradford-Smart's solicitor, Jack Rabinowicz, was critical of the judgement: "To allow bullies to drag a pupil out of a school just seems to be a distinction which gives schools and bullies the green light to make things worse."

The difficulty of dealing with bullying on the way to and from school was tragically highlighted with the murder of ten-year-old Damilola Taylor in November 2000. He was stabbed and left bleeding to death on his way home the day after his mother had visited the school to complain of bullying. On the day of the murder and in advance of any knowledge of the circumstances, the school's headmaster emphatically denied any connection between Damilola's death and bullying at his school.

Some claims have been successful. In November 1996, Sebastian Sharp won an out-of-court settlement of

£30,000 for four years of bullying whilst he was at Shene School, Richmond, London. Mr Sharp, who was represented by solicitor Jack Rabinowicz, said he was regularly insulted, kicked and punched by other pupils, who also tied him up with string in a four-year campaign starting when he was eleven. The London Borough of Richmond-upon-Thames said it wanted to contest the allegation vigorously but the Borough's insurance company "wanted to avoid a costly and time-consuming court process".

In many cases of out-of-court settlement, one has the suspicion that avoidance of court process has less to do with cost and time and more to do with preventing exposure of shortcomings.

Targets of bullying, for whom legal action is the last thing on their mind, if at all, find themselves confronted with threats of serious injury, and sometimes death, if they tell. The intense fear, helplessness and horror in the face of threats to physical integrity must never be underestimated or ignored. The school's defence that "we didn't know about the bullying because no one told us" does not hold water. The non-derogatable duty of care with its onus on proactive prevention and detection rather than belated reaction, lies wholly and exclusively with the responsible adults. Ignorance of the law is no excuse. The fact that bullying continues unnoticed and uninterrupted for months, and often years, is, ipso facto, evidence of negligence.

The Human Rights Act (1998) came into force in the UK in October 2000. Article 2 provides for the right to education. For the first time in the UK, citizens who believe their rights have been violated can pursue legal action in a UK court. Previously, action under the European Convention on Human Rights could only be pursued in a European Court at prohibitive expense.

A ten quid bullycide?

In an almost unheard of move, police were ordered to reopen their inquiries into the tragic death of a schoolboy when bullying torment came to light.

Seventeen-year-old fifth-former Neil Ross hanged himself in his own school grounds in Lochgilphead, Argyll, Scotland during the Christmas holidays.

The youngster's family has now found he was being bullied by another youth who'd falsely accused him of stealing £10 from his mother.

His father - also called Neil - said: "Neil was terrified. He told us of threats to his life but was even too frightened to let us go to the police and tell them about it."

The Ross family has struggled to find any reason for Neil taking his life. All they can come up with is the torture of a bully campaign against him.

Chief Inspector Harry Miller said: "The Procurator Fiscal (the Scottish equivalent of a coroner) has asked us for full statements and anything to do with these alleged threats."

The goldfish boy

Sometimes children feel bullied by their teachers.

Sensitive twelve-year-old Daniel Overfield hanged himself with his own dressing gown cord because he was so hurt by a bad school report written by his art teacher.

Recording the familiar but ambiguous verdict of misadventure at an inquest in Leeds in April 2000, coroner David Hinchcliffe said: "The comment went along the lines that Daniel had the attention span of a goldfish. It might have been in the back of his mind that he might get into more trouble because of the remark on the card."

Afterwards, Keith Burton, director of education at Leeds City Council, said: "The death has shaken the whole school. Any incident of this type clearly illustrates the fact that we all need to reflect carefully on the impact our words might have on the people listening to them."

Head of one of the biggest UK teachers' unions, ATL's General Secretary Peter Smith said: "There is a genuine issue here, speaking as a former teacher and a parent, of the extent to which sarcasm, however friendly it is, has a place in dealing with children."

The local education authority says the teacher at Corpus Christi Roman Catholic School, Leeds, who made the remark is "devastated."

They are taking no disciplinary action against her.

Daniel's Mum, Theresa, was so angered the day he carried home the report card containing the 'goldfish' taunt that she immediately marched to the school to confront the teacher.

It was when she got home from that meeting that she found Daniel hanging by the neck from the bunk-bed in his bedroom. He was pronounced dead in hospital three days later.

Daniel's case illustrates the cumulative danger of sarcasm and humiliation in a climate of fear, coercion and exclusion where pupils rapidly become disaffected through repeated negative feedback. Guilt, a more subtle and less conspicuous close cousin of sarcasm, can be just as deadly. Where there's a power imbalance and lack of control over personal circumstances, sarcasm can be deadly to self-esteem, as any victim of domestic violence will vouch.

Forcing pupils into unsuitable and unnecessary subjects for which they have neither aptitude nor interest can be seen as a form of institutionalised bullying, especially if children are subsequently branded as failures if they fail to get the requisite A grades in "approved" curriculum subjects in order to maintain the school's position in league tables.

Whilst the DfEE forces schools to focus their attention on OFSTED and league tables, teachers and children continue to die.

Chapter 12

Close shaves

Dark was the night when Jesus was born.
Blue was the head dress that Mary wore.
Bright was the star that shone down below.
Light were the wings of Gabriel.
Warm was the straw the baby lay in.
And green is what the kings were dressed in.
Light was the night when Jesus was born.
Lucy Forrester

They found Peter McQueen unconscious and near to death, lying alone in an alley in a pool of his own vomit. Emergency room doctors said that had he arrived just a few minutes later in the casualty unit, Peter would have been dead. But through Neil's journalistic work he lived to give advice against alcohol abuse to the sons of Prince Charles in one of Britain's biggest Sunday newspapers.

Slight, timid Peter had chosen to drink a potentially lethal booze cocktail rather than face the ridicule of tough bully boy "mates." He was twelve.

After days in a special hospital treatment unit, he was well enough to go home. But he wouldn't speak to doctors, teachers, or even his parents about his near-death experience.

We don't know why he shyly crept out of hiding in his bedroom in Blantyre near Glasgow and opened up to Neil. Maybe it was the cheap walkie-talkie set we'd bought him to keep in touch with his folks while he was out of the house and he wanted to say 'thanks.' Maybe it was because he found it easier to unburden himself to a stranger from a long way away who would be out of town tomorrow and never be seen again.

Whatever, he told us how the bullies from school had taunted him into stealing a £40 bottle of special whisky from his older teetotal brother's collection of single malts, how they'd mixed it in a large bowl with a bottle of cheap wine and then ordered him to drink it.

"I knew it might kill me," Peter said. "But anything seemed better than having to put up with them calling me a sissy if I didn't. I'd rather have died than put up with what they'd say. So I drank the lot. That's all I remember until I came to in hospital."

The cowardly bullies ran away when Peter collapsed. A local shopkeeper found him lying, as dead, in the alley gutter and rushed to his home where father, Tam, and his wife, Sadie, hurried to the scene.

Tam said: "He was completely white and his eyes had rolled back into his head. He was soaking wet and covered in bruises. He looked like he'd been run over by a car ... or beaten up. He reeked of alcohol so we took him home. We stripped him and tried to rouse him but he was icy cold. He didn't respond to anything. I thought I was going to have my third heart attack and my wife was completely hysterical. So we called an ambulance for him. We were sure he was going to die."

Ambulancemen put him on a drip and raced him to the local hospital. Peter was in such a desperate state that he was immediately transferred to a specialist unit in another hospital where he was put under sun lamps, wrapped in blankets and given plasma and drugs.

"Another few minutes," a doctor told Neil, "and he would have been dead of hypothermia and alcohol poisoning."

Sadie recalled: "His eyes were blood red in a deathly pale face. When he was well enough, he admitted drinking the stuff but he still wouldn't tell us who the bullies were."

Peter told us. Neil tracked them down. They came from a rougher area a mile away from the McQueen family's neat and pleasant home. They refused to talk. Peter made us promise not to name them. One thing we have learned is that children will only speak if they can call the shots.

Peter recollected: "That could have been the end of my life. I could have died. I'd have preferred that right then to getting called names any more. But being so close to giving up has taught me a lesson. I'm not going to let anybody walk all over me ever again. I'm going to make my own decisions.

"I might not be the best boy in the world, I might never play football for Scotland. But I've learned that I'm worthwhile and there are people like my family around me who care about me a lot.

"I gave advice to the princes in the newspaper to lay off the booze. My advice to anybody treated like I was is to say 'No. Enough's enough.' Find new friends who care about you and get on with life. Never give up and do something as stupid as I did." Peter smiled. A lovely wide smile.

"That's the first time he's smiled since ... well, you know," said his Dad.

Before Peter's near tragedy, another boy of twelve in Kent decided to risk death by downing an entire bottle of neat whisky rather than refuse the bully taunts. He was rushed to hospital with over four times the motorists' legal limit of alcohol in his blood-stream but was brought back from the brink. John Griffen from Sidcup lived to thrive. The bully was jailed for two and a half years for "administering a noxious substance with intent to injure, aggrieve or annoy."

Social Service workers are helping six-year-old Jake Martin cope with the aftermath of bullying. He threatened to take his own life because of bullying at school soon after Manchester's Marie Bentham was driven to bullycide.

Jake became ill and had nightmares after a campaign of verbal abuse.

Teaching staff dismissed his fears, according to his parents, Sharon and David, at their home in Nelson,

Lancashire. Social workers were brought in to mediate between Jake and his relentless tormentor.

Mother Sharon said: "It had started about a year before when one of the boys kept pulling his tie. Jake isn't the type to retaliate. I went to the school to complain three times. When he started a new class in August, the same boy started calling him names. That really hurt Jake."

Jake's sin? He wears a pair of round specs just like Steven Shepherd's.

"He bottled it all up. He was sick every morning. He carried on being sick for two months so my husband and I asked him what was wrong. He said it was all because he didn't want to go to school. He was frightened. He said 'I'll die. I'll kill myself.'"

The school head teacher now says the case is out of his hands and in that of the local Social Services department.

Bullying will not be tolerated

Daniel Jewell is also now living fear-free after the horrendous bullying which made his life hell was brought to an end by a judge who sentenced his three tormentors to three years' custody. Judge Ian McLeod sent a clear message from his courtroom in Southampton: "Bullying will not be tolerated."

Daniel, who's sixteen and from Totton, Southampton, wore glasses too. It made him just different enough to become a target for the thugs. Since the bullies were taken out of his life he has moved to a local technical college to start living anew.

His father, also called Daniel, said: "I hope this sends a signal to other bullies. I would like teachers to look extra hard at their policy toward bullying in their schools. This social evil must be stamped out."

The bully boys were sent to a young offenders' institution, convicted of grievous bodily harm when their campaign of intimidation peaked. The judge didn't buy their plea of not guilty to the savage beating of Daniel, repeatedly kicking and punching him even after he'd collapsed to the ground in a blind alley.

One of his attackers - showing little if any remorse - described the attack as "what normally happens around school." He said the trio had picked on Daniel because "He was a bit weird and a soft target."

After the attack, Daniel stumbled home and was rushed to hospital where doctors treated him for internal bleeding and told his parents he could have died.

Death potion

Kirk Tapp was twelve when he almost died by drinking a lethal "love potion" drug in the playground of his Birmingham school rather than say "no" to the bullies who forced it upon him. He fell unconscious within seconds and had to be rushed to hospital where doctors said the gamma hydroxybutyric acid, known as "liquid ecstasy" or "love potion" had almost killed him.

He knew from what other pupils had told him that the cocktail could kill. But he chose to risk death rather than the bullies' wrath.

His mother, Lynda, said: "They'd threatened to kick his head in if he didn't drink the stuff. We nearly lost him. It took twenty minutes just to bring him round. I was really scared.

"But when I discovered what had happened, my fear turned to anger."

Lynda and her husband, Roy, immediately transferred Kirk and his eleven-year-old brother, Clint, to another school. The bully blamed for intimidating Kirk into near bullycide was expelled. Kirk is now living life to the full without any fear of bullying in his new school.

Meanwhile, a thirteen-year-old boy from a mining village near Doncaster was saved from almost certain death after taking drugs to escape his tormentors. He'd been kicked, punched and called vicious names but refused to name his aggressors. The boy (who was never named by authorities) is now said to be excelling at school after recovering from his near-death experience.

The bullies have not been apprehended.

It must be your own fault

Deborah Scott's school life was made a misery by bullies who called her "Thunderthighs" and "Fatty" in the playground when she was in her early teens. Her body was a daily source of fun for the bullies who almost ended her life.

She made a desperate bid at bullycide. At the age of thirteen, she miserably wended her way home to her house in Edinburgh and swallowed forty of her mother's antihistamine tablets she found in a kitchen drawer. She told her parents who rushed her to hospital where doctors saved her.

After her bullycide bid, the campaign against her died down until, a few months later, sitting on a lawn in the school grounds, a group of girls suddenly surrounded her, tied her shoelaces together and pushed her to the ground. They tore off her T-shirt and snapped her bra. Then they held her by the arms, naked from the waist up, as a ten-minute free peep show for giggling boys. The same day, another girl dumped a plate of spaghetti over her head. Degrading graffiti about her was scrawled on school walls.

Her parents went so far as to complain to their MP and to Lord James Douglas-Hamilton MP of the Scottish Parliament's Cross Party Group on Children. But still the bullying went on. On her fifteenth birthday she was again stripped to the waist and dragged around the playground. The deep scratches on her back were so severe that she had to be taken to the school nurse who said that it must have been her own fault, that she'd provoked the bullies into the horrible attack. She spent eight months off school and was referred to a psychiatrist because of her terror of bullying - as though there were something wrong with her rather than the bullies.

Leaving school, Deborah also left the bully gangs behind her and became a slim, attractive hairdresser with a head held high and a new zest for life. The bullycide bid is part of a past which almost belongs to another person. She became so confident that, at twenty-four years of age, she even took her old education authority to court in Edinburgh claiming compensation for the hell she had been put through at school and the indifference of its staff.

The case was dismissed after a lengthy hearing. The Judge refused her justice only because so many incidents of bullying had not been reported to teachers at the time and so who, in their ignorance of the facts, could not be held responsible. The common code of silence between bullies and victims had worked against Deborah.

She told the Court of Sessions in Edinburgh: "I wanted to kill myself because I didn't think there was any other way out."

Judge Lord MacLean agreed that she had been tormented, taunted and attacked beyond endurance. He said: "Miss Scott is still deserving of much sympathy. Bullying within the school environment is hateful and it is insidious."

Her single official complaint had resulted in an intensified campaign against her for "clyping" [telling]. Her fear of complaining again lost her the case for financial recompense for the detriment which she was forced to endure because of others' failure to act.

Second chance

Rachel went the whole hog: sleeping pills, half a bottle of vodka and then a dive into the river. When she was spotted by a passer-by and ambulancemen were called, they thought her dead. She was eighteen with a file crammed with top school marks and a body filled with a deadly drug and alcohol cocktail.

She was lucky. The combination of lowered body metabolism from the booze and tablets and the chill winter waters had merely put her into a state of deep coma and, after three weeks in hospital in Warwickshire, she was recuperating at home with her parents.

Rachel, now living in another region and who does not want to be identified here to avoid contact with former schoolmates, had suffered racial, physical and verbal bullying from as early as she can remember until the day she left school with four A-levels and entered university.

"I was Jewish, I was fat, I wore glasses and I had a lisp. I was the dream victim for anyone who wanted to have a go. They called me 'Wachel,' 'Specky-Four-Eyes,' 'Lard-Arse' and 'Yid.' I can't remember a day of my school time when there wasn't something to bring me to tears.

"At first, I didn't tell my parents. I felt everything the others were saying was probably true. I was ashamed. I didn't want anyone telling me 'So what if you are fat, what if you have got specs, what if you have got a lisp and you are Jewish? I didn't want anyone else - especially people I loved - to agree with the bullies in any way at all. I couldn't tell teachers. I was frightened of retribution. I didn't know about such things as social workers or ChildLine. I just had to take it all and keep mum. It was driving me crackers.

"In secondary school, one of the teachers noticed what was going on and spoke to me in private. I told her I didn't want her to do anything about it because it might get worse because I'd also become known as a tell-tale. She told me it would probably blow over soon anyway. She didn't realise, you see, that I'd already been suffering for ten years by then. I felt I was just what the others were saying I was ... a useless lump.

"The only thing going for me was my school marks. I was pretty smart at my lessons. But even that became a problem. I got eight O-levels and they called me a swot. Then I got my A-levels. Sure, many of the worst bullies had left school by then, but there was still a group who'd have a go at me for being a smart-arse or teacher's pet.

"When I was accepted into university it was like a red letter day for them. You wouldn't believe the things they were saying about me. After that's when I snapped. I bought a bottle of vodka from an off-licence and used half of it to swill down a full jar of my Mum's sleeping pills. I vaguely recall walking to the river bank. I wasn't even wearing a coat even though it was very late at night and freezing cold. Then I don't remember a thing for days.

"I wasn't crying for attention or help. I really meant to do it. I know suicide's a sin and how much it would have hurt my parents and brothers and sisters. But I really wanted to end it all. Life was just too hard to cope with any longer. Too cruel.

"Coming to, though, in the hospital was a reawakening. Somehow, because I'd been given a second chance, I could see a new life opening up ahead of me. I'd already lost some weight whilst I'd been out cold. When I got dressed my clothes were loose on me. A young male nurse told me he thought my lisp was attractive. A doctor said I had lovely hazel eyes and suggested contact lenses might be less uncomfortable than glasses.

"All through my life, I suppose, I had unconsciously resisted changing because that would have been playing into the bullies' hands and there'd have been extra ribbing. But now I thought ... 'to hell with it. I'm going to university in a new city where no one knows me or my past and I can be what and who I want.' It was so easy to slim down, make a giggle of the lisp. And the doctor was right - the contacts were comfortable. I'd always been proud of my religion and it never became a problem at university.

Rachel is a college lecturer now, slender, pretty, coincidentally married to a non-Jew.

"One thing that helped me through was my great big, warm family. OK, I didn't tell them what was going on, but when I got home after a bully day at school it was like entering a new world of loving people who saw me as wonderful. But, in spite of that, I did snap and try to take my own life. Bullying can win out. Evil does sometimes overcome goodness.

"In my job now, I don't see any bullying. The students I work with are too mature and intelligent for that kind of nastiness, thank goodness. When I have children of my own? I don't know how I'll protect them. I just know I will. Please don't think that implies any criticism of my own parents. They saw me as just so perfect that it never crossed their minds anyone else could think otherwise.

"I know all those things I was taking to heart were just vicious lies from kids who were so insecure themselves they had to pick on someone they thought even weaker than themselves. I hold no animosity against them now. I pity them. But I'm not such a saint that I ever want to see any of their faces ever again.

"I've had to explain everything to my family and to my husband now. Since my attempt at suicide, there's been no hiding the truth. For a while my Mum and Dad even blamed themselves. No way was it at all their fault. You know, I realise now that I should have opened up to them all along. It might never have come to such a pitch.

"I feel so fortunate to have been given a second chance - a second life if you like. It could so easily have ended with a child having experienced a short life of daily misery instead of a happy woman who accepts every new day as a beautiful gift."

As is so often the case, Rachel did not have a broken or dysfunctional family, she had no psychological problems which required specialist treatment, she had no more than her share of physical difference and she did not wear her minority religious culture on her sleeve.

The only factor which drove her to near-bullycide was bullying itself.

Tribal warfare

A single schoolgirl giggle led to an intensive care unit and a desperate life and death struggle for teenager Caroline Worth.

That chuckle sparked off a vicious bully campaign against her at the local school and became such daily torture that the once brave and outgoing sixteen-year-old swallowed enough pills to kill two people.

Even as she stumbled, close to death, through the rooms of her rarely empty home, the thugs didn't give up their campaign of torment. They made crank phone calls and even hammered on the doors of the house as Caroline waited to die.

After her recovery the thugs followed her from school to a new college to keep up the brutal war of words, threats and violence.

Teachers at neither school nor college, say Caroline and her parents, lifted a finger to help. One even blamed Caroline herself for becoming the victim of the bully girls.

"I feel the same anger against the teachers as I do against the girls who made my life not worth living and who drove me to the very edge. They're as much at fault by doing nothing when it was well within their power to act."

At the time of writing, local education authorities had responded to her parents' detailed and passionate letters many months earlier with a mere acknowledgement of receipt and an apparently empty promise of an investigation.

Caroline is the second adopted child and youngest in the close family of five children. She's always been the pride of her four older brothers. Her mother, Mandy, is a teacher. But Caroline's adopted status, her mother's job and her medically diagnosed dyslexia and Attention Deficit Disorder (ADD) were no part of the campaign against her.

That took just one harmless but badly-timed snigger.

"Caroline recalls. "I was with my friends near the tennis

courts when a new girl of about thirteen appeared. I must admit she did look a little tomboyish. Someone called her a name - a 'Manbird' - and, unthinkingly, I giggled into my hand when my friend explained, because I'd never heard the expression, that it meant she looked like a bloke. I felt bad about giggling even at the time. I know I shouldn't have. It was an unkind reaction.

"I'd completely forgotten the incident by break time but the school bully decided to become part of the action. She asked me what I'd been laughing at and when I told her she pretended that the new girl was her little sister. Even though I apologised, that's all it needed for the whole group to turn against me. Not just that day but ever since. I didn't even give my friend's name for her protection. But my friend disappeared and left me alone to face the music. I could hardly believe she'd desert me.

"By lunch time a big gang of girls had gathered with the bully and approached me with their fists tightly clenched."

Putting on a brave face to protect her parents from worry, Caroline kept quiet about her ordeal that night. But the situation escalated the following day and, in tears, she told her mother who immediately rang the school where the Head of Year, although apparently being aware of the bullying, had not intervened. After that day, Mandy kept a day-to-day watch on the bitter schoolyard campaign, making it a point to be permanently at the end of a phone for emergencies.

Meanwhile, Caroline's agony increased. She said: "All my best friends dropped me and joined the fun. They were probably too frightened to do otherwise. I was excluded, hadn't got a single friend in the school. I quickly became the butt of every joke and evil jibe. I was called names, insulted, pushed, jostled and spat at until I couldn't take any more.

"They said the world would be a better place without me. One of the girls bashed my head into a mirror in the loo and threatened to change my face forever. Once, when one of them had spat in my face, I asked her 'do you really want me to die?' I was so upset I didn't even hear her answer. I just burst into tears.

"I needed security. So many people were against me. Mum and Dad did all they could to help but the teachers really didn't care. Soon, even the girls where I lived were ignoring me on the bus.

"I could feel the anger rushing over my body. When I approached one of my teachers with my problem, not only was he no help, he made matters even worse. He blamed the whole thing on me and even accused me of bullying. It was unbelievable. How could an experienced teacher blame the victim and not the bullies?

"Mum even gave up her teaching job early so that she could be at home for me when I returned from school."

Caroline - in terror of what lay in wait for her behind the school gates - had not suffered in silence. But, in spite of the stalwart help of Mandy and husband, George, nothing was done to help. Every school-day was hell. Then, one afternoon, she snapped.

"It was during an English lesson," she said. "Some of the girls were at the door laughing at me. The teacher demanded 'are you concentrating?' No. I wasn't. I was crying. I was jostled and mocked as I got on the bus in tears after school and was still weeping when I got off near my home.

"The house was rarely empty at that time of the day, but Mum had popped out for a short while to get some photographs developed. Still in tears, I scoured the bathroom cabinets and gathered up every pill I could find - forty-seven in all. Thirty-eight of them strong paracetamol. I sat on the carpet by my bed and pressed out four pills at a time, washing them down with a glass of water. I was in a daze waiting to die. That's all I wanted, just to die in peace."

The heartless bullies wouldn't even allow her that sad escape from the nightmare which had become her life.

"The phone kept ringing and going dead when I answered it. It was the girls. I was sure of it. They even came to the house, knocking on the door, shouting things like 'have you done anything?' It was as if they knew they'd pushed me over the top and were suddenly afraid. I didn't answer. I just lay in bed shouting to myself, shouting into the pillow."

Caroline's mother returned home to find her apparently in a calm sleep. It was not unusual after a tormented school day for Caroline to snatch forty winks, so she merely tussled her dark hair and quietly closed the door to tiptoe back downstairs. George got home half an hour later and was surprised to find his daughter still asleep. It was only on waking her that the couple realised something was very wrong with their daughter. They questioned her gently and Caroline opened up. "I'm so sorry," she sobbed. "I've taken tablets."

Dazed - working almost on automatic pilot - her frantic parents leapt into action and within minutes Caroline was being sped by ambulance to the local county hospital where, only thirty minutes later, doctors were fighting to keep her alive with emergency antitoxin treatment. Mandy and George stayed at her bedside until the early hours of the morning and were back to keep their vigil by the crack of dawn to find Caroline - now out of immediate danger - had been transferred to a children's ward.

"It was horrible," Mandy remembers. "We were hugging her and the ambulance seemed to take a lifetime to arrive. I just didn't know what would happen next. People all looked normal. The same as ever. But, at the same time, something had changed forever."

Caroline survived her bullycide attempt and returned to school later only to face renewed taunts ... but determined to ride them out, even informally counselling younger victims like her own cousin.

"When I came to and realised I wasn't going to die," she said, "all I felt at first was a deep loneliness. But I'm one of the lucky ones and snapped out of it. I'm so lucky to have the support of loving parents and family. The whole terrible time so near death has taught me the world and how to cope with it.

"I'll never let anyone bully me again. My mind is quite clear on that.

"I've learned that school is no playground. It's a very tough place and you are ultimately left alone there with your problems. I should have had proper protection there. But I didn't. The staff who pretend they are available to help just aren't there for you when you need them. School told my mother that the situation was being handled. It wasn't. Nothing helpful was ever offered. The bullies remained on the loose and they are still out on the town to this day. I could meet them any time and be victimised again if I were alone.

"I don't hate the bullies, I pity them. They need help. Some of my original friends realised what they'd been a part of and we're friends again now.

"Some girls still try to bully and exclude me. Some of the girls even turn up at my weekend job to taunt and threaten me. There's no escaping them. I get upset, of course, but I won't let it get on top of me again. I even find I can sometimes communicate with the bullies."

In a well-considered and detailed letter to the local county education authority - passionate but non-hysterical - Mandy complained bitterly about school failings which allowed the bullying to go on and on and which almost drove her daughter to the grave.

She wrote: "The school - at its own admission - did not seem able to control the ferocity and passion of the bullying and, themselves, described the atmosphere as tribal. Caroline was isolated, teased, mocked, physically assaulted, threatened and victimised."

Mandy pointed out that she and her husband had been in close touch with the school since the start of Caroline's trial and made regular appointments with the head of Caroline's year. Each time Caroline telephoned from school to tell of another bout of torment, Mandy telephoned the head for advice and was simply told to collect her from class and take her home.

Mandy added: "She's a brave, spirited girl and has never been weak or passive. But we were anxious that the situation was bordering on chaos in school at that time.

"There was no safe haven from the unremitting bullying and isolation. Despite my constant intervention the bullies were not apprehended, the situation was not thoroughly investigated and Caroline felt utterly let down by the school staff. By this time we were taking her to school by car to avoid the gangs of girls who waited for her to get off the school bus. The school seemed to be quite unaware of the seriousness of the situation and my daughter's desperation.

"She continued to show remarkable bravery by not giving in to the constant harassment of these girls - until 9 November 1998, which was a particularly horrifying day. She impulsively planned, once and for all, to blot out the horrendous experiences. Tragically she took an overdose. Enough to kill two people the doctors told us. It was a nightmare scenario and the full picture of just how badly she had been treated began to emerge.

"There had been nobody available or willing to protect her, even though staff were aware of the bullying. The head teacher was dismissive and defensive from the outset and seemed quite obstructive and callous. At no time did he ever take Caroline's concerns seriously. At the critical time he had not even introduced himself to her, though she had been in his school for eleven months. When we had stabilised Caroline's recovery at home and I felt strong enough to meet him he would not discuss the situation openly or frankly and was quite cruel in the way he spoke to me at this vulnerable time. He subsequently even refused to meet my husband at all.

"The bullies were not helped to face the situation they had caused, no reconciliation was ever attempted and the head refused any further dialogue with us. He decided that it was all in the past. It certainly was ever-present to us at home as we tried to re-establish ourselves in the aftermath of such a horrifying near-death experience.

"The terror will stay with Caroline for a long time to come, no matter how hard she's trying to put it behind her. For instance, we recently visited my aged mother in hospital. The drip in her arm reminded Caroline of the drip she had when she was being treated. It was enough to make her break down in tears."

After her near-bullycide Caroline could not face going near the school but asked for a meeting with the head teacher and her head of year to describe the evil which lurked there. The sympathetic school nurse had arranged a neutral venue at the local medical centre.

Caroline's request was turned down.

At the beginning of a new school year, talented Caroline was told that she could not sit her CSE Drama examination without returning to the school of her nightmares for classes. She courageously did, but only with a qualified teacher, paid for by the Home Tuition Service to act as bodyguard and lead her through a bully-gang of girls. The result of her bravery is that Caroline passed all her examinations with straight As and is now on an advanced course in Art and Design.

She is still dogged - even in college - by some of her original tormentors in spite of an official police caution against one of them who threatened her life. The caution was organised by her parents - not the school.

In a letter to us, Mandy says: "The school seemed not to care that all the unfinished business of these bullies was like an ill-extinguished fire that was set to flare again at the slightest provocation. We have tried in vain to get a response from the chairman of school governors and the head teacher refuses any dialogue with us.

"I met the School Liaison Officer and painstakingly described our feelings about the whole affair to her. Although she seemed sympathetic at the time, nothing useful came of that meeting - I could have saved my breath. The whole affair has been sorely mismanaged.

"If an articulate person with a background in education cannot manage to get even a reasonable response what would happen to one without this?"

As Caroline and her family awaited response to their letter of complaint and an investigation to be launched into the bully campaign, the school's 55-year-old headmaster surprised the community last year when news broke of his sudden resignation after an unpublished OFSTED report.

No official reason was given for his quitting after seven years in the post and several years before his planned retirement.

Suggestions were made that the blame should be laid on the school's inability to acquire sports college status.

We only know (because he will not return our calls) that he told a colleague on the local newspaper: "It is due to a variety of factors. When OFSTED happened there was a view that something radical had to happen within the school."

Even after his resignation the former headmaster was offered a position of responsibility within the local education authority. Reports from Tim's Advice Line suggest this is common practice, with incompetent teachers and heads with reputations for bullying landing plum jobs with the LEA or as school inspectors. One wonders on what basis the appointments are approved.

Chapter 13

From ragging to riches

The Ugly Duckling

There once was an ugly duckling,
Feathers all stubby and brown,
The other birds, in so many words,
said get out of town.
Get out of, get out of. Get out of town.
He went with a quack and a waddle and a quack,
a flurry of eiderdown.

Poor little ugly duckling,
Wandering far and near,
At every place, they said to his face,
Get out of here.
Get out of, get out of. Get out of here.
And he went with a quack and a waddle and a quack,
And a very unhappy tear.

All through the winter time,
He hid himself away.
Afraid to show his face.
Afraid of what others might say.
During the winter time in his lonely clump of weed
'Til a flock of swans spied him there and very soon agreed.
"You're a very fine swan indeed."
"A Swan? Me, a swan? Awe, go on!
"You're a swan!
Take a look at yourself in the lake and you'll see!"
"Why, it's ME! I AM a swan! Whee!

I'm not such an ugly duckling,
feathers all stubby and brown."
In fact these birds in so many words said
"Tsk, the best in town.
Tsk, the best, tsk the best.
Tsk the best in town."

Not a quack, not a quack, not a waddle or a quack.
A glide and a whistle and a snowy white back,
a head so noble and high!
"Who's an ugly duckling? Not I."
© 1979/80 Frank Music Corporation

In 1952, popular songwriter Frank Loesser wrote this piece for Danny Kaye for his famous musical version of the life of Hans Christian Andersen. Based on Andersen's 19th century children's tale, *The Ugly Duckling* could be seen as an allegory of bullying.

From survival to success

Too often, experts say, children victimised by bullies, even though never reaching the extreme of bullycide, have their lives permanently damaged by their horrifying childhood experiences.

They live timid adult lives in perpetual fear of new bullies taking up where the school-day thugs left off. Some are fortunate to find that elusive inner strength and preserve their self-respect. And some come out bigger than they had ever hoped in their wildest childhood dreams.

Amongst those who survived to succeed are:

SIR RANULPH FIENNES, 55, EXPLORER, had contemplated bullycide: "I went to Eton and was bullied very badly. I was an attractive boy and it was the norm for any boy considered a pretty boy to be wolf-whistled at by others. They'd sit on their window ledges above, whistling and shouting 'tart ... tart.' My father had died before I was born and I'd been raised in an all-female family. Such things were never explained. I had no idea why they were whistling at me or what a tart was. Such remorseless nastiness squeezed every last trace of self-confidence from me.

"At one point, I stood on Westminster Bridge and contemplated throwing myself off. I didn't go through with it, but I can understand why some children feel so bad that they think about suicide.

"By the end of the first term, I learned that one answer was to show the scowl the whole time, look at the pavement and make yourself part of the brickwork. I also took up boxing, which helped give me more of a macho reputation. But the bullying ruined chapel for me. The place was designed so that half the boys faced the other half across a central aisle. No way could you concentrate on the service.

"It lasted for about two years. Eventually, I must have told my mother, and she took it up with the masters. They dealt with the matter without exposing my identity. I think that's very important today in cases of bullying.

"After that, things improved and I began to enjoy my time there. Looking back, I can see that Eton built individualism. You either conformed or realised there was no way you could conform, it strengthened your ability to be an individual. I'd been reared by women. Perhaps I did need to toughen up."

SIR CLIFF RICHARD, 58, EVANGELIST, ACTOR, AND ONE OF BRITAIN'S MOST SUCCESSFUL POP SINGERS: "I looked different and came from a different background, and as soon as people realised I came from India, the other kids began to say 'when are you gonna go back to your wigwam?'

"I used to get jumped on regularly and had to just fight back all the time. There were groups of kids that would gang up on me. That happened a lot to start with.

"I remember rubbing one boy's hand raw to the bone on the ground after being jumped on by four of them or something like that - it makes me cringe to think of it - but when you're in a situation like that, who knows what we could do? Could you shoot somebody if they were about to knife you? Could you shoot somebody or knife somebody who was about to kill your child? The answer is probably 'yes.' It's a fact of life. But it's not something I think I'd want to wholeheartedly recommend."

TESSA SANDERSON, 43, OLYMPIC CHAMPION JAVELIN-THROWER: "I went to a mixed comprehensive. A good school with good teachers. But there was this boy who we used to call 'the Cock of the School' who'd boss everyone else around and push in front of the queue. The abuse was stuff like, 'hey, nigger! I'm talking to you, Blackie.'

"Guys would call me things like 'coon' and 'golliwog'. In those days silly-looking golliwogs were on the jam jars and we black kids hated them. There was pushing and prodding to make you respond, to make you get really aggravated. "I think the very worst thing about being a black kid at school is the names. Bullying is not just about the physical. I think the majority of black kids at my school were set upon a lot mainly because, at the time, there was a lot of racism and people weren't mixing so closely. But I've always been 100% proud to be West Indian, to be black. I could have built up a hate for the average white person. I'm glad I didn't."

LAURIE TAYLOR, 62, SOCIOLOGIST AND BROADCASTER: "At my schools it was the teachers. Some cultivated an atmosphere of fear. When children bully other children, in some cases they take the lead from the teachers, who pick on a kid to get cheap laughs. All through my school career, there were teachers who put pupils down, and the boys who were bullies were never as bad as the teachers themselves.

"My parents sent me to a Catholic boarding-school when I was six or seven. I believe they thought I would find my vocation in the priesthood. I was a thin, gangly boy and one of the teachers nicknamed me 'Boney' It was the Latin master. We were going through the forms of 'bonum', the word 'good' in Latin. One of its forms is 'bone'. The teacher said 'Now boys, you'll never forget this: think 'boni' and think of Laurie Taylor.

"There used to be what we called a Tickling Hierarchy. The attractive boys would be tickled and cuddled by the Fathers. But there was this unattractive crowd who never got a tickle or a cuddle. There was nothing avuncular about this tickling priest. The tickling probably had all kinds of unpleasant overtones, and I was probably very lucky not to be a favourite of the tickling priest. But, at the time, there you were in boarding-school, feeling homesick and thinking 'I wish I could have a cuddle.'

"Some of the other boys and I formed an alliance of the weak. We'd meet before class and hope 'Perhaps he won't shout at me today ...' Afterwards, if you'd been picked on, the other unpopular boys would try to cheer you up. "At the age of eleven I went to secondary school in Liverpool. Although there was strapping and caning at this school, too, I recall I got myself adopted by a gang of working-class Liverpool boys and they gave me some protection.

"Of course, teachers can also be the victims of bullying by pupils and it's often the libertarian teachers who come in for this, the teachers who didn't bully us and cared the most came off the worst because we kids saw them as a soft touch."

SIR JOHN HARVEY JONES, 75, FORMER CHAIRMAN OF ICI AND RECENT TV TROUBLESHOOTER: "I was a natural target for bullying. The school believed in corporal punishment - as well as the headmaster beating children, the prefects, who were aged about eleven or twelve, were also allowed to beat people. And the bullies beat people. Everybody beat people. I used to get my head ducked into basins of water. I would be beaten continuously with slippers and even sticks. I'd be held down and beaten.

"At the time, I accepted that I was bullyable. Years later, when I came to write my autobiography and recounted this, I got a number of letters from people who'd been at the same school. They shared with me the fact that they had also been bullied. For three years, the bullying was more or less unabated. Three years at that age is a lifetime."

MARTYN LEWIS, 54, AUTHOR AND NEWSCASTER, CHAIRMAN

AND FOUNDER OF YOUTHNET UK - which among other things offers on-line advice to children about bullying: "The fact that I was born in Wales may have played a part. Some people in Northern Ireland (where he lived as a child) welcome people from outside, but my tormentors were a clannish group. I didn't tell my family. For some reason I felt ashamed that it should be happening to me. It lasted only a term. I developed a dreadful stammer which, no doubt, alerted my parents to the fact that something was wrong. They found out from some other source that I was being bullied and moved me back to my former school. The stammer stopped.

"Now, whenever I believe I'm right, I refuse to be put off. Whilst I would not liken my colleagues to bullies, it's almost as if for me the alternative to being in control is being bullied."

CRAIG CHARLES, 35, ACTOR AND COMEDIAN: "When I was about fourteen or fifteen, there was a gang called The Lawrence Road Loonies. They had 'LRL' on the back of their jackets and polished heads and big boots with buttons. They used to come to the local disco. I had to leave before the disco was over because, otherwise, they all started piling out, wanting to jump up and down on me and my brother's head.

"So we'd leave about half an hour before it ended. As soon as the slowies - you know, the slow dances - were on, we'd nip over the wall. Many girls didn't wanna dance with black guys, so I never got any slowies anyway. Over the wall and away before the lights came up."

WAYNE SLEEP, 51, DANCER: "I was in the junior school and I had this little girlfriend who was from Hartlepool and she used to protect me. I used to run into the girls' yard when they started ganging up on me. My first real experience of almost hatred was when the kids at school found out I was doing dancing classes. They started calling me a sissy.

This was when I was seven or eight.

"I think the jealousy arose because I knew what I wanted to do at a very early age. These other kids didn't know what they wanted and their only view of dance was seeing it sent up on Benny Hill on the TV in a pair of tights and with floppy wrists."

LIZ KERSHAW, BBC RADIO ONE STAR came in for bullying because she was fat as a child. She escaped the beatings only because her father was headmaster at the school in Rochdale, Lancashire, where she was being tormented. The bullying stopped when she was moved to a new school. She said: "I simply had no friends."

SIR RICHARD BRANSON, 50, BILLIONAIRE AIRLINE BOSS, RECORD BOSS, ETC: he revealed being sexually bullied on his first day at public school. He was forced into a senior pupil's bed and bullied into a sex act. The £12,000-a-year school in Buckinghamshire became the centre of a major child abuse sex scandal in 1994 when school officials had to call in police after expelling a fifteen-year-old boy for bullying others into sex. Branson got over it. He's now said to be worth four times more than the Queen.

He said: "I told my parents matter-of-factly and they said 'best not to do that.' I never did again in my entire time at boarding-school."

THE LATE PETER COOKE when asked by Michael Parkinson on his chat show how he'd spent his time at boarding-school: "Mainly trying to avoid buggery, I suppose"

JAMES MACPHERSON, 38, ACTOR AND STAR OF TV'S TAGGART: He filled the toughest police boots in British TV, but in real life, as a kid, he lived in daily terror of the schoolyard thugs. Macpherson, who plays Detective Inspector Mike Jardine in the hard-hitting ITV drama, used to lie awake at night, terrified of the next day's playtime ordeal.

"I had six months of hell," he said. "I wanted to roll over and die. I was just fourteen years old and it still affects me to this day. One guy in particular made my life a misery. He carried a cut-throat razor and I knew that, if he got me, I would carry the physical scars for life. He had already cut somebody else up with his razor. I was in no doubt he could do it again.

"I saw him recently. He's a pathetic character now. But what I went through from him still haunts me. It's the whole male pride thing. Sometimes I wish I had done something instead of just running away."

Another bully targeted Macpherson simply because he didn't like his laugh and one "hard-case" threatened to urinate over him if he didn't hand over his lunch money.

"I met the guy a few years back and he said 'you don't remember me do you?' I told him 'Yes I do. You tried to pee on me at school.' He was with a lassie he was trying to impress and he didn't know which way to look, he was so embarrassed.

"I was very tall at school and most of the bullies were short and stocky and crazy. Maybe they just didn't like the way I looked, I had the wrong face. But the bullies are all fairly sad characters now. One was just out of jail and the other was short, bald, and pathetic so revenge has been taken."

Unavoidable violence

A famous chart-topping female 60s and 70s pop star from Glasgow, who asked not to be named because she's trying to put memories of the city behind her, told us: "I could show you the scars on my body. I can't show you the scars on my mind. I had to fight every inch of the way - physically fight, scratch, tear, bite and punch - just to get by day by day. Not because I was pretty and could sing but because the others were ugly and could only grunt. Sorry, there's not a tiny spot of pity in my heart for the bully ... let them go to hell! And, yes, I tried bullycide."

Adult targets of bullying reluctantly but regularly reveal their fantasies about disposing of their tormentor, The fantasy sometimes involves a weapon. However, being contrary to their moral values, such thoughts bring more guilt than relief, and few act out their fantasies, despite the temptation. These visualisations are, in fact, both a safety valve and a measure of the severity of psychiatric injury.

When responsible adults fail, it is left to the target to take action. Having been drilled throughout childhood that it's wrong to resort to violence, child victims find themselves in a dilemma. Sometimes, in a manner consistent with the integrity and high moral values that attracted the bully in the first place, the dilemma is resolved when targets direct the violence at themselves.

In many cases, when the victim has had enough and finally asserts their right not to be bullied by responding with force, it is often the victims who are punished for being violent.

Bullies are losers. They may be top dogs at school, but only by virtue of their propensity for violence and authority's propensity for inaction and denial. With school behind them, many bullies find their lack of communication skills, lack of interpersonal skills, and lack of all skills doom them to a life of failure. The antisocials and socialised psychopaths may appear to succeed but their lives are always unsuccessful over the long term.

What the authors find amazing is the incredibly long time that targets of bullies put up with the bullying by peers and older children, often overlooked, ignored or denied by the responsible adults, who sometimes, wittingly or unwittingly, join in. Targets of bullying often have an integrity and strength of character that can withstand years of abuse, torment, and physical assault - unlike the bully, whose weak inadequate personality becomes immediately obvious when they run crying to teacher the first time a target fights back.

Some people say that bullying makes you stronger, or you succeed because of the bullying. In fact, people survive, achieve and prosper *in spite of* the bullying. Their success is merely delayed.

Not everyone survives bullying. Even when the body does survive, sometimes the spirit has been dealt a death blow.

Chapter 14

Seconds out

Sticks and stones may break my bones
But words can also hurt me.
Sticks and stones break only skin
While ghosts are words that haunt me.

Pain from words has left its scar
On mind, and heart that's tender.
Cuts and bruises long since healed;
It's words that I remember.
Anon

Psychologists say that in rare cases an intimidated child will crack and react to the campaign against him, not by taking his own life, but by killing his tormentor. Some of the school spree killings in America, where the right to bear arms is enshrined in the Constitution, are likely to be carried out by targets of bullying who, without support and with their pleas ignored, have been pushed over the edge by years of unaddressed torment.

There's evidence that courts, newly aware of the pressure intimidated victims are under, treat hit-back killers leniently, as though agreeing that they killed in defence of their lives. In other words, they killed to prevent their own inevitable bullycide.

Whatever the reasons, bullying results in unnecessary and sometimes fatal injury which, had the danger signs been heeded, could have been prevented.

Damien Olive and Okera Clarke had been friends but as the years passed, the boys thought of by neighbours as near-brothers developed a new relationship. Clarke, time after time, beat up the smaller and slightly younger Damien.

Damien was beaten with chains, robbed of his pocket money and even dangled over the balcony of a five-storey tower block.

Recently, at the age of sixteen, Damien could take no more. Eighteen-year-old Clarke and a posse of youths grabbed him at a bus stop outside school and Clarke held him in a head-lock whilst another bully battered him with a rounders bat as dozens of bystanders looked on.

With a single lunge Damien plunged a knife he had taken from his mother's kitchen into Clarke's chest. The bully's lung was punctured and he died in hospital two hours later.

The Crown Prosecution Service decided not to prosecute Damien, of Acton, London, for murder and accepted a plea of guilty to manslaughter on the grounds of provocation. Judge Peter Beaumont QC set him free after hearing of his years of torment and sentenced him only to an eighteen-month supervision order saying: "Damien is not a danger to society. This was wholly exceptional."

His defence, Helena Kennedy QC, said the bullying campaign against him had been so horrific that "He suffered nightmares and flashbacks about what Clarke had done to him. He was more sinned against than sinning."

Judge Beaumont looked at Damien in the Old Bailey dock and quietly said: "You were outnumbered. You were losing. You were held in a head-lock while you were being hit by a rounders bat by a third person and struck on the shoulders and head. It was only then you lashed out with the knife you had in your pocket and it was a single, unaimed blow with the consequences which followed."

More telling than anything in court were the later forgiving words of bully Clarke's mother, Karen. She said: "I wanted Damien to go free. At the end of the day it was a tragedy of two friends that went wrong."

An unnamed boy was new at the school in Stoke-on-Trent, Staffordshire, and instantly became the target of cruel jibes. One day, as another fourteen-year-old, Anthony

Holland, engaged him in a tug-of-war over a box of crayons during a maths lesson, the smaller new boy struck out.

But the schoolboy's traditional punch in the nose went tragically wrong. It was a freak blow causing compression of the spinal chord as in a car crash whiplash injury. Anthony died almost instantly.

A coroner later recorded a verdict of misadventure and said: "Usually only dignity is hurt when a boy is given a bloody nose."

In Birmingham, fifteen-year-old school bully Sean Keyes warned fourteen-year-old Rustum Ali that he was a "dead boy" if he had the nerve to turn up for classes at the city's comprehensive school. Ali had the nerve to arrive and was immediately attacked. When someone handed him a knife, he used it on Keyes, killing him.

He admitted manslaughter but was given only a three-year youth custody sentence by Mr Justice Otton at the local crown court. Otton said Ali had suffered "gross provocation."

The unbeaten

His nickname was Chocolatedrop. A tiny, skinny, brown-skinned kid in a tough school dominated by white boys whose favourite pastime was playing the bully game.

They were the fighters and little Naseem Hamed made the perfect punchbag.

But Naseem - now a British boxing legend who has retained his World Featherweight Title against all-comers - wasn't going to spend his life being kicked around. The bullies became the losers and Naz became Prince Naz MBE, the champion who can say "I've never been beaten."

Out of the ring he spends much of his time counselling young bully victims and campaigning for an end to the kind of vicious torment which so often ends in bullycide.

He's redoubled his efforts since the recent birth of his son, Sami. He said: "His skin colour, who I am and what I do for a living makes me concerned he may be bullied. That's why my family and I are going flat out to get the message across - bullies are weak, bullies are the losers of life."

The bullies saw Naz, quite literally, as a knock-over. He was devoutly Moslem, black, and the kind of size you'd think would have him blow away in a strong breeze. Most of the bullying was verbal. But Naz wouldn't give in to it. He had backup from his close-knit, deeply religious, hard-working family and eight brothers and sisters. More importantly, he'd already made up his mind to become one of the world's winners.

"I'd decided to be rich and famous. There was no doubt in my mind. I'd just stare the lads out. Give them that smile folk think is mysterious. And, I'll tell you something for nothing - I'm still standing. Where are the bullies now? They were the weaklings, not me. They were cowards hanging around in gangs like jackals looking for a weaker animal to feed off. One they thought couldn't fight back. They're knocking around street corners now, lost.

"I knew I was better than them. I was. I've proved my point. But, don't get me wrong, I'm not a special human being. Anyone can do what I've done. I don't mean necessarily becoming a boxing champion. What I mean is that anyone can fight for their own self-esteem, self-respect and come out a winner in life."

Naz has the showbiz image of a Mohammed Ali without the extra few inches and pounds. Ali had muscles in places where Naz doesn't even have places. But that's all razzmatazz, according to him.

"Really I'm just an ordinary guy who changes the baby's nappies and spoons food into his mouth. I'm just one of the lucky ones who found a way, with help from my family, not to let the bullies ruin my life. I'm no macho man. I have always had an inner strength. No one was ever able to beat that out of me. Please don't think I'm arrogant - that's just the face I wear for the job. I'm just a guy doing his very best and loving Eleisha, my wife, and Sami, my son, and my family and friends almost to distraction."

"You see," he says, "boxing isn't bullying. It's sport. It's two well-matched equals who admire each other and agree to pit their skills. There's no hatred. No animosity. In fact there's a lot of warm respect. I would never dream of using what I have to intimidate anyone else."

Naz, who's 28 and who, although born in the UK, comes from a Yemen background, doesn't mind being called The Prince or Champ. But his favourite appellation is "Aba". That's what his baby son calls him in Arabic. It was his first word. That's what many of the children he has helped and encouraged out of being bullied might be calling him now.

Kids like young Elliott Stephens, so belittled by the thugs, that he tried to scrub his black skin white, then got a surprise meeting with Naz and can now face the bullies with the words: "I'm proud of who I am. The Prince told me why."

When Nabeel with older brother Riath and younger Naz took up boxing they found another, though less insidious, form of bullying in the gym.

"It was just by chance that Naz chose boxing. It could have been any sport. He just felt he had to excel in something to show his value as a man. We could fight back then if we needed to. But boxing was our sport not, firstly, a way of learning to hit back. That would have made us as bad as the bullies themselves. Like a kind of Kray Triplets. I'm sorry to have to say this but there weren't many Asian kids at our school and the bullying all seemed to come from the white boys. My sisters never had any problems with bullying because of us older brothers being around. But, strangely, when we went to an Arab school later, there were never any problems for any of us. It was more a kind of gathering than a school of competition between children.

"We were a very energetic family. Dad had an open-all-hours newsagents and grocery corner shop. Six in the morning until nine at night were opening times. The entire family chipped in. We never employed anybody, it was purely a family business. But still there was energy to spare. We had so much energy in fact that we maybe needed the gym to diffuse some of it. We did have anger about bullying but we could let that out at the gym, too. It was controlled, you see. If only the bullies could have done the same.

"A little - but not all - bullying was verbal. It could become physical, sometimes we fought back and came off best. My own parents even came in for intimidation. We lived in a National Front area. We got our windows smashed and what have you. That was when we were younger. Our parents were raising nine kids and working fifteen or sixteen hours a day in the shop. It was tough for them. We still own the shop premises but it's not open now. Things have changed.

"The bullying stopped - not because we could instil fear because of our boxing - but because we could command respect for the effort we had made. I remember at assembly one day when I'd won my first amateur boxing fight and I had to pick the award up in front of all the kids. I got some kudos that way. A little bit of respect and self-esteem goes a long way.

"I've met a couple of our old bullies. All of them have gone downhill. They're either on drugs or whatever. Nothing going for them now they're no longer the Big-I-Am. If you want to be a loser, be a bully. All the people I know who were bullies are losers. They're confused and insecure.

"Everyone's different and must handle the situation in their own way. If you're eleven or twelve and there's a bigger lad threatening you, of course you're going to be scared. Kids need somebody to back them up. We had the family to support us. But you must never show weakness no matter what the situation. Bullies thrive on that. We learned when we could box that we were left alone because bullies are the biggest cowards on earth.

"They'll never pick on someone they think might give back as good as they get. They hardly ever work alone. They're cowards. They work in packs like wolves. They prey on the weak ... the others they steer clear of.

"I have never been able to bring myself to make friends with a former bully but I have spoken to them. I think it might be right to say that the bullies have been bullied themselves at home or wherever. They should have had the strength of character to overcome that and not pass the buck. I've found that if you grow up in a decent family, you tend to be decent outside. What happens in your household is probably what moulds you."

Nabeel takes up the story: "It wasn't like school, bullying, niggling every day. It was the bigger boys who'd say 'you little, shitty crap you.' Under those circumstances that was all a bit of hype. A kind of showbiz. No harm was meant. No offence was taken. It just gave you the ambition to be that bit better in the sport. I wouldn't even call it bullying. It was all a part of the game. The jibes soon ended and we made pals. There was no real anger there. In fact the best thing we ever did was blow our anger in the gym. There's no anger left after a heavy session of training.

"Naseem is actively doing things against bullying now. We know bullycide does exist. Elliot, the young black kid who tried to scrub himself white, after a chat with Naseem, came out a changed and beautiful person with such a grin saying: 'That was a World Champion who said that to me. I don't need anybody else telling me. Naz has been through it all and look at him!'

"What course might he have taken without that talk? I can't say for sure we're saving kids. But we're trying our best to point them in the direction of a dignified, valuable life.

"Jabbing a finger at colour difference is a horrible way of

bullying somebody. We were lucky in that way, having such a big, proud family. Kids on their own who just sit in their room panicking with their fears get to the stage where they're terrified of going to school.

"Looking back on the horrible verbal bullying we suffered, I often wish we had told our parents. Especially our father. I mean, that would be an older person who you trust implicitly who can give you that boost you need. Who can tell you about your worth. My Dad was brought up in a village in Yemen. It was hard there and when he came here to Sheffield he could handle most things that came his way. We're all so proud of Naz ... but also of Dad and Mum and each other and how we've come out at the other end of intimidation.

"We were brought up to show respect. My father always said 'leave a good name behind you. Don't let anything tarnish that.' It's the soundest advice Naz and the rest of us have ever had. He's a proud man, our Dad. He deserves to be.

"Another thing is that, in bullying, there's no race really. It's just one of the handy excuses bullies use. Anything that makes you different makes you a target. A bully is a bully no matter what nationality, culture, religion. You go to any country, human nature never changes. It's all the same. There'll always be some little difference to give the bully his mad reason for terrorism.

"What Naz is putting over to the kids is: here's a little fella of five foot four who knocks people out and he's against bullying. We don't need a title to our campaign: just that message. Nobody is small enough or different enough to have to suffer bullying. There is never a need for bullycide. There's always someone somewhere on your side to help pull you through if you seek them out. The message itself packs a punch!

"Kids relate to Naz more because of his size ... he's no bigger than most young teenagers themselves. They feel safe with what he has to say. He's not intimidating. He's quietly spoken in private and - not just because he's my brother - he's a lovely, down-to-earth man. When you see him before a fight, he's preparing himself mentally and saying all kinds of things loudly about his opponent. But they kiss each other after a fight. The job's done. If only we could do that with our bullies, eh? If only they had the same set of ethics.

"He sees kids in hospitals. He's a patron of Teenage Cancer Trust and his office door is always open. The anti-bully side of it is only just building up. He's totally committed. People don't really know him properly. They just see him as how he is in the ring. Naz wins and he wins outside the ring because he's always there for the kids. Prince Naseem fights for other people, not just for himself."

The three boxing brothers all have kids about the same age "And we're going to make sure they stick together as we did", said Nabeel. "They won't become victims. We all know the signs of victimisation. We would never allow any bullying against any of our own ... or anyone else's if we can help.

"Today we'll remember in our family prayers what Mohammed, Christ, and others said so well ... treat others as you'd like to be treated yourself. There's no space in the world for the bullies who have never taken this beautiful idea on board. The morality being preached by all our religions is that which Naz and our family live by ... be kind to each other and have respect for everyone.

"You know, after the McCulloch fight, they hugged all the way to the changing room. They brought their kids in and shared them. They had a great time. Nobody lost, you see. They'd only been playing the game that pays the bills. One had a higher score during the match, that's all. It wasn't a fight. It was a sporting contest among equals."

Prince Naz would give one simple piece of advice to those to whom he is a guru, a role model and a hero, says

Nabeel. It is simply this: "Go through this life with dignity. Never let it enter your head to lose. Don't become a bullycide. Leave the bullies where they belong, kicking their downtrodden heels on a street corner wondering why they are now standing alone."

Flying into the record books

Brian Jones is a man with an ordinary name and an extraordinary history. He has lived life with one nightmare and a single dream.

He tried to drown himself as a kid in his early teens because he'd been bullied that far. That accounts for the nightmare he cannot shake almost forty years later, how close the murky pond had come to ending his young life.

Brian was a near-bullycide. He meant to drown in that pond. He found, though, that he couldn't resist another breath of air, surfaced, drenched and gasping and aching with shame.

His courage, though, like his dream, lay elsewhere. In March 1999 he became, with co-pilot Bertrand Piccard, the first to circumnavigate the globe non-stop in a hot air balloon, beating contenders like Richard Branson to the coveted world record.

Here he's speaking out fully for the first time. He feels he's earned the right to cast off the lifelong shame of being a victim and to tell it like it was.

On his website Brian echoes the word of higher-up astronauts "While Bertrand and I were drifting high above the earth in our small capsule, we became very aware of the fragility of our planet and of the people who inhabit it."

Brian spoke to us because he strongly believes, as we do, that his words of encouragement might mean that fewer children will be bulldozed into bullycide.

He told us: "Nobody could help me because nobody knew. I was so utterly ashamed of believing I was some kind of wimp I was just too embarrassed to talk about it."

Brian had been to a private fee-paying school with only forty pupils before finding himself thrust into a big new comprehensive with 1,300 tougher kids already in place.

Life suddenly became hell. He played truant, faked illness and lied to avoid answering another school bell. His studies suffered so badly that he gained only one GCE O-level so wasn't qualified to apply for the job of his dreams - piloting an RAF jet.

Undeterred, he learnt to pilot a glider at sixteen.

He joined the RAF as a clerk, spent two years studying in his spare time and eventually got the five extra O-levels he needed to achieve his ambition.

In 1986 he snatched at the challenge of ballooning. "The thing about flying - why it has such a special place in my life - is that for the first time, when I took off in a glider, I distinctly remember that comfortable feeling of having no fear. I had an immediate affinity to that.

When Brian came back down to earth in Orbiter Three, he'd gained the confidence to no longer worry about any description of his experience incurring the label of whinger, wimp or failure. As a history-maker he's determined that his two daughters and four grandchildren will never suffer as he did.

Brian reminisces: "I'd have been thirteen or fourteen years old, I suppose. It seemed to me that there was only one single bully - but he wanted to be the Big Guy and he had a gang of henchmen.

"I'm not quite sure why they picked on me. OK, I was very small when I was at school. At the earlier private school I enjoyed science. Perhaps they thought I was rich or posh or something.

"What is extraordinary to me is, looking back on it, how much I loathed school.

"The bullying when I was in the comprehensive was much worse than merely physical. It was the ongoing threat of the physical. When I look back on it now it sometimes seems just ridiculous and childish fear. But at the time, that's the only thing kids know about and understand. It's about all the constant insults - there wasn't a punch-up every week. It was extremely rare for me to be involved in a fight. To the others, their fun was just in instilling fear.

"I didn't complain to teachers or approach my parents. I was too ashamed. You *are* ashamed of yourself in the position I found myself in. It's so humiliating when you feel you must really be a wimp.

"I did have friends. From a certain form onwards the classes tend to split into different subject groups so you're among people more like-minded. I'd still be forced by my personal bully, before the teacher arrived, to stand up in front of a whole class and address him as 'My Lord And Master.' I had to go through that humiliation.

"My parents, nobody, they just didn't notice what I was going through and I was so utterly ashamed of myself that I couldn't bring myself to explain to anyone else."

Brian was the first during our research to introduce the element of shame in a victim.

He shared his memory of near bullycide with us: "Did I get to the stage where I considered suicide? Yes, very much. When I concentrated I was convinced I'd have to kill myself and I took it to the point where I seriously tried to do it. But it was too difficult to go through with.

"I tried to drown myself in a pool. That's not an easy thing to do. Then I wrote a letter to my folks saying I was running away. Tried to get to Scotland but only reached just North of Bristol and was picked up. I was still contemplating killing myself and all because of bullying. Suicide would have been a cry of shame from me.

"I decided to start playing truant from school and as a truant you get into all sorts of lies about where you've been and what you've been doing. Then it all catches up with you and people find that you're hiding the truth.

"My parents, when they realised, took me to a child psychologist and then went to the head and my form master. The thing is, you feel you've failed Mum and Dad by admitting you're being bullied. You make up any excuse to deny it. I would never have told the truth. Never. Because of the shame.

"The experience of bullying lasted until I was sixteen. It's left a deep scar.

"I needed to prove I wasn't the wimp everybody thought I was."

"I don't know quite how the bully experience relates to my success in the air. While I was on duty in the balloon and my fellow pilot was taking his turn to sleep, the bullies never crossed my mind. I saw the fragile earth and thought of its fragile inhabitants but I was above it all.

"There was a touch of - not so much revenge at leaving the bullying behind - but of getting away from detail, of the feeling that I'd let my parents down in terms of lack of education.

"I'm in my fifties now and remember that what's so important is the destruction of self-esteem when you're young and the terrible, unwarranted embarrassment. I still don't know why I became a target or why the bully became a bully."

This wasn't at the front of Brian's mind as one half of the first duo to circumnavigate the world. It's when he touched down that he realised something had happened that had changed his life.

"The spark, I think, was over North Africa, looking down on a landscape which was unbelievably beautiful and feeling ourselves the luckiest, most privileged men in the history of the world, then realising that there were kids down there starving to death and grown-ups trying to kill each other and realising what a crazy world it really is."

Chapter 15

Grim start to the millennium

"Things are going to get a lot worse before they get worse."
Lily Tomlin

As awareness of bullying rises, so media coverage grows. Here we include stories that have made the news during the first year of the new millennium and which show that little has changed since Steven Shepherd's fateful walk.

Nothing changes
Danielle Goss died with her cellphone in her hand. This new hi-tech weapon meets the two essential criteria bullies demand which have come to light in this book: secrecy and ingenuity. There's no fun in pulling pigtails in the playground any more.

For Dani, the dawn of a new millennium was just another day of horror, tormented by calls from the bullies who waged war against her.

Her cowardly antagonists gave no reason for their campaign of hate. They just told her they wanted her to die.

Dani became the first bullycide of the 21st century, ending her life on the second day of the new millennium as revellers still celebrated life, and as American scientists predicted that a baby born in that special week could expect to live to be at least one hundred. Dani was fifteen.

Kevin Donald, news editor of North News in Newcastle, followed the case of young Dani Goss on our behalf.

He reports: It was bullying for bullying's sake. The girls who tormented her never gave a reason for her suddenly becoming their helpless target in the late months of 1999. All her family and we can think is that she was easy prey. She was, quiet, sensitive and, probably more than anything, she would never stand up for herself.

She didn't even report her problem to the school. It's doubtful they could have done much anyway, for at school there was never a sign of bullying. The thugs used the cellphone as their weapon of hate.

Dani, like so many others in her position, spared her family the whole truth. Their only inkling of the hell she was going through was when she sobbed that she wanted to die and, then, when they found her dead with her cellphone clutched in her hand with a final-goodbye note.

Coroner William Duffy recorded an accidental death verdict at the inquest in August. He said that he felt her notes expressed her massive distress but that he wasn't convinced she'd meant to go that far, maybe just to cry out her suffering.

Dani died at the house of her Grandmother, Anne Fenwick, on a nearby housing estate. The last painful memory Mum Diane has of her daughter was a first and last Millennium kiss on 1 January 2000.

After the inquest, Diane said Dani had told friends that she was being "put through hell" and was planning to take her life.

Diane continued: "I didn't see the warning signs. I looked for them, but I didn't see them. Sometimes youngsters hide the way they feel. They don't like to open up about the way they are being treated.

"Dani didn't tell me her troubles. We could talk openly about everything else. She didn't express the real extent of the misery in her heart and how deeply these people were hurting her.

"What happened to my Dani should serve as a warning to other parents. Bullying must be known before it can be tackled.

"The bullying had taken its toll secretly over a cellphone. It had a terrible effect on her. Just a couple of days before she died she'd phoned me in an awful state, screaming and hysterical. She'd been chased by two girls and had nasty phone calls all through the day. But the main way to get at her was by the funnyfone. Some calls were threats, others were sneers and wishes that she would die.

"She was a sensitive kid. She took all this to heart. She told me they called her a psychopath and that really hurt her. She was quiet, maybe a little shy. That's all. I just can't pin down a reason for her becoming a target.

"She may not really have intended to kill herself. It could have been a cry for help. But, either way, the bullying caused it. I just wish she'd told me. I can't believe she's gone. I don't know how I'm going to live without her.

"Dani had been so badly threatened sometimes that I kept her off school. Then they picked up on her mobile and it became long-distance bullying over the airwaves. She told me she didn't want to live because people wouldn't leave her alone. She was frightened. But I didn't realise how frightened and I didn't realise that the death wish was more than an empty threat. Kids sometimes say things like that and wake up the next morning in a completely different mood, forgetting they'd even spoken the words.

"No one can believe how she was secretly being forced to the very edge - and then over it. Teachers from her school have visited me in tears. These bullies will have to live for the rest of their lives with what they did to my girl. They will suffer."

Dani was doing well at schoolwork and was determined to pass all the exams she needed to become an air hostess.

An autopsy showed she'd consumed enough alcohol to put her over the drink-drive limit before swallowing a lethal dose of painkiller pills. She died with her mobile in her hand. They traced the last incoming calls to a town centre phone box. Everyone's convinced it was another evil taunt. The last words Dani heard were words of hate.

She left a couple of notes. One was for Diane and her partner, Kevin, and to a pal, Ashley. It read: "I'm sorry. I love you all very much. I hope I live, Mam and Kev. Thanks for your support, Ash. Thanks for everything."

The second note said: "If I live, I'm sorry. If I don't, love you Mam and Kev and Nana. Life is good with you. But I'm sick of life with friends. Love Dani."

Some "friends"! Her mother told us she did have friends at school. But these weren't the "friends" Dani was talking about in her last note. In fact her real friends were so devastated by her death, the school brought in grief counsellors to help them overcome the trauma.

The now ubiquitous mobile phone is proving irresistible to bullies. In October 2000, Wirral coroner Christopher Johnson recorded a verdict of suicide on 15-year-old schoolgirl Gail Jones from Tranmere on Merseyside.

She had taken an overdose after a campaign against her culminated in her receiving up to twenty hate calls an hour on her cellphone.

In an ironic twist, Gail recorded her own bullycide message on her telephone. Father Glyn said: "She tells us how she feels towards us and hints that the calls had driven her to do what she did. It really got to her and she could take no more."

Cellphone bullying has increased substantially over the past year. Liz Carnell, founder of the website Bullying Online which throws a lifeline to despairing parents, said that use of the instrument for torture was virtually unknown before December 1999 when cellphones found their way into Christmas stockings for the first time. Her organisation now averages two calls a week from children tormented via mobile phone. Sometimes these involve death threats.

Gail's father begged her to throw away her phone but relented when police suggested they could use technology to track down Gail's tormentors through incoming calls. The bullies were more effective than the police though.

Glyn told the inquest: "We can only guess she got a last call in the middle of the night and it pushed her over the edge. Whoever did this will probably never be caught. I hope they can live with themselves."

More au fait

Teenagers are better informed about the world around them than their parents ever were according to Georgina Pattinson in the Birmingham Post. Harry Potter's antics and Adrian Mole's naivety may have delighted readers but in real life teenagers today are much more complex than their fictional heroes. A government survey shows that children are growing up faster but are weighed down by what used to be purely adult concerns.

While Adrian Mole fantasised about sex and Harry Potter has still to discover it, one-quarter of children now have sex before the age of sixteen, thus opening up a new battlefield of potential bullying by rivals. The UK has the highest rate of underage pregnancies in Europe.

Esther Thompson, an outreach worker with the Youth 2 Youth website, sees young people exuding confidence but without any real confidence to back up their image. The website's list of common stresses includes a 68% experience rate of bullying at school.

More violent females

Delegates from schools, local authorities, charities, social services and children's homes heard the full horror of female violence at a congress in Glasgow in September 2000.

A Glasgow University study of 800 Scottish girls aged between 13 and 16 showed that violence was now so commonplace it was considered the norm. Whereas forty years ago boys were responsible for eleven times more violence than girls, girls were to blame for one in three attacks by 1995. Girl violence in Scotland has doubled in the last ten years.

Ten percent of girls interviewed admitted to being routinely violent. Seventy percent said they regularly stood by and watched bully attacks. Forty-one percent had been on the receiving end.

Ninety-eight percent told researchers that violence was now accepted by teenaged schoolgirls as a natural and everyday part of life.

Professor Betsy Stanko, who heads a European Social Research Council project researching violence, described the new Scottish figures as "staggering."

The conference was addressed by a group of girls who described attacks with iron bars and knives. Delegates were told of the kidnap and brutal, systematic torture of one young girl over two days and nights by a gang of schoolgirl thugs. Delegates also heard of children being forced to drink urine, having faces rubbed into dog excrement, hair being set alight, and one girl leaping 60 feet from a building 200 yards from her home to escape a mob of more than 20 bullies. She survived with serious injuries.

It's a rap

Sally Morris discussed the less-than-innocuous influence of rap song lyrics on teenage behaviour in The Times on 7 July 2000.

Bullying by girls, she wrote, is getting nastier and more violent. Maybe a rap song is inciting them?

Girl-on-girl bullying has increased by 50% in the past three years. Now teachers and educational psychologists are concerned that a chart-topping song by American pop duo Daphne and Celeste will encourage bullying schoolchildren to believe their behaviour is acceptable.

The song U.G.L.Y. has such lyrics as: "You got eyes like a pig and your nose is big" and "You're so fat and ugly with a belly full of flab, when you wear a yellow coat people shout out 'cab'".

Ted Cummings, head of press for Universal Island, Daphne and Celeste's UK record company, denies U.G.L.Y. encourages bullying.

Hereward Harrison, Head of Policy for ChildLine isn't in the business of flogging records. He told Sally: "The name-calling in U.G.L.Y. is just the sort of thing that young people call ChildLine about every day."

It used to be a cliché of teaching that boys sorted out their disagreements with a thump and girls resorted to more subtle forms of manipulation. But girls are becoming more and more physically aggressive.

Gaby Shenton, assistant director of Kidscape, told Sally that besides the increase of girl-on-girl bullying reported to her organisation, the nature of female violence is changing; girls now use knives and push their victims in front of oncoming cars and lorries instead of just threatening violence as had been the traditional way of oppressing the physically less strong.

The rise in girl bullying is linked to the erosion of traditional masculine and feminine roles. Where years ago you could pull the occasional pigtail or whisper nasty names, you still had to appear a "nice" girl to win respect in a wider society. Now, influenced by outspoken and often brash role models, girls perceive that aggression can apparently pay off.

Victims bullied for a year are six times more likely to contemplate or commit suicide than their peers and four times more likely to suffer lifelong lack of self-esteem. Research from Norway shows that boys who bully are four times more likely to end up with criminal convictions. It is vital to attack the girl-on-girl problem here before the same patterns are established.

Catherine Howard, a regional education adviser for the NSPCC in the Midlands, says that girls are clever at distinguishing and that teachers and adults are not. "We know," she says, "that about 85% of bullying is a group activity with a ringleader, assistants and reinforcers. We try to break down the group power by re-individualising the members, many of whom are privately unhappy with what is going on. When a girl is being bullied, we ask each member of the bully group what she is going to do to help her and then follow up her commitments. Once they realise they can make their own decisions and not follow the ringleader, the power is gone.

"Some schools exclude troublesome bullies, but this often simply shifts the bullying from school to outside territory where there is even less control."

Kidscape has a simple but effective piece of advice: Shout "NO" loudly to attract attention. Bullying thrives on secrecy.

Sally Morris spoke with Dieter Wolke, Professor of Psychology at the University of Hertfordshire, who told her there are two types of bully: the manipulator and the victim-bully. He said: "The manipulator might repeat the words of this song [U.G.L.Y.] in a controlled way because it would amuse her to taunt other children. She is sharing the joke with the singers.

"The victim-bully is sometimes a bully, sometimes a victim. When she is playing the bully role, she will hold a child down while the manipulative bully does the beating. As a victim she will use the song to get at someone. She is impulsive and impressionable and likely to be influenced by pop icons.

"Hers is a more casual and more dangerous approach to bullying. Typically she will anger easily and say such things as 'why you lookin' at me?' She will have a higher risk of psychiatric problems later than the manipulative bully, who is likely to become a future manager."

Girls are proving that they can become just as tough and threatening as the very worst boys and sneakier with it. Dr Mike Eslea, a senior lecturer in psychology at the University of Lancashire, told Sally: "Ten percent of boys will admit to being bullies but girls never do. Either they're more dishonest or don't even realise what they're doing."

Desperate to die

In an all-too-familiar tragedy, Andy Loudon from the Daily Mail reported in June the case of a troubled teenager who tried to escape bullying by starting a new life at boarding-school but could not shake off the torment blighting her life.

Alexis Cantor tried to hang herself, cut her wrists, took an overdose and finally jumped to her death from a high university building an inquest heard. She was seventeen.

Alexis had been missing from her Liverpool home for three days before her body was found with a note lying beside her on a low projecting roof of the UMIST building in Manchester.

Her stepfather, Anthony Myers, told how bullies at Liverpool's King David High School had made her life hell.

He said: "Alexis had been talking about not wanting to live. She was being bullied at school and decided to make a fresh start at boarding-school. She had excellent GCSEs and had been accepted to study at Stonar School. But after just two days there she tried to hang herself and slit her wrists.

After her early suicide bids, Alexis left the £11,000-a-year Wiltshire school to live with her mother, Barbara, and her stepfather in Mossley Hill, Liverpool.

Soon after the move she took a massive paracetamol overdose but survived that attempt. Only with a final horrific death leap was she able to end her torment.

Statistics

Denis Cassidy is co-editor of Cassidy and Leigh, one of the UK's most experienced freelance press agencies. He is also co-founder of the National Association of Press Agencies whose members include all major freelance news services in Britain. Denis confirmed what other agencies have told us: "You're right. Bullycides are slipping through our fingers because we can't afford to speculate expensive journalistic time on the off-chance that something valuable might come up. We're all also suffering from a breakdown in communication with coroners' officers.

"My rough, off-the-cuff advice would be this: take your figure, double it at least and you'll still only be exposing the tip of the iceberg. I'd say your figure of sixteen UK bullycides a year is very conservative based on knowing as a professional what we must miss."

Denis relayed the case of a girl who was bullied at school who hanged herself after returning home on the last day of school term just four days after a classmate had taken his own life.

Minutes after she crept into her bedroom in West Byfleet, Surrey, Kate Williams, who was just fifteen, was found by her stepmother hanging by the neck and dead. She'd already tried an overdose of pills.

Her natural mother Yvonne Bunn, 46, said after the June inquest into Kate's death: "I can only hope that this will send a message to other children - if there's something on their minds they must tell someone about it."

Apart from being bullied in the playground, Kate had one particular bully girl to contend with according to her father, David.

Bullying north of the border

Scotland does seem to be a bully black-spot. Scots children's campaigners recently warned that more Scottish children are being bullied at school than ever before.

A ChildLine survey published to mark the tenth anniversary of the charity ChildLine Scotland said that bullying among children aged ten had increased in the decade their organization had been in place. Over the same period bullying of a physical sexual nature had doubled.

The survey, which warns that 3,000 children suffer physical and domestic abuse in Scotland, follows a spate of suicides and attempted suicides by young Scots.

However, ChildLine has become a victim of its own success according to new statistics which show that as many as two out of every three children calling for help hear an engaged tone.

When the Glasgow office is closed at night, callers are automatically transferred to London headquarters where, often, the only voice they hear is that on a recorded message asking them to try again.

In the ten years since they opened, ChildLine in Scotland has helped almost a quarter of a million children on its shoestring budget. The charity's director north of the border, Anne Houston, fears for those who are so disappointed at not reaching immediate help that they don't call back.

It's impossible to say what happens to the no-reply kids but we have seen the ChildLine help numbers in the diaries of bullycides.

ChildLine Scotland needs to raise at least £750,000 each year. Already the crisis has prompted calls in Scotland's new parliament for an emergency cash injection.

ChildLine founder and veteran broadcaster Esther Rantzen, speaking at the charity's birthday celebrations in Glasgow, said that bullying was the biggest single reason for distress calls to ChildLine. She said: "On the one hand, this increase in calls about bullying is encouraging. It suggests that children now realise they don't have to put up with it.

"But it also shows that adults are not taking it seriously enough if they must call us because they can't rely on the grown-ups around them. We must work together to end the pain that bullying causes."

She said in an interview with the Scottish Sunday Mail's Victoria Mitchell: "The brutal facts are that desperate children who have nowhere else to turn are unable to talk to our counsellors because we don't have the money to open enough lines. Although year-on-year we counsel more children, it's still not enough.

"Government ministers or ordinary people who care about children must be aware that we save lives, we send abusers to jail, we protect children from bullying and we also talk to them when they are deeply distressed.

"We know there are children whose lives we could be saving who cannot get through to us. All because we don't have enough money. We are terribly cheap and we are terribly good value for money. About thirty pounds can save a child's life.

"We need to be twice as big. Even as you're reading, there will be children desperately trying to get through and not able to."

The situation could be even worse. Of the 20,000 calls from primary-school-age children in 1999, one-third concerned bullying. However, research published by ChildLine in October 2000 revealed that 52% of all children throughout the UK under the age of 11 have never heard of the service.

Sandra Brown, founder of the Moira Anderson Foundation and author of the award-winning book *Where There Is Evil*, takes the view that the high levels of bullying in Scotland are because of the very traditional education system which for decades encouraged children to be seen and not heard.

"Entrenched attitudes in the playground", she says, "mean that you don't clype [grass] on peers. Only when physical assaults clearly get out of hand do kids go to janitors, heads, or other teachers. Still not enough recognition is given to the grinding down of the spirit involved when severe psychological warfare is going on.

"I think parents in Scotland have been far more likely to see the staff as experts and let them deal with problems (although they don't) and not challenge the school or question their policies. I can think of several schools still without Parent Teacher Associations even in the year 2000; this history and lack of investigation has allowed bullying to flourish unchecked."

School violence

Investigative reporter Hamish MacDonell in a July issue of the Daily Mail exposed the scale of violence in Scotland's schools, citing a study which showed 200 pupils were excluded from school *every day* during 1999.

Head teachers were forced to use their ultimate sanction of suspension or expulsion 35,000 times in a bid to curb the growing culture. One-third of suspensions were the result of aggressive behaviour and assaults on other pupils or staff. The statistics were the first such figures compiled in Scotland.

In June a thirteen-year-old Glasgow girl, Stephanie Govan, tried to kill herself after six months of bullying. Her attacker was suspended for just three days before returning to carry on the bullying.

Police reports during the summer of 2000 have detailed how children as young as nine are carrying knives to school and that the incidence of assault in the playground is increasing alarmingly.

Glasgow was the blackest bully spot. Over twelve months 8,000 children, 10% of the classroom population, were excluded from school.

Deputy Education Minister Peter Peacock was reported by Hamish as saying he wanted to discourage school heads from expelling pupils and reduce the number of expulsions by one-third because exclusion would hurt their later lives.

He came in for immediate flak from teachers and parents for failing to give support to victims and well-behaved students.

Paul O'Donnell of the teacher's union NASUWT warned that discipline would collapse if disruptive children were not removed. He told Hamish: "If they're put back in the classroom, the message to other children is clear - if you misbehave, nothing will be done. Discipline will go to pieces."

Tory education spokesman Brian Montieth read the report and concluded that some schools in Scotland were "a battlefield."

Donna Watson had this story to tell in the Daily Mail in June. We reprint her words with her kind permission and that of the family involved.

"A grieving teenager was found hanged outside her family home just weeks after a close friend committed suicide.

"Lyndsey Walker, 16, was found hanging from a clothes pole in the garden of the family home in Airdrie, Lanarkshire, by the local postman.

"Her close friend Neil Miller had hanged himself just nine weeks before.

"The death was the latest in a spate of teenage suicides and suicide attempts in Scotland in the first week of June.

"Lyndsey, friends say, had been badly bullied at a previous school. Ten young Scots under the age of seventeen have now taken their own lives in just over twelve months."

Claire Anderson, 14, hanged herself from a bunk bed in Elgin, Morayshire in June 2000. Claire was the second child to take her own life in Moray. Eighteen months earlier, Derek Craib was only ten when he hanged himself less than a mile away.

Greig Ryan, 15, from Fallin, Stirlingshire used his own dressing gown cord to hang himself in his bedroom. Gary Agnew of Drumchapel, Glasgow was just twelve years old when he hanged himself in 1988. At the Royal Hospital for Sick Children in Glasgow an eleven-year-old boy is still fighting for his life at the time of writing after being found hanging at his home in Dunblane.

There has been a 13% increase in the overall suicide rate in Scotland alone since 1988. This only reflects those deaths officially recorded as suicide.

Bullied children are often popular youngsters with everything to live for, Roz Paterson wrote in the Scottish Daily Record. But behind the facade, young suicide victims live with a sense of emptiness and self-loathing.

Karen Strang, who runs a UK-based membership organisation called 'Education Otherwise', has taught her eleven-year-old son, Alban, at home in Stirling, Scotland since he was born. She believes a key reason for parents opting for home tuition is bullying.

She said: "Schools often do not admit it is happening or they say that it isn't a problem. Parents cannot accept this and see their child suffering." Research from the University of Durham puts the number of home-educated children in the UK at around 150,000 (1% of the 5-16 population) and predicts this will reach 3% within a decade.

In July 2000 an Irish couple was fined £10 for refusing to send their son to school. James Duffy and his wife, Lucy, say that fourteen-year-old Rory is a victim of bullying and prefer to educate him safely at home.

They will appeal the conviction under the ridiculously outdated 1926 School Attendance Act after their twenty-fifth appearance in court in a legal battle with the State.

Mr Duffy said: "No matter what, it is better than sending our son back to the bullies. The police have done nothing about it. We'll fight on."

Children who are gifted and don't fit the mould because they are "too clever" can find themselves the target of bullies' envy and jealousy as well as the target of institutionalised bullying.

One parent told us: "Our daughter Stephanie suffered frequent migraines and school refusal from the stress of it all. The Education Authority refused to allow the school to advance her on to more stimulating work as they said they were an "equal opportunities" authority - by which they meant all children had to be treated in exactly the same way rather than according to their needs. Stephanie saw an educational psychologist and a consultant about her migraines, and both agreed she was understimulated and that this was the cause of her unhappiness and problems.

"We gave up fighting for better support for her when she was nine and moved her to an independent school. Within three weeks she was a completely changed child, her migraines vanished (and she's never had another one since), and she started enjoying school for the first time in her life. For her things have turned out well because we were able to find the right school for her, and find the grants and scholarships to pay for it, so she hasn't had to miss out socially."

A Scottish hotline set up to aid bullied schoolchildren has been swamped by calls ... from teachers.

Of every 500 calls, 120 are from school staff complaining of victimisation by pupils. A similar proportion of calls are from parents of bullied children.

Anti-Bullying Network Manager Andrew Mellor said: "The teachers are concerned about workplace bullying from pupils, parents, and management."

Barbara Clark, Assistant General Secretary of the Scottish Secondary Schoolteachers Association, commented: "Our members are complaining more frequently than ever before about being bullied by colleagues and line managers."

Racism and homophobia

Fifteen hundred London schoolchildren were handed pocket guides on how to handle bullying based on racism, sexism, and homophobia as part of a radical anti-bullying drive by Lewisham Council in mid-July. The booklets tell them what to do if they suffer or witness bullying and advise: "You don't have to suffer this kind of hassle."

The forty-page guide lists helpline numbers and anti-racism plans for schools. "Lewisham schools want to challenge such unacceptable behaviour," the guide tells its readers. More than half of all Lewisham schoolchildren are black or from ethnic minorities. Many are asylum seekers.

Four out of every ten gay schoolchildren attempt suicide or resort to self-harm by cutting themselves or burning their skin with cigarettes, a study published in July reveals. Those suffering bullying are more likely to quit their education at the minimum age of sixteen rather than face further torment, although their grades match those of straight students.

Ian Rivers of the College of Ripon and York St John interviewed 190 lesbians and homosexuals who were bullied at school. He found that more than one in six suffered Post Traumatic Stress Disorder, (PTSD), nightmares and flashbacks, and used medication to cope with life after school. Analysis of a smaller group showed gays would use any excuse to absent themselves from school. Only on in ten had a good attendance record.

The study, presented to the British Psychological Society's Lesbian and Gay Conference on 18 July 2000, said that, even though GCSE examination results were equal in gay and heterosexual school communities, not a single gay who admitted frequent absence to avoid intimidation went on to pass A-levels.

Halting the horror

At least three teenagers deliberately injure themselves or attempt suicide every hour in Great Britain.

After the suicide of a seventeen-year-old schoolboy this summer the charity, Depression Alliance, had this to say: "The statistics are frightening. Not only are there more than two million children attending GPs' surgeries with some kind of psychological or emotional problem, but there are 19,000 suicide attempts by adolescents every year. That's more than one every thirty minutes. On top of that a recent study by the Mental Health Foundation says that children are becoming less resilient and less able to cope with the ups and downs of life."

Befrienders International, the UK-based umbrella group for the Samaritans' lifeline organisation, is to work with children in Denmark and Lithuania to help develop a programme to teach life skills with which to combat bullying and bullycide.

The Samaritans organisation is keen to draw attention to the epidemic of bullycide and attempted bullycide. The charity believes that at least half the UK population knows someone who has self-harmed. The number of young boys who have taken this horrific escape route has doubled over the past ten years, they believe.

Director Chris Bale said: "People have been working on coping skills with ten-year-olds for some time. We wanted to go for something far, far earlier."

The countries chosen for the study have among the highest suicide rates in the world and, if the Reaching Young Europe project is a success, results will be applied to help combat bullycide in Britain.

Bullying of the disabled

Raymond Duncan of the Daily Herald in Scotland told us that bullying is the main reason disabled children move from inclusive schools to special schools.

Raymond's research is based on an Edinburgh University study and is the first of its kind to take on board the views of disabled children themselves rather than the opinions of parents and professionals. The study maintains that bullying is caused by less visible social factors than by the obvious physical disability of victims.

The University study, funded by the Economic and Social Research Council, was conducted in mainstream and special schools as well as in homes and leisure venues in

Scotland and the North of England and involved more than 300 children with a wide range of physical disabilities.

"The children brought their own unique understanding of what it means to be 'disabled'" said academic Nick Watson of the University's Department of Nursing Studies, co-author of the report.

"We need to listen to disabled children more and encourage them to put forward their own solutions to problems."

Watson said that many disabled children had spoken about their experiences of bullying which was the one thing they all had in common.

The report highlighted the fact that almost all school support staff were female leaving boys lacking male role models and male assistance, a phenomenon already noted in UK primary schools following heightened sensitivity to child abuse issues and a growing number of false claims of abuse.

This summer, school inspectors issued a highly critical report on an East Lothian, Scotland, education unit for problem pupils, reports Scottish colleague Frank O'Donnel. Behaviour of teenagers at the East Lothian Leavers' Unit is so bad that the report called for staff to be issued with mobile telephones to call for emergency help.

Poor leadership and understaffing at the unit, formerly situated in the grounds of Musselburgh Grammar School near Edinburgh and now in the village of Tranent on the Firth of Forth, also found an atmosphere of low expectations.

Pupils took frequent cigarette breaks, swore at teachers, and became violent, according to HM Schools' Inspectorate. The unit was awarded the lowest rating possible on more than half of the thirty performance measures.

Inspectors called for the education authority to take urgent steps to make the place safe for students and staff.

Politicians expressed shock at the findings and the Scottish National Party blamed government failings.

The report said: "Pupils formed a volatile group. There was a high level of aggression between pupils and occasional outbreaks of violence." In interviews, pupils reported that they felt unsafe and were exposed to abuse by their peers.

A restricted curriculum also damned students to leaving without worthwhile qualifications.

Meanwhile south of the border a summer directive by the Boarding Schools Association, English Education Authorities, and school inspectors will be binding on all the UK's public boarding-schools. The directive demands - among other improvements - that all must immediately put anti-bullying policies into action. Staff will now be given training in counselling and social work skills.

Prince Charles, who attended the spartan Gordonstoun in Northern Scotland, described his school life as "hell." He sent his own sons to Eton.

Attractive to bullies

Bullies seize on any opportunity to tease and torment their target. Infirmities, medical conditions, and disorders are vulnerabilities that can be exploited. To the bully, a visually-apparent condition such as facial disfigurement is especially attractive.

A child may be born with a facial birthmark or cranio-facial condition, or they may develop skin conditions. Others become scarred through burns, dog-bites, or accidents. Disfigurements affecting the face or hands are the most obvious, but summer clothes, swimming and getting changed for sport can trigger staring, curiosity, and unwelcome taunts.

Teacher Jane Francis is School Specialist at the charity Changing Faces which helps children and adults deal with facial disfigurement. She told us: "I like teachers to use a broader term than bullying like 'unkindness' or `nastiness'. That brings in name-calling and ostracism and other things which can be very subtle and difficult for teachers to recognise, but which can be terribly hurtful."

Jane is another who brought up the question of the recent hit pop song U.G.L.Y. She said: "It's a kids' song and on the whole, teachers don't know it. But just humming a few bars from the song within earshot of a child who is disfigured will stick the knife in, so to speak. The teachers will never know what's going on and if the targeted child reacts, she or he'll be told they're imagining things. We try to educate teachers as to the level of subtlety they must be attuned to when a child is noticeable and vulnerable because of something about the way they look."

In discussing pupils' experiences of school, Jane commented: "Sometimes teachers seem to be acting on the theory that, since the child is going to look like this all their life, they are just going to have to get used to being called 'Scarface' or whatever. This may even be a genuinely well-intentioned attempt to toughen the youngster up for what the teacher envisages will be a difficult life ahead.

"In some cases children are so hurt they just can't face school any more and simply drop out. For them it's a catastrophe. They're as intelligent as anyone else but they'll end up without any qualifications. The child and their parents and the LEA may decide that home tutoring is the only solution. In the short term it can help. But sooner or later they must face the outside world, a college course, a job - and above all a social life, some friends to just hang out with."

Jane gave another example of how things can go wrong at school. "Another well-intentioned approach to helping a child whose appearance is unusual involves school staff in 'treating all children the same'. Staring, comments and questions are felt to be wrong because no child should be picked out in this way. Teasing and name-calling are prohibited and punishable. No one is allowed to say anything about what anyone looks like - and a child can go through the whole of their primary education with their disfigured appearance being 'not an issue'. Then after transition to secondary school they suddenly face all kinds of difficulties. Staring and comments from kids they've never seen before - and teachers too. Questions they've never had to answer before so that they are dumbstruck and embarrassed. They're left feeling confused, hurt and angry - easy prey for anyone looking for someone to wind up."

In other situations, teachers seem to have taken the view that, since they themselves can hardly see their pupil's scar or blemish, the child is bringing the teasing upon themselves by fussing and worrying about nothing. Denial can be a useful strategy for a person unable to deal with others' problems but for the individual it can be disastrous.

"Our work in schools is based on the social-psychology of appearance and disfigurement", explains Jane. "This enables us to offer effective interventions and strategies for supporting a pupil who looks noticeable."

Unfortunately, many adults forget the sharpened sensitivity that was unique to their teenage years.

Little big girl
Kirsty Wilson is a little girl with a big heart and a big future who is overcoming childhood thoughts of bullycide.

Kirsty was born with a condition called pseudohypoparathyroidism which means her bones were so soft and weak that even trying to walk would break her fragile legs. It also condemned her to life as a near dwarf. She was lucky though to have escaped the mental retardation which is often an added symptom of the syndrome.

Her condition, however, resulted in her life being made

hell from the day she started school.

She's still in a wheelchair and still a target. The day of our interview she was so ill and in so much pain it was likely that she'd be back in hospital again before the sun went down in Lanarkshire, Scotland, where she lives. But in spite of this, she giggled and laughed through our chat.

She told us: "I'm going to put all this bullying behind me. I'm going to forget everything I've been through and those kids who made my life a misery. I'm going to have a birthday party when I'm eighteen with lots of good new friends, maybe even a boyfriend by then. And I'm going to start a new life."

She's fifteen now, just four feet and one inch tall and less than four years past the day when she whispered to her parents' closest friend and next-door neighbour, Irene: "I can't take the bullying any more. I want to kill myself."

When Irene - shocked by the child's resolve - told Kirsty's parents, Linda and Tam, it was the first time the couple realised the extent of what their eleven-year-old daughter had been going through since the day she'd started primary school six years earlier. They leapt into action.

As with most cases in this book, Kirsty's school denied the existence of bullying, and even implied that wheelchair-bound Kirsty was a bully herself. They took no action, despite her attackers going to the extreme of torturing Kirsty by dragging her from her chair and jumping on her brittle legs as she lay helpless on the ground.

The doctors have started with an operation this summer to repair her legs. No one will know if the bullies made her condition even worse by their cruelty. With the help of family, loving neighbours, and a handful of friends, Kirsty is busy re-empowering herself. Life, even with the bullying still in swing, has become an exciting adventure to her as she puts thoughts of bullycide behind her and has learned to see her hell as anything but eternal torment.

She told us: "I'm even forgetting why I got to the stage

where I wanted to kill myself. I just remember I was serious about it. I'd started to believe the things the bullies were saying about me. I'd started to accept I'd be physically attacked at school every single day.

"Even in secondary school I'm bullied - physically and mentally - but there's something in me now that tells me it won't last forever. I'll climb out of this chair one day. I'll be at college with a bunch of good friends. I'll be playing my keyboards and working on art and drama. Life's coming. I've made up my mind to survive in spite of everything."

Mother Linda recalled: "It all started when she was just a tot of five. They were calling her 'poisoned dwarf' because her medical condition meant she was so short. 'Little Fat' was another nasty nickname. They were pushing her around, knocking her over, and jumping on her legs.

"When we found out what was going on, she'd been suffering in silence for years. But we got no help from the authorities or the school. I can't count the number of times I went to the school to complain. Nothing was done.

"There were whole gangs of girls and boys bullying her. The school chose to ignore it, to deny there was any bullying there.

"She's at the local academy now and there they at least try to protect her and bring the bullies to account. But it still goes on. We've been very close to keeping her away from school at times but we've never had to do it. Kirsty isn't a weak girl. She won't turn her back on a problem.

"This school is so much better. I think even if we hadn't told the staff, the bullying would have been noticed.

"She's got lots of support from her teachers and the family and our neighbours. There's even a young boy up the road who looks after her.

"Trouble is there's always something for the bullies to find fault with in Kirsty. She's so short, she's overweight because she's in a wheelchair ... they can always find some lame excuse to make life a misery. But if we'd changed schools, it wouldn't have helped her. She'd have found the same thing in another playground, on another school bus.

"We've seen a change in the last year. She's somehow shaken depression. To think that when she was only eleven she spoke the worst words a parent could ever dread: 'I want to kill myself.' All we could do was give her sympathy and go all out to change things.

"We even approached the bullies themselves and got nothing but abuse. Like they were even bullying us. I went to their parents who just wouldn't believe their children could possibly act the evil way they did."

Kirsty told us she used to look in the mirror and see a pretty face reflected there. When asked if she still sees that pretty face, she giggled in embarrassment. She does. She's just too bashful to admit it. She's growing up and growing up well. Kirsty might gain an extra eight inches in height if treatment is successful

"I've been through a tough time but I'm coming out at the other end. I feel encouraged. Things are getting slowly better and I can see a future. You know, even the time when I felt suicidal has faded from my memory.

"They're still calling me names. But now I never believe what they say. I've learned to ignore it and just let them get on with it. I'm not too bad on the keyboard unless something's really hard to play and I'm going to study art and drama at college."

"And," says Kirsty, "I think the operations which might improve my physical condition have helped encourage me. I'll climb out of this chair one day.

"I've got some friends now - but there's a wee problem. Most of them smoke and they sneak around the corner at school for a crafty cigarette and don't see what's going on and can't help me when the bullies start in.

"I don't hate the bullies. I just don't like them. Not one has ever apologised for what they've done to me. If one ever did, I think I'd just say 'all right' and turn my back. I don't want them as friends. I could never forgive them for how they've ruined my childhood. Mum and Dad wouldn't forgive them either. I've been bullied every school day I can remember.

"My school pulls the bullies in now one by one and somebody will stop for a week or so ... then it just starts again. They never change. But I'm happy the teachers and the staff are at least trying for me - one teacher in particular.

"That teacher has regular chats with me to ask how I'm going on."

Brown-haired, blue-eyed Kirsty was still waiting for word of whether she'd have to go through another gruelling hospital experience. She didn't give a hoot. "I've been there so often, I'm used to it," she said. "It can only make things better. Bullies in the school yard only ever make things worse."

Chapter 16

Voices heard

*"I really started to believe I was ugly, some
kind of beast. I became ashamed."*
An interview with Princess Diana shortly before her death.

I don't want this to happen to others

Lucy Forrester committed the most horrific bullycide Britain has ever seen.

But her sacrifice and her scream for justice was heard and has already saved others.

As Lucy was being laid to rest, two self-confessed bullies clung to her mother, Elizabeth, and sobbed their shame. Elizabeth held them in her arms. There were tears. But there were no recriminations.

Four hundred attended the memorial service in Congleton, Cheshire. Elizabeth and her husband Richard didn't let Lucy's final, fatal statement fade with the flowers scattered near her cremation site. They heard, listened and understood Lucy's dying cries and launched a charity to help not only bully victims like their daughter, but the bullies themselves.

Lucy's legacy is VISYON - Voluntary Initiative Supporting Young People's Ongoing Needs. Five years after her death, with three full-time workers and ten volunteers, it costs £60,000 a year to run.

Lucy's was not a dysfunctional family. No divorce. No neglect or unemployment poverty on the sidelines. Her environment was loving, caring, close, and with never a deaf ear turned to the slightest problem of Lucy and her two elder sisters.

Lucy described her torment in diaries she later destroyed

... but tellingly left open on her bed for her Mum to read the tales of name-calling, insult, and violence at school.

Lucy's suicide was not her first try. She'd attempted bullycide five times in her 16 years.

She took a coil of the copper jewellery wire she used in her junk-gem hobby, spun it into a thick strand and attached it to a metal bracelet on her wrist. Then she hurled it over the 24,000-volt live electric line at the local railway station.

Onlookers saw her turn into a pillar of fire. Doctors tried their best to save her after the terrible 75% burns she'd sustained. But six days later Lucy died.

The last words on her lips were: "Mum I know you love me. I wasn't attention-seeking. I really meant to do it."

Lucy had been severely depressed for almost two years because of the bullying campaign against her. Maybe she was too pretty. Maybe she was too bright. Perhaps it was her striking red hair that singled her out as a target. Her parents had done everything in their power. They spoke to her teachers, brought in doctors and psychiatrists and even accepted drug treatment. A spell in full-time residential care was demanded, but Lucy died whilst on the five-month-long waiting list.

She'd fibbed to her parents about going shopping in the small market town of Congleton, Cheshire and went to the local railway station instead. There she electrocuted herself. It wasn't the first time she'd tried. At the previous attempt the wire had been too short to reach the overhead cable. Months before she had taken a massive dose of sixty paracetamol pills but her body had rejected them and she'd survived.

"We tried everything we could," says father Richard. "We knew she was suffering too much to bear. We even sent her to a strict Roman Catholic School, even though we're not Catholics, in the hope that the discipline there might mean less bullying.

"Nothing helped. There is nothing I can think of now that we hadn't tried. I'm not blaming schools or neighbours, family or anything else. I can only blame bullying. The syndrome - not the individual bullies."

Lucy's parents feel so strongly that Lucy's story must be told that they travelled to Neil's South of France base to discuss the horror.

Mother Elizabeth said on the anniversary of Lucy's death: "The way she chose to die was so horrific that she could never have been merely crying for help, she was making a statement. I think she was trying to speak out in the loudest way open to her and demand action against bullying. I wasn't surprised when she finally did it. It was something she knew she was being driven towards. I hope we did all we could. But she was on the ultimate downward spiral."

Since Lucy's death, Elizabeth and Richard have certainly fulfilled Lucy's wishes. With the experts and volunteers they employ, they have counselled hundreds of kids, bullies and victims alike. Their phone lines are seldom free. Their doors are always open.

"There's a rush," said Elizabeth, "to switch services from hospitals to communities but no one has yet worked out what is really needed."

Before she died, without residential care, Lucy had to stay at home and rely on a visiting teacher for her school lessons. She angrily sent away a psychiatric nurse and it was down to Mum and Dad to mount a 24-hour suicide watch to make sure Lucy didn't make another attempt on her own life.

Friends helped but there were moments when Lucy stayed alone to brood on the schoolyard bullying which had made her life hell. There seemed to be a glimmer of hope when Lucy brightened up and smiled for the cameras on a family holiday in Wales. That was just a few days before she died.

A child psychiatrist who saw Lucy every couple of weeks

said: "There were no skeletons in this family's closet. They were close-knit and loving. They did everything possible. There was something else."

"Bullying", says Elizabeth. "She was a pretty redhead. She stuck out in a crowd. By the time she was just fourteen she was being harassed and bullied at school. She was sensitive. She was a perfect victim.

"Richard and I are trying our best to give her life and death value by just saving one more child through our organisation. I can never believe that we have ever done enough."

The only verdict open to Coroner John Hibbert was suicide. He said "This was an horrendous tragedy and I have heard some evidence of some serious gaps in the support that ought to be given to young people in a depressed state."

Elizabeth insists: "This wasn't a cry for private help. It was a cry for general action. I hope Richard and I and Lucy's sisters and our helpers have heard her statement and are not letting her down. Maybe we can't beat bullying immediately. But we can keep it in check until we can. We can stop bullycides.

"Denial of bullying is the first thing we must overcome. My daughter used to cuddle me every night. There were no problems at home. She loved and was loved. All I've got left to blame is this horrible syndrome of bullying. Perhaps she was susceptible to depression. But it was bullying that pushed her over the edge."

Elizabeth later wrote to us: "Our conversation has awoken many thoughts about young people who are in distress. I write from a mother's perspective. Richard and I are both 'middle class' and have enquiring minds. When Lucy became ill (through bullying) I endeavoured to find care for her - she was almost sixteen when her condition became serious. She was denied care by the paediatric services but was not yet eligible for adult services. She took an overdose and was admitted to the local adult psychiatric ward. It was inappropriate in the extreme. She was sharing a ward with adults who were seriously ill and their behaviour was excessively disturbing.

"From that time she was seen by an excellent child and adolescent psychiatrist, who saw her weekly or fortnightly, depending on her condition. She was referred to a residential unit and was on a waiting list. My feeling was 'she needs therapy now' and weekly visits to hospital were wholly inadequate. Lucy withdrew into a shell. I begged for art and drama therapy - any therapy in fact which might reach Lucy. At that time I decided that if Lucy ever recovered we would actually campaign for a freely accessible, non-judgmental, confidential service for young people. We did. But not until she was already dead.

"When Lucy died, two other children of her age killed themselves about the same time under similar circumstances. The facilities for their age group were almost non-existent. Case loads for the community psychiatric nurses were high, but also their skills didn't cover this age group. The action I've taken with Richard in setting up VISYON came from a great desire to stop what happened to us happening to anyone else. Our hopes exceed our means but we have expanded and continue to work hard for the young people in our community.

"We miss Lucy. It should never have happened. But if we can just save one single child from going down the same path by offering early recognition and intervention, every penny spent at VISYON will have been worthwhile."

At the sharp end of VISYON and its full-time staff, based in Congleton, is Salli Ward, its Youth Care Manager.

"We're successful. We've never lost a child to bullycide." Salli pauses and says quietly: "It's tragic but true that had we been in place the week before Lucy died, she could be alive today."

Salli's favourite approach with the seventy or so kids she

has on her books at any given time is drama therapy which, she says, breaks down inhibitions and allows children to open up and speak about their bully problems. They role play together and act out thoughts and feelings until the barriers are down and Salli can tap their innermost fears as a friend rather than a remote adult counsellor. Together, Salli and her bullied battlers laugh until they talk and other members of staff use a range of other methods to slash through the fatal silence of their young clients.

After Lucy took her life rather than face another day of torment, Salli answered the Forresters' advertisement for a leader for their organisation.

She said: "It was only later after I'd been given the job that I found out what they had been through, that they'd lost a daughter to bullycide, and began to understand the reason for their total commitment. I think Lucy's story unfolded over an informal evening of wine and biscuits."

Salli took up the job of saving young people from bullycide in July 1997, almost three years after Lucy's death. She now reckons bullying is the main factor in the misery of at least 20% of the young people who come to her for help, many suicidal, and a major factor in another 40% or more. Although highly qualified and experienced, she admits her skills were honed at home. That's where, she says, she learned to teach what she calls "The Coping Strategy."

"I feel a great responsibility to Lucy", Salli continues. "Hers was no childish cry for attention. She chose to die in the most painful way to make a statement. She was saying 'help the others like me!' I feel now as though I know her, though we never met. She stands beside me in spirit and helps me along. I wanted to name our centre after her. Elizabeth and Richard said that wasn't necessary. I can see why now. Lucy is such a huge part of it that she doesn't need her name over the door. She runs this place. Her experience is what guides us all. What she went through is saving others.

"To say that bullying in Lucy's case was the last straw that broke the camel's back is too simple. She was intimidated into taking her own life. It was *the* factor. There was no other. She was needled by other kids because of her good looks, intelligence and, perhaps, because of the very happiness she experienced at home. Those three things made her different from many others and the jealousy, uneasiness, or lack of acceptance of those others was expressed through bullying - verbal and sometimes physical.

"She carefully chose her own way out with so much pain that she was obviously demanding help, not for herself - she knew her life was forfeit - but for others in her position. What a girl she must have been. I really wish I'd known her in life.

"What she's helped me do is to let kids know there's somebody out there - an adult but still a friend - and that's going to stay with them through the rest of their school life. Bullying is inextricably linked with self-esteem for the bullied *and* the bully. We are completely confidential here at VISYON. But we do realise that bullying itself needs an environment of secrecy where power relationships become the order of the day.

"Here we treat all the children in the same way. They might have just a two-day problem, but even that might be enough to make them take their lives or have their futures permanently damaged. All children should be happy. But, because of many things, even by the time they get into school, many young heads are in a muddle. They haven't developed coping strategies. I believe kids are born ready to cope and with their self-esteem intact. If they get the message early on that they're loved and wanted, worthwhile and valuable, they're equipped for life. But there's this huge thing that gets in the way of that and that is bullying.

"If bullying hits the right - sorry, the wrong - child at the vulnerable time it wipes out that beautiful love and need they'd felt before in the close family group. It's not only children from dysfunctional families who can suffer bullycide ... look at Lucy.

"It's difficult to profile the 'typical' victim. I've got one sixteen-year-old girl in mind, a petite, blonde Scot who has so much in common with Lucy in that she has no out-of-the-ordinary difficulties. She has a loving Mum and a Dad. She has a brother she thinks the world of. Nothing at all is wrong in the family or her social history. She is suffering purely and simply from bullying and has done for several years. She's attractive. I suppose the only thing that identifies her as a victim is that she was a bit of a tomboy a few years ago. Short hair and trousers. That kind of thing. She doesn't want to conform and be the same as everyone else. Being different, that's enough, you see.

"They used to shout at her 'Are you a lesbian?' and it's driven her to distraction. Thing is, had she changed her looks, the bullies would have found another reason for having a go at her. She'd become a victim and they wouldn't let her off the hook no matter what. She did try to get more feminine - nail varnish and whatnot - and they started calling her 'girlie'. She's working on our coping strategies and hasn't yet got to the stage Lucy did. But sometimes those coping strategies fail her and she sits down and thinks 'this is just too awful and I don't want to carry on.'

"Her bullying is just verbal and that's bad enough. Even a bad glance hurts her and no teacher can do anything about the complaint of a dirty look. She feels hopeless, a failure. She's started to feel guilty: maybe I am ugly, maybe I do look like a boy, maybe there's something wrong with me and that's why they bully me. Maybe nobody loves me. Maybe I don't deserve them or even to be here.

"But through therapy she is coming to realise that really she's a nice person, certainly not ugly or a lesbian. There's nothing strange about her. She's learning the biggest message 'I'm a loved and valuable person.' She's not out of the woods yet. But now she will never become a bullycide."

"We have all the time we need to listen. We make that time no matter what the clock says. I see them on good days and on bad days. I approach each case holistically and there's no alarm bell to signal the end of what they want to say.

"Bullying works in secrecy, my job is to blow that secrecy wide apart before schoolyard bullying becomes, like in Lucy's case, bullycide."

Salli herself came in for bullying at school but overcame it by treading the fine line: "I became neither a swot nor a divvy [dummy, idiot], I kept in with the in-crowd but remained an individual. Somehow I managed to steer the middle course. It worked for me. I try to encourage my young clients to think for themselves and make their own decisions. Even swots and divvies have a right not to be bullied.

"I do remember at school when the regular teacher was away and the stand-in was always late that there was a group of girls doing physical bullying against a couple of lads. They'd take them into the stock room and do horrible things to them. People would watch and do nothing - guilty bystanders as you say. I remember feeling dreadful. I wasn't part of the bullying but I wasn't part of the solution either. The image sticks with me. I knew what was going on. I knew I should have done something but didn't. I feel guilty even now because I did nothing.

"My husband - he's a youth worker - went to a boys' school and there was 'peer competition' I think. There was an established pecking order and you had to stay within that. Top of the pecking order was a teacher with a cane.

"Sometimes, even when the bullying might stop, you must still take your child out of his school because there are too many bad associations. They can never adjust to it in their head and the best thing is to get out to a new environment with a new confidence."

Salli and husband John drove to Romania with supplies for starving children a few years ago. She said: "It's amazing. Coming back to the little town of Congleton here to start my work was more difficult than arriving in Romania. It takes such a long time to be accepted as the friend of the children who might have taken Lucy's path to bullycide.

"I'm seeing one young lady right now. She has a terrible history of intense bullying. She tried hard to end her misery with an overdose. It didn't work, thank God. She also self-harms, cutting herself and things. This girl is 22 now. She'd been bullied two or three times a week, sometimes every day. She was really desperate.

"I'm very worried about her. Every time I leave her I don't know if I'll ever see her again. She's passed the bullying now but she is still open and vulnerable. She constantly says 'what did I do wrong?' She thinks now what is there to live for? She's so severely damaged. She can intellectualise, she studies psychology but it still hurts. Hurts to the heart. She has loving parents but she tries to hide the extent of her pain from them.

"VISYON is the last resort for so many. We stand between bullycide and life. We're the last line of defence. I know it's working because we've never, ever lost a child to bully-induced suicide.

"The person I've been telling you about comes to see me, she told me, because there is only me she can tell how bad it feels. She can't tell her parents because she thinks it will upset them. She can't go to a psychiatrist because she's afraid she'll be admitted to a psychiatric ward and labelled for life. She wants to pretend to everyone else that she actually feels OK ... but she can tell us that she's going through hell.

"Most of the kids who go through bullying at any significant level say they want to end their lives. Fortunately when they come to us they haven't yet given up all hope. They can still be looking down the road to life.

"Bullycide is often spontaneous. The desire to take one's life might be only a temporary thing which would pass with the right support. If help is available then and there these children could survive.

"I know from my job that young people don't ask an awful lot of you. All they ask is that you listen to the pain they carry. Accept them for what they are. Don't judge them. Don't come down heavy on them. Especially don't try to make them someone else.

"Some go to psychologists, psychiatrists, and other experts and some have a good experience but others just don't ever want to go back. I keep thinking 'what are these people doing wrong?' Surely within ten minutes you can form a trusting relationship, something that's going to go somewhere and save a child from the ultimate horror of bullycide.

"Tell you something else: kids expect you to be imperfect. I am. Imperfect I mean. They can relate to me. They can open up. They want to see the cracks in our adult persona. They want to see us as contemporaries. Friends speaking and hearing at their level. They don't want to die for their feelings. They want to be saved. We're here to make sure their voices don't come from the grave.

"Had she come through VISYON's door or had we shared a cuppa, we could have saved Lucy, I believe. That's why we're here. Lucy gave us what we have. We work for others just like her. What was missing for Lucy was somewhere else that wasn't home. Somewhere she could open her heart without hurting those closest to her. A bolt hole. We're a bolt hole. We're an open door.

"Richard and Elizabeth set VISYON up because they knew, had it been in place earlier, Lucy would be alive and happy today."

Nicky Hudson's own story

The bullying started really bad when I was about eight years old. There was always the main bully, but others picked on me too.

I tried to deal with it myself as I didn't want to worry Mum and Dad.

My friend, James, used to tell Mum he was fed up with the bullies too. They occasionally picked on him as well.

I used to get so frightened about going to school that when it was nearly time to leave I would run away somewhere to hide until I knew I could come back and stay at home. Mum sometimes took me in late.

Playtimes used to be worse, but it did happen in class sometimes. I knew it was no good to keep telling the teachers, I didn't want them to think I was a wimp or something.

One morning I ran off in my night clothes and my Grandad found me. Mum promised that she wouldn't make me go to school. Then the headmaster came and must have talked her into it. He always did.

One day they kicked and pushed me around the playground so much that in the end I hit a bench really hard. At first I didn't say anything but it hurt. I told a teacher. They must have rung my Mum because she came and took me to the doctor.

I stopped telling Mum. I told James not to tell her either. I thought at the time she didn't care. She made me go to school when she knew I was unhappy. Looking back now I know that she did care, she wanted me to be happy.

I felt my life wasn't worth living. I wanted to die. To get away from it all.

My Mum told me I had been ill. I can't remember. A big

piece of my life is missing.

I had a tutor called Eric. I liked him. He made me feel good about myself and took me on small trips. Then they took him away because they wanted to try me somewhere else.

I wanted to stay at home and let Eric teach me but they wouldn't let me have him back. One week they said I could have him, the next, they rang Mum and said I couldn't.

They sent someone else but I haven't met her, I just do the work she brings.

I would rather be at school and be happy like other kids my age but I can't face it. I don't trust anyone, not even now. Mum and Dad have meetings with an education man every few months in our home, but nothing is ever solved.

Mum now supports families all round the country, in fact she spends most of her time on the phone. She never gets much time to herself and always worries about the phone bill but I'm pleased she does it.

I do worry about the future, but hope, one day, to play professional football. I like being in goal best but don't mind playing out field.

Mum, Dad, and I go to watch Peterborough United every home game. It gives me something to look forward to. I have met the players and Barry Fry, which I am very pleased about. Football is the only thing that keeps me going.

Forty red balloons

Nicky Hudson had a professionally diagnosed stress breakdown at ten years of age.

Eight years on the scars and wounds of bullying are still raw and show little sign of healing.

His is the by now familiar story of unrelenting infant and youthful viciousness and institutional inadequacy. It does have its up-side because - as in Lucy Forrester's case - his parents have turned his and their tragedy into a ray of hope for others.

The bullies stole Nicky's early promise of a full, happy, successful life and turned him into a bullycidal recluse who became so mistrustful of the world he would not even speak to his parents for half a year.

It started when Nicky was attending his local school near Peterborough. He was well dressed by parents Linda and Fred, perfectly groomed, happy at home and bright as a button. Maybe that's what was "wrong". Perhaps the very fact that he was so obviously well loved and cared for was what singled him out as the victim by others less fortunate.

Linda told us: "I think it was all down to jealousy. At the time, there was no school uniform and we did our best. I'm not saying we got him everything he wanted, we've never had a lot of money, but our two kids have always been the most important thing in life to me and my husband. We both came from big families and thought - because we only had two - we should provide for them as well as we could.

"I'd never known Nicky to brag about this. It's just that the others must have spotted it and maybe thought he was being treated better at home than they were.

"It started when he was eight. He came home with bruises all over his body and his behaviour changed. He got more aggressive at home. He'd always been a very placid and an easy-going little boy. We noticed the changes but didn't really understand them until he admitted that something was going wrong. He told us he'd been getting bullied for some time, both verbally and physically.

"This went on for the next two years with me going up to the school at different times and them saying they were going to sort it all out. I felt they were concerned and really thought they would get the problem under control. But they didn't.

"Then came one morning when Nicky woke up and just decided, this was it, he couldn't face going to school any more and ran away. We even got the police in to help us find him. We did, the following morning in a dyke not far from our house, drenched through and freezing."

Unlike Steven Shepherd, Nicky was rescued, but his protest fell on deaf authoritarian ears.

"The headmaster came down but we'd brought Nicky home with the promise that no way would we force him to go back to school. The headmaster told him that if he didn't go back he'd be taken away from his Mummy and Daddy. So we did take him back in the headmaster's car and I stayed with him right through the day.

"We thought then that the school would look after him and that he would be safe. But as soon as I wasn't there, the bullying started all over again. I got a phone call from the headmaster saying Nicky had suffered a bad accident. I thought he'd maybe slipped and broken an arm or a leg and rushed straight over. But no. I found he'd been attacked again by the bully gang. He'd been kicked and punched and they'd cut up his private parts. The doctor cleaned him up and said he didn't think there'd be permanent physical damage.

"But there was permanent damage to Nicky's heart and soul.

"Nicky was always talking about taking his own life. It had become a misery. Not worth living, he thought. I got the LEA involved myself and they sent people to the house. The only result was that Nicky lost confidence in all adults. He didn't even trust me and Fred any more.

"And then, at ten years old, he had a nervous breakdown. He just shut down. He didn't even speak to his Mummy and Daddy for six months. Not a word. A knock on the front door and he'd run behind the couch and hide. The local psychiatrists didn't seem to have come across anything this serious before. They didn't know how to handle it."

Slowly with his parents' care, love, and patience, Nicky began to show signs of improvement and at eleven made his own decision to re-enter the world and attend secondary school. But his old tormentors had also moved to the same new school and the brutal campaign against him began again as though the horrific climax to his earlier suffering had never happened.

He just opted out and stayed like a hermit in his home for four years with his mother and father fighting the authorities for the right to his sanctuary there. For a time, the LEA provided a home tutor but as the cost is high eventually demanded he get back to the classroom.

Linda told us: "They sent him into what they call a 'sin bin', a little school actually set up for children who've been expelled from other schools.

"He's always threatened to kill himself right through it all. And I mean seriously. Life wasn't worth living for him. Even now at eighteen, he still bears the scars. He's very damaged. I don't think he'll ever recover from the hurt and the pain. He can't work because his education was destroyed along with his childhood. His potential for life was utterly wrecked. More than anything his self-esteem was trampled on and smashed to pieces. Not only will he not realise his early potential and the promise he had before becoming a bully victim, he's achieved nothing. He wants to but he's got no outside confidence."

Linda, Fred and Nicky are still struggling with the fight to repair the damage. Along the way, Linda and Fred found the strength to help other lives being smashed to smithereens or ended. They opened a helpline called Parents And Children Unite (PCU) for other bully victims. They've already saved many young lives from ruin and bullycide. When their home telephone number is carried in a magazine or newspaper they get up to a hundred calls a week whilst letters pour through the door.

"I felt I had to do something. It's hard work - just me and my husband at night time. But we've never regretted it. I'd like to think we've saved lives, I've had quite a few calls from kids on the brink of bullycide. I'll actually go to their homes to meet them or even meet them in private on a street corner. I've got a girl of fifteen who phoned me to say she wouldn't be alive today if it wasn't for us. There are others. The thought that any child commits suicide because of bullying is horrifying."

Many children - as ChildLine and Kidscape and others attest - find it difficult or even shameful to talk of their lives as victims. Linda encourages many of her callers to write it down instead. They pour it all out that way so that on a follow-up call, Linda knows the whole story and is better equipped to advise.

As much as the Hudsons detest bullies and bullying, there's an ear at the end of the line for victimisers too and many bullies have called for help in straightening out their own lives.

"Some of them," says Linda, "say they hate themselves for what they are doing. I must admit I get a little bit stern with some of them when they say they had to become bullies because they'd been victims themselves. In that case, how can they possibly become a tormentor knowing what the other kid must feel? It's a lame excuse. I've asked many others why they pick on a particular kid and they just cannot answer. The real problem is not in the victim but in the bully himself.

"I've been able to turn some of them around by insisting that they imagine themselves in the victim's place. One called back and said that when he'd done just that he was really frightened, was sorry and would never be a bully again. But I must say that the bullies who do call me are not entirely typical. They already feel ashamed of their behaviour and want to do something about it. The majority don't even see the evil of their ways and will be heartless bullies all their lives."

Linda was one of the first in her community to realise the existence of bullycide, although she had not, until we contacted her, heard the word or realised the scale of the epidemic. With local backing and the help and support of

Peterborough Football Club she inflated one thousand white balloons, representing innocence, one thousand blue balloons, representing the sadness of victims, and forty red balloons representing UK children she knew had committed bullycide since she started her helpline. They were released at half-time during a Saturday match.

PCU and VISYON are two responses to tragedy, but such Herculean efforts are always short of funding. Recently, VISYON has had good news and bad. Manager Salli has moved on but the charity is now expanding thanks to a grant from the National Lottery, thus ensuring that Lucy's sacrifice continues to help avert similar tragedies.

From dealing with thousands of cases of adult bullying, Tim reports that, like the families in this book, the most common wish of survivors is "I don't want others to suffer like I've done."

Chapter 17

The happiest days of your life

*A nation without a conscience is a
nation without a soul. A nation without
a soul is a nation that cannot live.*
Winston Churchill

Never again should anyone be in doubt about how it feels to be the target of bullying.

To wake up each day knowing that you *have* to go to school, knowing there's no way of avoiding it, knowing that the moment you set out for school the bullies are there, waiting for you to arrive, waiting to call you names, to tease you, torment you, humiliate and mock you, embarrass you in front of friends, push you, punch you, slap you, pinch you, spit on you, kick you, and ... you daren't think about the rest, or the possible consequences.

Don't the bullies behave like perfect darlings whenever a teacher approaches? Aren't they polite and deferential, until the teacher is out of sight, then the kicking, punching, spitting, tormenting starts over, school books are damaged (how am I going to explain that again?), homework defaced (ditto), projects sabotaged, food spoilt, possessions pilfered, personal items desecrated, clothes ripped, school uniform torn, dinner money stolen, pocket money extorted. Just another normal day. Like yesterday. And the day before. Like tomorrow. And the day after that.

Why have my friends deserted me? They used to support me, now they join in with the bullying. Can't they see the hurt they cause? Are they too frightened? Don't they realise that if we stood together we could defeat the bullies?

Not one teacher takes the slightest interest, preferring to

believe the glib excuses and assurances of the bullies. Why are they taken in so easily? No point in telling teachers, they don't care, they're under enough stress as it is, anyway. It'll just make the bullying worse and the bullies more covert then it'll be even harder to be taken seriously. How can the head teacher tell parents that "we have an effective anti-bullying policy" when the head is the biggest bully in the school? How do these people get to be in positions of power? I can't escape school for at least four years. I have to attend otherwise I'll be treated as a truant, the authorities will give me hell, my parents will give me hell, the head will give me hell, the teachers will give me hell. *Who will believe me anyway when I say I'm being bullied?* There's no escape. What I need is a permanent solution so that I don't have to endure this never-ending pain. Ever.

Psychiatric injury

As well as those unfamiliar with the injurious nature of psychological violence, bullies and their supporters perpetuate the fallacy that "sticks and stones may break my bones but names can never hurt me." Whilst the effects of a single taunt may not hurt, daily psychological violence and threats of violence are a form of abuse which, in the absence of support especially by those in authority, result in inevitable psychiatric injury. The delight, or gratification, that bullies gain each day from tormenting their prey is reminiscent of the actions of a torturer. Bullies, too, have the power of life and death over their victims.

Recognition of psychiatric injury (for example Post Traumatic Stress Disorder, PTSD) is low, even within the mental health professions where psychiatric injury is misdiagnosed and labelled as mental illness with which it is frequently confused. Facilities for treatment of psychiatric injury are scarce for both children and adults, and often non-existent. The sudden transition from normal school and family environment to enforced incarceration in a psychiatric unit with patients suffering serious and severe long-term mental health problems makes trauma worse rather than better. Bullycide itself is almost always misdiagnosed.

In many ways, psychiatric injury resulting from verbal or emotional or psychological abuse is more damaging than physical injury. With the latter there's visual physical evidence which is difficult to deny. The former, though, leaves no obvious visible trace (except to those skilled in recognition) and whereas a physical injury is likely to heal, trauma can endure, blighting self-confidence throughout life. Psychiatric injury caused by bullying and abuse, whatever its source, prevents people from realising their potential. There's no known cure for a broken heart.

Bullies and abusers control and subjugate their victims by stimulating shame, embarrassment, guilt and fear. Most insidious is the seed of self-doubt that bullies plant with sustained accusations of worthlessness. In truth the criticisms are a projection of the bully's own sense of worthlessness but, prevented by the bullies from undertaking their studies, the allegation becomes self-fulfilling.

Society teaches deference to authority and unhelpfully encourages people to accord higher priority to the opinions of others (witness the current test- and appraisal-crazy culture) rather than teaching individuals how to value themselves and trust their own judgements. In this climate, bullies are able to persuade their target to believe it's their fault by stimulating that guilt feeling of "what did I do wrong?". The answer the target and others are least likely to think of is, of course, "nothing". Except, perhaps, to be in the wrong place at the wrong time.

Psychiatric injury is not limited to the target of bullying. The effects on parents, family, and friends can be just as devastating, especially if the bullying culminates in bullycide. Even attempted suicide leaves its mark given the stigma that society attaches to the act. However, suicidal thoughts are not a sign of mental illness or mental instability; they are a reliable measure of psychiatric injury.

Accountability

In the aftermath of tragedy, society displays an overwhelming need to identify someone who can be blamed. Scapegoating and vilifying an individual might satisfy the primitive lust for revenge but it doesn't solve the problem which, because it remains unidentified and unaddressed, recurs. With bullycide, because of the lack of understanding, it is just as likely to be the victim who is blamed. Effective solutions are those which identify both individual culpability *and* deficiencies in systems which have allowed the tragedy to occur.

The majority of teachers are hard-working individuals who dedicate their lives to educating the next generation. There are some teachers who bully but it's surprising how often these get promoted despite their unsuitability. The problem, as so often, lies further up the management chain.

A serial bully is a bully who makes a lifetime career of cruelty. The teacher who is a serial bully is hated by the pupils although young people haven't developed the verbal skills to articulate their dislike. Their perception, though, is uncannily accurate; in one case, a bullying headmaster was nicknamed "Psycho Sid". Another earned the title "Mr Pervert".

The most common reaction of the head teacher in the cases described is either "there's no bullying here" or "we've investigated and the problem is resolved". However, schools in which bullying is rife are really saying "We are happy to fail and to be seen to fail in our duty of care, we have undertaken no research, no training and no collection of resource material, neither do we have any intention of doing so. We are content to fail to provide a safe secure environment in which pupils can study and grow". These schools are bullycide black spots.

Bullies are people who act outside the bounds of society and will regard the absence of an anti-bullying policy, or failure to implement a policy effectively, as encouragement and approval of their antisocial behaviour. Failure by a school to implement an effective, active anti-bullying policy is a breach of duty of care. Consequent legal action will centre on negligence and the provisions of the new Human Rights Act.

Children who are targets of bullying become demoralised, demotivated, and ultimately disaffected. They may develop a lifelong hatred of school and, as a consequence, a lifelong hatred of learning which reminds them constantly of pain and betrayal. Schools must understand that bullying prevents children from completing their studies which leads to lower grades than the child would otherwise have achieved. This results in the school appearing in a lower position in league tables than would otherwise be the case. Bullies are responsible for and in charge of this downward slide.

When children feel comfortable, safe and happy they'll learn more, be less aggressive and more cooperative, and grow up to be more mature adults with greater coping skills. They're also likely to earn higher income (and thus pay more tax), be less likely to need social security benefits, and are likely to enjoy better health and thus need to use fewer NHS resources. The links between mental well-being and physical well-being are only just being explored.

Bullying is about choice and personal responsibility. Bullies choose to bully. When called to account, bullies pour forth a plethora of excuses, many derived from sociological explanations for the alleged causes of violence such as deprivation, abuse, poverty, etc. It is important not to be beguiled and misled by these excuses, however convincing. Bullying is always a personal choice;

a bad choice, but a choice nevertheless.

Environment and circumstances are likely only to *influence* the expression of violence, not be a *cause* of violence. The child who is a bully sometimes does have a dysfunctional home life and may have a lot of pent-up aggression, but not always. Many children suffer less than optimal home lives but do not resort to bullying. Like abuse and sexual abuse, bullying is independent of class or financial status.

One should not be too quick to blame the parents, either. Whilst bullying runs in some families, many good families are driven to despair by one wayward and defiant child who resists all attempts by parents and authorities to ensure behaviour remains within the limits of acceptability. Such families often find there is nowhere to turn for guidance and support.

When called to account, bullies identify and reveal themselves by exhibiting a characteristic response for the purpose of evading accountability. One can learn to recognise the response and resist being manipulated.

The bully will typically parade the "denial - counterattack - feigning victimhood" ploy that has enabled them to escape judgement and sanction. Denial is forthright and delivered with certitude and self-assuredness which is plausible and convincing. This is followed immediately by a counter-attack, falsely accusing their victim of some misdemeanour. The accusation is based on distortion and fabrication. Attention is switched to the target who then becomes the focus. Further false allegations maintain the focus until everyone has forgotten the original question or has had their interest in the original question usurped.

In the unlikely event of denial and counterattack being insufficient, the bully switches into victim mode and turns on the tears whilst claiming to be the one being bullied. The waterworks are designed to evoke expressions of sympathy and thus manipulate people's emotions (especially guilt); many are fooled by this ruse but once accountability has been evaded, the bullying restarts.

It's not only the bully who tries to blame his victim. Sometimes the responsible adults will also blame the victim, for this absolves them of responsibility and diverts attention away from their failings as accountable adults.

The most common responses of schools to allegations of bullying are to either deny it or to take ineffective action which makes the bullying worse. Sometimes, the plight of the victim is highlighted for the whole school to see. In one case a child was assigned a teacher as a minder and, in another, a child was given a mobile phone to call for help any time she felt bullied.

Research by national charity Parentline Plus in November 2000 revealed that nearly half of the 400 parents questioned in a survey felt that schools and teachers did not take their concerns seriously. Around 28% of parents felt that their child's school was not at all interested in serious problems like bullying.

When attempts to deal with bullying are half-hearted, the bullying goes underground and may evolve from physical to psychological. The outcome will be the same. Bullies may vary their attacks so that the violence is committed on the way to and from school. This allows some schools to claim that what happens outside school is outside the school's jurisdiction and thus outside the school's responsibility.

In April 2000, eight months after it became a legal requirement for schools to adopt an anti-bullying policy, teachers' union ATL published a survey revealing that a third of all schoolchildren are bullied each year. A quarter have been threatened with violence and 13% have been physically attacked.

Selection

The cases in this book demonstrate that one doesn't have to be a stereotypical "victim" to be picked on. Bullies are aggressive and dysfunctional with an overwhelming need to bully. Anyone will do.

When bullying is reported, or violent incidents or suicide hit the headlines, the reason the child was bullied is often highlighted as a principal cause of the bullying. In fact, the reason is always spurious and specious.

Table 4: Reasons for being bullied
Physical fat, thin, tall, short, glasses, crooked teeth, spots, big ears, small ears, sticky-out ears, ginger hair, any colour hair, speech impediment, accent, disfigurement, good looking, not good looking, not interested in or competent at sports **Preferences** wearing the "wrong" clothes, being shy, quiet or timid, having different likes or dislikes **Sexuality** being pretty, being handsome, being gay **Origin** skin colour, different culture, mixed culture, part of a minority, different **Beliefs** being religious, being non-religious, different religion **Vulnerabilities** physical: less strong than the bully emotional: parents splitting up, bereavement, sick sibling, sick parent(s), caring responsibilities, etc personal: immigration, relocation, displacement, English (or the national language) not first language being happy or unhappy at home disabled or learning difficulties **Other** parents are "different" (eg police, Salvation Army, etc) poor or rich parent in prison or away long-term being "different" - whatever that may mean anything

These excuses have one thing in common: they are all irrelevant. Each is a deceptive justification for the bully to indulge in a predictable pattern of violent behaviour. The target is simply a useful object onto whom the bully can displace his or her aggression.

If a child is picked on because they are allegedly "fat", then losing weight will make no difference. Similarly, wearing the "in" fashions will not alter the course of events; the bully contrives another excuse. Acknowledging the reason (eg telling overweight children to diet so they won't be bullied) unwittingly accords the bully validity and justification which is unwarranted. The focus instead needs to be on why the bullying child needs to bully.

People who are bullied often have a number of personal qualities of which the bully is jealous and envious; these are described in Table 5.

Table 5: Personal qualities of targets of bullying
independent dislikes gangs and cliques forsakes classroom politics not interested in power and control sensitive intelligent resistant to provocation unwilling to use strength to defend him or herself low propensity to violence academic abilities and interests imaginative, creative artistic interests and abilities, talents in music, art, literature, poetry, drama, etc empathy and concern for others easily forgiving high integrity low assertiveness refuses to resort to lying and deception for personal gain

Personal qualities

The main reason shared by all targets of bullying is that they are *in the wrong place at the wrong time.* This becomes self-evident when you understand the bully's compulsive need to bully, and that bullies always need a victim regardless of who it is. Investigation often reveals predecessors, and if the current victim becomes unavailable, someone else becomes the target of the bully's wrath.

Table 6: Profile of bullies
aggressive
physically strong
easily and willingly resorts to violence
poor communication skills
low self-esteem
insecure
may have a dysfunctional home life
thrives on control and dominance
thinks it fun to torment and hurt children who are less physically strong
cowardly
exhibits attention-seeking behaviour and needs to be respected but can't distinguish between "respect" and "fear"
needs to impress
disrespectful and often contemptuous of others (both children and adults)
immature
jealous and envious
divisive and dysfunctional
disruptive
academically below average
underachiever
often lies
cannot and will not accept responsibility
uncaring
lacks empathy
exploitative
manipulative

Bullies aren't always obvious. They're not always

scruffily dressed with bulging muscles and bigger than their target. Often they are bigger but only because they're too cowardly to pick on someone their own size or larger. Size is not everything; the critical factor is propensity to violence

Stereotypes of victims are sometimes perpetuated by the use of negative words to describe victim attributes. These are shown in the table. The word "victim" allows bullies and their supporters to tap into and stimulate people's preconceived notions and prejudices of "victimhood", ie that victims are "weak" and somehow bring the bullying upon themselves. "Target", by contrast, correctly highlights the bully's deliberate act of choice and selection.

Table 7: Positive elements within stereotyping	
victim	target
swot	studious and scholarly; enjoys learning; academically a high performer and achiever
loner	independent
isolated	has no need or desire to join cliques or gangs; has little or no need to impress
weak	physically less strong than the bully; unwilling to meet violence with violence; low propensity to violence

Whilst it is often the target who is regarded as "weak and inadequate", in fact it is always the bully who is weak and inadequate, as evidenced by the need to bully. People of strong character and high integrity don't need to bully.

Despite common perceptions, those who commit bullycide have a high degree of integrity and a strength of character which may not be recognised. Often they have withstood abuse for months, sometimes years; this is in contrast to bullies, who, when given a taste of their own medicine, immediately run whingeing to someone in authority.

Although bullycide ends the pain for the victim, the act of

suicide is far from painless. Every bullycide should scream out to us that life as the target of a bully is a fate worse than the most horrible early death. For the bereaved families, the suffering has only just begun.

School environment

There are few programmes that actively help an aggressive child learn to deal with their aggression. Many schools, under pressure of budgets, lack of time, overburdened with work (especially tests and tick-sheets), rising class sizes, suffering lack of leadership, lack of LEA backing and lack of government support, either ignore the problem (in which case it gets worse), punish the bully (in which case it gets worse), punish the target of bullying when they stand up for themselves (in which case it gets worse), or expel the bullying pupil (in which case the problem is passed to someone else). All of these are short-term, short-sighted non-solutions which fail to address the cause of the problem.

Schools need to create an environment where children understand from the moment they start that bullying, aggression, and violence are not acceptable. It is often the absence of such an ethos that potential bullies perceive as acceptance of their aggressive behaviour. A policy is a start, but it must be a proactive policy, not just a rule book which is dusted down in the head's study after aggression has resulted in injury or worse.

Children need to be taught at the outset to show dignity and respect to other children regardless of whether they are "in" or "out", and to be proactive in their relationships to other children, especially those who "do not fit in", for whatever reason. Conformity is high on the list of children's priorities and rejection, for whatever reason, is particularly painful. Some children do not learn the best interpersonal skills at home, and this is where schools can play an important role.

A whole-school policy should also support both parties. The target is taught assertiveness skills (this will not solve a bullying problem but enables a child to learn verbal self-defence and assert their rights), whilst the bully is taught how to deal with their aggression and how to interact socially and responsibly with other children and with adults. Physical punishment is inappropriate for it reinforces the bullying child's view that violence is an acceptable solution to any problem - if you don't like what someone else is doing, it's OK to hit them. Violent subjugation has been the dominant force for thousands of years but society is only just beginning to recognise its inappropriateness. The bullying child needs support and mentoring whilst being helped to understand that violence is not acceptable. Supervision will need to be proactive and continual.

Those children who are non-violent, not physically strong, or physically small, are always vulnerable; their needs are often overlooked, as are their talents.

All children need to be empowered to act wherever and whenever they see bullying. This will go a long way to precluding the bully recruiting a gang of both willing and unwilling collaborators.

Many children will try bullying at some time. However, most will realise that it's a wrong way of behaving and quickly grow out of it, especially when they are helped to see why it's inappropriate and then encouraged and supported in learning better ways of behaving.

The bullying child's parents may lack parental skills because they were brought up by parents who lacked appropriate behaviour skills and their parents were brought up in that climate, and so on. The cycle has to be broken, a function that schools can fulfil.

Helping parents adopt better parenting skills can make a major difference if this is done tactfully. The challenge is to achieve this without infringing civil liberties and without appearing to be patronising. Placing parenting skills on the national curriculum would bring significant gains, although the results would only show up one or two decades later. In general, governments are not keen to spend money on pursuing policies whose payback may accrue to successive governments of a different political persuasion.

In the absence of leadership by those in authority, many who are doing the most to tackle bullying are families whose child has given their life to draw attention to the issue. Motivated by loss, they devote themselves selflessly without thought of political or financial gain so that others will not have to suffer as they've suffered.

Almost everyone we talk to has experienced bullying at some time in their life: at school, at work, at home, or in the community. It has been experienced sometimes in more than one place, and sometimes in all four. Many people remember the horror of school bullying as if it were only yesterday. They remember the intense feelings of helplessness, of being trapped, of being alone, and of the responsible adults' failure to recognise and deal with the abuse.

To tell or not to tell

Bullying thrives on secrecy, and targets of bullying find themselves in an impossible predicament: to tell or not to tell. Telling will make the bullying worse whilst not telling means it's going to continue. The bully speciously exploits the idea that telling is grassing and anyone who tells is a squealer and a snitch. The consequences of telling, especially an inappropriate reaction by the responsible adults, can be dire not only for targets but those close to them, as recently-graduated pupil Dee Turner relates:

"My boyfriend and I decided to tell our parents what had been going on and this was when the headmaster got involved. We were assured we had done the right thing by telling someone, and this was the beginning of the end of all this. In fact it was the worst thing that could have happened. These people were spoken to and warned that my boyfriend and I were not the only ones involved any more, and that there would be consequences if similar pranks were to continue.

"Of course the whole thing was played down, the headmaster being more worried about the school's reputation than the things that were going on. We didn't have to wait long for our pay-back for telling on them.

"I thought it would be a scratch down my boyfriend's car, or even letting the tyres down, but in fact it was far worse. They smashed in my boyfriend's Dad's car window as it sat in front of the school. I had that horrible gut feeling when I was called out of class. I cried for hours. I felt so vulnerable. I wasn't just scared for myself; we were scared for our families."

Differences between child and adult bullying

There is much overlap between child and adult bullying, but there are some significant differences.

Firstly, adults are responsible for their behaviour whereas children are below the age of responsibility. However, bullies have a greater understanding of responsibility than they give the impression of having. They simply *choose* to reject the controls which normal people develop.

Secondly, adults are selected for bullying because they are good at their job and popular with people. The child who is bullied tends to be socially less popular than most children; however, closer inspection reveals that many children side with or appear to side with the bully because they know that, otherwise, they themselves will be bullied. They become assistants and reinforcers. Children who are bullied often exhibit a degree of interpersonal relationship (with fellow pupils and adults) beyond their years although this may not be recognised, perhaps because it is based on empathy rather than bravado or fast talk or charm. The bully, by contrast, is a deeply unpopular child with whom other children associate through fear rather than friendship.

Thirdly, children are still in their formative years, and if a child is exhibiting bullying behaviours, effective interception can help many bullying children learn better ways of behaving and interacting with other children. However, bullies with a conduct disorder (the precursor to antisocial personality disorder) or psychopathic personality are less likely to be amenable to this approach.

By the time people emerge from adolescence into adulthood, their behaviour patterns are set and only time or a traumatic experience can alter these patterns. However, people who are likely to be bullied have a considerable ability to learn from experience and apply that knowledge positively. People who are bullies or prone to be bullies have limited ability - and willingness - to apply knowledge gained from experience (especially in interpersonal and behavioural skills) and will often exhibit bullying behaviours throughout life. Their learning ability is dedicated to improving their faculty for bullying and evading accountability.

Selecting a safe school for your child

In recent years politicians have broadened parental choice in respect of schools; however, the government's focus has been exclusively on league tables. Whilst all parents want their children to gain the best exam results, the importance and relevance of OFSTED and league tables should not be overplayed.

In order for a child to flourish and succeed, the school must demonstrate that it understands and deals with bullying; one of the best indicators is substantive evidence that pupils and teachers are happy. Otherwise your child will, at the least, be prevented from achieving anywhere near his full potential. At worst, your child might not survive to discover their potential.

If playground bullying is rife then staff room bullying will also be in evidence, as indicated by unusually high rates of the following:

- turnover of teachers
- turnover of secretarial and administrative staff
- amount of staff sick leave
- number of days when supply staff are engaged
- number of different supply staff engaged
- number of stress breakdowns of staff
- number of suicides and attempted suicides amongst staff
- number of suicides and attempted suicides amongst pupils
- number of ill-health retirements
- number of early retirements
- number of grievances started
- number of uses of disciplinary procedures (verbal and written warnings issued)
- number of suspensions of staff
- number of dismissals of staff
- number of times the employer is involved in employment tribunals or legal action against employees
- poor attendance record of pupils
- number of pupil exclusions
- amount of damage to school property including graffiti

Prospective teachers can use the figures to gauge how happy they are likely to be at the school and whether their career will flourish or flounder. The figures also indicate how wisely national and local taxes are being spent.

When selecting a school for your child, avoid any school where the head teacher or staff claim "we don't need an anti-bullying policy, there's no bullying here". It is in these schools that bullying is most prevalent. Check that the school's anti-bullying policy is effective; some schools' policy serves only as window-dressing. Ask the experts: talk to the pupils and ex-pupils in private and in confidence. Talk to the children who are artistic, gifted, non-sporting, of high integrity and non-aggressive - these are the ones most likely to be targeted by bullies. And talk to parents, especially those whose children have been at the school for some time.

Chapter 18

End of term report

*"Never be bullied into silence. Never allow
yourself to be made a victim. Accept no one's
definition of your life; define yourself."*
Harvey Fierstein

Television doctor and medical columnist Miriam Stoppard
became acutely aware of the scale of Britain's bully
epidemic on meeting Kidscape founder Michele Elliott
fifteen years ago.

When her own newspaper, The Mirror, reported the
parenting fears of Posh Spice Victoria Beckham and her
football star husband, David, she published her own
advice on how to deal with the problem of playground
torment. (The Mirror, 31 August, 2000).

Victoria and David had just announced the birth of baby
son, Brooklyn, and already, Victoria recalled with dread
her own school days. She told The Mirror: "I just pray that
he finds a good set of friends when he starts school.

"I know that children can be awfully cruel sometimes.
When I was growing up, I was the victim of some really
nasty bullying at school. Nothing would hurt me more than
to see Brooklyn suffering."

Dr Stoppard observed: "Victoria's words echo the
thoughts of hundreds of thousands of parents across
Britain who dread their child being picked on." She then
told us: "It's a serious issue and one I've been made even
more aware of through my close contact with Michele
Elliott and Kidscape."

Dr Miriam advised her readers: "There will always be a
few who like to make other children's lives a misery, and

they seek out victims. The bully will always find something about a person to focus on - wearing glasses, having big ears, being in a wheelchair. They may taunt you for being good at exams or for being shy, too fat, too thin, being the wrong colour or wearing the wrong clothes.

"Bullies use differences as an excuse for their behaviour. But this difference isn't the problem. Bullies - who are insecure, jealous, cruel, angry and unhappy - have the problem.

"It's hard to imagine what a child goes through each day at their hands. There's no escape and asking for help may be impossible. It's not surprising the victim may start to act strangely."

Miriam believes parents can spot a bully problem when:
- a child becomes withdrawn and shy
- grades deteriorate at school
- no apparent friends
- refusal to say what's wrong
- fear of walking to and from home
- crying to sleep
- nightmares
- becoming distressed
- refusal to eat
- unwillingness to attend school.
- suicide attempts

Echoing advice from others, Dr Miriam suggests:

For child targets:
- Laugh at or ignore comments and teasing. Remember these people want to frighten you, so humour and silence might throw them off. If you keep it up for a while, they'll probably get bored.
- It's hard for a bully to continue bullying someone who won't stand still and listen. Say "No" really firmly, then turn and walk away. Don't worry if people consider this 'running away'.

- If a group is bothering you, look the weakest one in the eye and say: "This isn't funny," then walk away.
- You can sign up for a self-assertiveness course which will boost your confidence and self-belief.
- Stay with a crowd - bullies usually pick on kids alone.
- If you can get bully gang members on their own, ask them why they feel it necessary to gang up on one person.
- It may help to call one of the bullies and ask how they'd like it if this were happening to them. It will only work if you have some sort of relationship with that person.
- Seek the advice of your parents and, if they have any ideas, give them a try. You need their help and support.
- Tell a friend what's happening and ask for help. It'll be harder for bullies to pick on you if you have a friend at your side for support.
- Stop thinking and acting like a victim - you don't deserve this. Walk tall, pretend you are confident, even if you're not.
- Ask yourself "How would I act if I wasn't so frightened of them?" You'd smile. You'd stroll. You'd be casual. So do it.
- Keep a diary of all events - time and place and what's said. Give it to your parents and have them contact school governors and use the diary as evidence.
- No school governor will tolerate bullying and will make sure the head and teachers deal with it. Teachers have a duty to act against bullies.

How can school help?

- Your school should have an anti-bullying policy which tells you how to report bullying. If you're not sure, ask your teacher or head of year.
- Kidscape has a model anti-bullying policy which you can get by sending a large self-addressed envelope.

An anti-bullying policy should include:

- Encouraging anyone who's been bullied or who sees bullying to tell about it.

- Having bully boxes where students can place anonymous reports about what's happening.
- Holding student meetings where problems like bullying are discussed and dealt with.
- Ensuring there are specially trained students to help others, or teachers assigned to help with bullying problems.

What to do?

Bullying has plagued the human race for millennia. It's not going to go away overnight. However, the deaths by bullycide of at least sixteen children in the UK every year impel us to take action.

With thanks to ChildLine, Kidscape and others, we've pulled together the following advice:

Message for children

✗ *Don't* put up with it.

✗ *Don't* keep quiet; this is the worst thing you can do, and it's just what the bullies want.

✗ *Don't* be fooled by the bullies into believing you can handle it by yourself; you can't (no one can, not even adults), and there is no shame in recognising this.

✗ *Don't* give up.

Do...

✓ tell someone who can help. Ask them to talk through with you what they plan to do about it before they do anything.

✓ keep a diary of every incident that's relevant to the bullying; this journal will help establish the patterns by which bullying reveals itself. It's the patterns (frequency, regularity, incessance) which reveal intent. The diary will also validate your experience and help you maintain your objectivity and sanity.

✓ understand that you have a **right** not to be bullied, harassed and abused.

✓ call helplines, visit websites, and contact organisations

which offer help to children suffering bullying.

✓find out as much as you can about bullying - the earlier you recognise it, the more likely you are to achieve a successful outcome.

✓recognise that all the bullies' criticisms are false.

✓learn to trust your own opinion of yourself and overrule the bullies' opinions.

Message for parents

✗ *Don't* put up with it.

✗ *Don't* expect your children to tell you they are being bullied; kids feel responsible for what is happening and blame themselves. Children have an overwhelming desire to protect their parents from pain which means that parents are often the last to find out.

✗ *Don't* wait for children to bring up the subject of bullying before you talk about it; children worry about bullying more than anything else, so take the initiative.

✗ *Don't* ignore, deny or dismiss reports of bullying; bullying almost never gets better and almost always gets worse.

✗ *Don't* tell your child to ignore it.

✗ *Don't* dismiss verbal bullying as 'only teasing'. Persistent teasing is psychological violence which can result in bullycide.

✗ *Don't* just tell your child to stand up for himself or herself. Even adults find it difficult to defend themselves against the antisocial behaviour of sustained bullying.

✗ *Don't* blame your child for what is happening; responsibility for bullying is 100% with the bully and a system which fails to address the problem.

✗ *Don't* suggest, however obliquely, that your child must have done something to initiate, invite, or deserve the bullying; it's not the case.

✗ *Don't* immediately march up to the school and demand an end to the bullying; you will not be taken seriously.

There's a school grapevine which will make matters worse for your son or daughter. Any school where bullying is rife is likely to give top priority to protecting its image and fending off possible legal action.

✗ *Don't* expect the school to miraculously bring an end to the bullying.

✗ *Don't* expect the bullies to stop bullying any more than you'd expect a hyena to voluntarily become a vegetarian. Bullies need to be helped, encouraged, and if necessary forced to adopt acceptable standards of behaviour.

✗ *Don't* expect any quick answers or solutions.

✗ *Don't* put it off - the sooner the bullying cycle is interrupted, the more likely you are to be successful.

Do...

✓ find out as much as you can about bullying - the earlier you recognise it and take considered action, the more likely you are to achieve a successful outcome, and the less will be the damage to your child's health, confidence and esteem.

✓ your research on bullying - start with the resources section at the back of this book; send for literature, visit websites, and gather as much information as you can. Do this before your child becomes a target.

✓ read Kidscape's book *101 ways to deal with bullying: a guide for parents.*

✓ read other books on bullying.

✓ obtain information and advice from more than one source.

✓ ask your child's school for a copy of their anti-bullying policy.

✓ think of bullying if your children feel unhappy or upset.

✓ look for signs: clothes or possessions disappearing, damage to clothes or possessions, sullenness (a sign of psychiatric injury), uncommunicativeness, avoidance behaviours, unusual changes in behaviour (check for bullying before attributing these to puberty, adolescence, hormones, or whatever), secretiveness, changes in speech patterns (eg developing a stutter), tics, bed-wetting, sleep problems, excessive worry, avoidance behaviour, panic attacks, depression, suicidal thoughts, panic attacks, self-harm, unexplained truancy, changes in circles of friends, changes in diet, unexplained loss of interest, changes in academic performance, unexpectedly low marks, etc.

✓ encourage your child to tell you everything.

✓ take your child and their experience seriously; childhood can be tough and the bullying experience will determine the happiness or otherwise of years to come.

✓ explain what bullying is and why children bully.

✓ explain to your children that the reasons bullies give for picking on you are false.

✓ instil in your child that they have a **right** not to be bullied, harassed, molested, blackmailed, assaulted, abused, etc.

✓ talk to your children about what is the best course of action; they will have important things to say about what they think is best. Although it is perfectly natural to be furiously angry on your child's behalf and want to call the bullies to account, it is not the time to let feelings affect judgement.

✓ the obvious: say daily that you love them and care for them and tell them they are brave to tell.

✓ keep telling your child that he or she is valuable as a person.

✓ keep at it; bullying can be hard to stop.

✓ encourage and help your child keep a journal.

✓ keep your own journal of everything you and your child do.

✓ think of things your child can enjoy doing out of school and away from its stresses.

✓ consider if classes in self-defence, karate, or similar

can help your child develop self-esteem and self-confidence.

✓ consider whether your child needs to talk to someone else to get help with their confidence and self-esteem.

✓ try to help your child make other friendships outside school and family.

✓ complain to the school if the problem persists and write formally if this does not work; keep your cool while you're at it or the tables may be turned and you'll find yourself labelled as a bully - feigning victimhood is a common tactic of bullies in their attempts to abdicate and deny responsibility.

✓ let the school know that you expect them to discuss with you and your child what they plan to do to put a stop to the bullying, and to be kept informed about what has been done and the outcome.

✓ ask the school, in writing, to provide you, in writing, with details of what they are doing and what they will do to address the bullying.

✓ make an appointment with your child's teacher to discuss the bullying and if necessary make follow-up appointments to monitor progress.

✓ talk to other parents to see how widespread the bullying is.

✓ try and talk to the bully's parents if this is possible - not all bullies come from dysfunctional families. Bullying thrives on secrecy. You might not realise your child has become a target but likewise the bully's parents may be unaware their child is an aggressor.

✓ point out to the school the detrimental effect that bullying is having on your child, and other children, and how this will lead to lower grades and thus how bullies will drive the school down the league tables.

✓ have a good idea of the legal position in case the school does not take you seriously. Keep this in reserve in case other approaches fail.

✓ pursue every avenue.

✓ recommend this book to parents, teachers, education employees, and everyone who has contact with children in any capacity.

Questions for school staff

Do you have a whole school anti-bullying approach in your school which everyone understands and is committed to?

Do you make children aware as soon as they enter your school that bullying is not acceptable? How do you achieve this?

Do you have a specific staff member responsible for overseeing anti-bullying work? Is this person trained?

Have you mapped the scale, extent, and location of bullying in your school through a questionnaire?

Do you have any anti-bullying literature off the shelf and used effectively?

Does your policy forbid harassment and discrimination on the grounds of race, gender, disability, culture, ethnic origin, religious belief, sexual orientation, etc? How is this policy policed?

Do all staff feel involved and are they treated equally?

Are members of staff trained in group approaches?

What curricular work focuses on bullying?

Do you provide support, mentoring and counselling for targets of bullying?

Do you provide support, mentoring and counselling for bullies?

Are children in your school directly involved in helping to prevent and stop bullying?

Are the children in your school empowered to take action in the event of witnessing bullying, and are the children aware of what they can and cannot do?

Is the head teacher a good role model? Does he or she have good interpersonal skills and is he or she approachable?

Do the teachers and other staff make good role models?
Are staff approachable, safe, and reliable?
Are non-teaching staff offered training in preventing bullying in the playground and off school premises?
Do the school governors take a keen interest in activities to prevent or deal with bullying?
Have you identified those areas of school premises where bullying most often takes place and which adults are least able to monitor? What have you done to address this?
Is your playground a fun, safe area with lots of activities?
Does your policy proactively deal with bullying on the way to and from school?
Do you have contact with other organisations that deal with safety and welfare, eg social services and the police?
Do you make and maintain contact with peers and professional bodies and keep abreast of best practice?
Are you pushing the Local Education Authority and Department for Education and Employment for practical guidance and leadership in addressing bullying?
Do you value diversity in children, especially those whose talents and interests lie outside the National Curriculum?
Do you accept that some children will be inclined towards subjects such as art and poetry that might cause them to be more likely to be targeted by bullies?
Do you do everything to make school an enjoyable experience for both children and adults?

Changing the culture
Bullying can only be successfully tackled when both staff and children are genuinely committed to a whole-school anti-bullying ethos such that:

- everyone knows and understands what bullying is and discusses openly why they think bullies bully
- everyone knows and understands that bullying is unacceptable
- incidents of bullying are nipped in the bud

- the bully is called to account in a firm but supportive manner without physical punishment (if the bully were subjected to physical punishment then it would reaffirm in his mind the acceptability of violence to achieve objectives)
- the bully is subsequently supervised and supported in learning more appropriate ways of interacting with other children
- all children are taught how to be assertive
- all children are taught how to spot bullying and intercede or report it
- all children are empowered to help both target and bully

Our suggestions are not exhaustive and our final recommendation is to keep researching the subject and keep up to date on developments, especially with organisations who work on the front line.

Conclusion

Each bullycide is an unpalatable fact that a child has died as a result of the deliberate actions of another in an environment where the responsible adults have failed to provide a mechanism for reporting, intervening, and dealing with physical and psychological violence. The excuses of "we didn't know" or "we didn't understand" are no longer valid.

Over the last decade, teachers have come under fire from all sides, including heads of department, management teams, deputy head teachers, head teachers, governors, local education authorities (LEAs), the UK government's Department for Education and Employment (DfEE), the Office for Standards in Education (OFSTED), parents, and children themselves. All of this has occurred during a time of unprecedented demands by governments to "raise standards". However, this obsessive focus on exams results means that the teaching of life skills has been eclipsed. Most importantly, there appears to be almost no formal support for teachers to deal effectively with bullying.

Consequently, few people know how to tackle bullying. There are few legal avenues. Law is not a solution, neither does there appear to be any leadership from DfEE. But, above all, bullying is sustained by the attitudes of society and it's those attitudes that have to be changed. Building on the work of Kidscape, ChildLine, The Suzy Lamplugh Trust, ABC, VISYON and the countless other organisations making a difference, this book is an attempt to bring that about.

Suicide often induces doubt. As the coroner indicated of Danielle Goss: "[I] wasn't convinced she'd meant to go that far." No strangers to mysterious death, coroners are often moved to report that "we will have to accept that we will never know what was going on in [the child's] mind". David Tuck's suicide elicited the suspicion "...that this was a cry for help".

Bullycide: death at playtime is an answer to all those cries for help, recorded or otherwise. We heard Marie Bentham, our youngest case at only 8 years old. We heard Denise Baillie, at four weeks the shortest case. We've described the sustained campaigns mounted against Kelly Yeomans and Katherine Jane Morrison, and we've detailed the final unbearable moments of Steven Shepherd in the strawberry fields at Newburgh and Lucy Forrester at Congleton railway station.

At least sixteen families will lose a child to bullycide this year. Schools, and especially those with managerial responsibility for education, must do better.

We must all do better.

Resources

Reports and publications

Why Me? Children talking to ChildLine about bullying, Mary MacLeod and Sally Morris

Long-term effects of bullying, Michele Elliott and Gaby Shenton, Kidscape (published in *Bully Free*)

Preventing school bullying, Professor John Pitts, Home Office Report

Still running: children on the streets, The Children's Society, 1999

I didn't come here for fun, Save the Children Scotland and Scottish Refugee Council, 2000

Don't suffer in silence, DfEE anti-bullying pack for schools, 1994, see www.dontsufferinsilence.com

Action Against Bullying: a support pack for schools, Scottish Council for Research in Education, Edinburgh

Bullying: a guide to the law, Children's Legal Centre, University of Essex, see www2.essex.ac.uk/clc/

Books

Bully Free, Michele Elliott and Gaby Shenton, Kidscape, 1999

Beyond Bullying, Gaby Shenton, Kidscape, Bracher Giles and Martin, 1999

101 ways to deal with bullying: a guide for parents, Michele Elliott, Hodder

Keeping safe, a practical guide to talking with children, Michele Elliott, Coronet Books, 1994

The Willow Street Kids: Be smart, stay safe, Michele Elliott, Pan Macmillan

The Willow Street Kids: Beat the bullies, Michele Elliott, Pan Macmillan

Bully Wise Guide, Michele Elliott, Hodder, 1999

Bullying: a practical guide to coping for schools, Michele Elliott, FT Prentice Hall

Don't pick on me, Rosemary Stones, Piccadilly Press, 1993

Bullying: a resource guide for parents and teachers, Vivette O'Donnell and the Campaign Against Bullying, Attic Press, 1995, http://indigo.ie/~odonnllb/cabullying/

501 ways to be a good parent, Michele Elliott, Hodder and Stoughton, 1996

Books for adults

Bully in sight: how to predict, resist, challenge and combat workplace bullying, Tim Field, Success Unlimited, 1996

Bullying at work: how to confront and overcome it, Andrea Adams with Neil Crawford, Virago, 1992

The verbally abusive relationship: how to recognize it and how to respond, Patricia Evans, Adams, 1996

Post Traumatic Stress Disorder: the invisible injury, David Kinchin, Success Unlimited, 1998

Supporting children with Post-traumatic Stress Disorder, David Kinchin and Erica Brown, David Fulton Publishers, 2001

Why zebras don't get ulcers: an updated guide to stress, stress-related diseases, and coping, Robert M Sapolsky, Freeman, 1998

The gift of fear: survival signals that protect us from violence, Gavin de Becker, Bloomsbury, 1997

When she was bad: how women get away with murder, a controversial and explosive look at female aggression, Patricia Pearson, Virago Press, 1998

Where there is evil, Sandra Brown, Macmillan, 1998

The history of childhood, Lloyd de Mause (Ed), The Psychohistory Press, 1974

Bad Boys, Bad Men; Confronting Antisocial Personality Disorder, Donald W Black with Lindon C Larson, 1999

Inside the criminal mind, Stanton E Samenow PhD, Times Books, 1984

The mask of sanity: an attempt to clarify some issues about the so-called psychopathic personality, Hervey Cleckley, C V Mosby, 1976

Without conscience: the disturbing world of the psychopaths among us, Robert Hare, Pocket Books, New York, 1993

Organisations and websites

See also www.bullycide.com and www.bullycide.net

Kidscape has lots of leaflets, booklets and help for parents of children suffering bullying. They can also train teachers, children and parents' groups in dealing with or preventing bullying. Send an A4 stamped (80p) addressed envelope marked *Anti-Bully Pack* to Kidscape, 2 Grosvenor Gardens, London SW1W 0DH, Telephone 020 7730 3300, see www.kidscape.org.uk

ChildLine is the UK's free 24-hour national helpline for children and young people in trouble or danger, Tel 0800 1111, see www.childline.org.uk

The Suzy Lamplugh Trust is the national charity for personal safety: 14 East Sheen Avenue, London SW14 8AS, Tel 020 8876 0305, see www.suzylamplugh.org

Get connected, an initiative of the Suzy Lamplugh Trust, a free confidential helpline that puts young people in touch with the right help, Tel 0800 096 0096

Anti-Bullying Campaign, 10 Borough Hill Street, London SE1 9QQ, Tel 020 7378 1446

Parentline Plus offers support to anyone parenting a child, Tel 0808 800 2222, see www.parentlineplus.org.uk

VISYON supports young people aged 14-25 under stress in Congleton Borough with a range of services from one-to-one counselling to group therapy work. HQ is at 43A West Street, Congleton, Cheshire CW12 1JY, Tel 01260 290000, see www.visyon.org.uk

Bullying Online at www.bullying.co.uk throws a lifeline to despairing parents whose children are being bullied and who don't know what to do

Parents and Children Unite (PCU) against bullying within schools, Tel 01733 208048

National Child Protection Helpline (NSPCC), Freephone 0800 800 500. A 24-hour helpline for anyone concerned about a child at risk of abuse (including bullying), including children themselves. See www.nspcc.org.uk

Lucky Duck Publishing, 34 Wellington Park, Clifton, Bristol BS8 2UW, Tel/fax 0117 973 2881. Information, leaflets, videos and books on managing behaviour in schools. For details email luckyduck@dial.pipex.com

Advisory Centre for Education provides information for parents, school governors and teachers. ACE Ltd, 1B Aberdeen Studios, 22 Highbury Grove, London N5 2EA, Tel 020 7354 8321, see www.ace-ed.org.uk

The Children's Legal Centre, University of Essex, Tel 01206 873820, see www2.essex.ac.uk/clc/

Young Minds is the children's mental health charity; see www.youngminds.org.uk

Bully OnLine at www.successunlimited.co.uk provides insight and information on bullying and related issues
Child bullying: www.successunlimited.co.uk/child.htm
Home tuition: www.successunlimited.co.uk/hometuit.htm
Links to organisations and websites dealing with child and school bullying: www.successunlimited.co.uk/links.htm

UK Department for Education & Employment (DfEE), see www.dfee.gov.uk/bullying/pages/home.html

DfEE Parents' Centre, see www.parents.dfee.gov.uk

Teacherline - for stressed teachers, Tel 08000 562 561, see www.teacherline.org.uk

Scottish Anti-Bullying Network, Moray House Institute of Education, University of Edinburgh, Holyrood Road, Edinburgh EH8 8AQ, Tel/Fax 0131 651 6100, see www.antibullying.net

Scottish Council for Research in Education (SCRE), 15 St John Street, Edinburgh EH8 8JR, see www.scre.ac.uk

Websites

Youthnet UK's TheSite.org at http://ned.thesite.org.uk

Brian Jones and the Breitling Orbiter 3 capsule at www.orbiterballoon.com

Youth 2 Youth at www.youth2youth.co.uk

Moira Anderson Foundation at http://members.aol.com/sandra7510/

Changing Faces at www.changingfaces.co.uk

Bullying: a survival guide, BBC Education at www.bbc.co.uk/education/archive/bully/help.shtml

Copyrights and credits

Strawberry Fields with the encouragement of the late
   John Lennon's family, and current copyright holders of
   Northern Songs, the music publishing company originally
   set up by Lennon and McCartney.
Ugly Duckling © 1979/80 Frank Music Corporation.
   Reproduced by kind permission of Robert Webb, Archive
   Dept, Music Sales Library, Bury St. Edmunds.

Centre photographs
1.   Steven Shepherd, © Wigan Heritage Service
2.   Steven Shepherd's Uncle and Aunt, Jimmy and
     Marjorie Jolly, © Bill Batchelor
3.   Stanley Holland today, © Bill Batchelor
4.   Steven Shepherd's school pal Stanley Holland in a
     police reconstruction, © Wigan Heritage Service
10. Neil Marr pauses by Steven Shepherd's grave,
     © Bill Batchelor
11. Targets of bullying are excluded and isolated,
     © Martyn Snape
13. Peter McQueen with his Mum and Dad, © Newsflash,
     Edinburgh
15. PC Fred and pals, © Martyn Snape
16. Prince Naz before his fight with Wayne McCulloch,
     © News Group Newspapers
17. Elliott Stephens with Prince Naz, © News Group
     Newspapers
22. Peanuts cartoon, © 1993 United Feature Syndicate,
     Inc. Reproduced by kind permission of Knight
     Features.
24-26. Caroline Worth expresses her pain and anguish
     through her art, © Clarey Art
27. Lucy Forrester, © Bill Batchelor
28. Lucy's parents, Richard and Elizabeth Forrester who
     set up VISYON in Lucy's memory, © Bill Batchelor

29. Salli Ward, former Centre Manager at VISYON,
    © Bill Batchelor
30. Congleton Railway Station, scene of Lucy's bullycide,
    © Bill Batchelor

All other copyrights acknowledged.
Thanks to all proofreaders, including Jennifer Studdard and Sue Little.

Special thanks to:

Jo Brand for writing the Introduction.

Bill Batchelor for his help in compiling the bullycide picture file. British Press Award winning photographer Bill works as a freelance press photographer for national newspapers in the UK after retiring as chief photographer of the Manchester Evening News. Bill worked on the local evening newspaper in Wigan alongside author Neil Marr during the hunt for Steven Shepherd.

Cover picture:
First-prize winning photograph by British Press Photographer of 2000, Ian Torrance, on the Macedonian border. A bemused child, his face pressed against the dirty, rain-spattered window of a refugee bus suffers the ultimate bullying of war. Ian does not know if the child survived his ordeal. Reproduced by kind permission of an old pal. © Daily Record and Sunday Mail Ltd, Glasgow.

Additional research by Brian Gallagher.

Index

Comments and feedback

Email to
 timfield@successunlimited.co.uk

Send via Bully OnLine
 www.successunlimited.co.uk

Or send to:
 Success Unlimited
 PO Box 67
 Didcot
 Oxfordshire OX11 9YS
 UK

Thank you for your comments.

Bullycide: death at playtime

Order Form

Please send me .... copies of Neil Marr and Tim Field's
BULLYCIDE: DEATH AT PLAYTIME at **£16.50** per copy in the UK,
(rest of Europe £17.35, outside Europe £19.95)

Please send me .... signed copies of Tim Field's
**BULLY IN SIGHT: HOW TO PREDICT, RESIST, CHALLENGE AND
COMBAT WORKPLACE BULLYING** at **£14.85** per copy in the UK,
(rest of Europe £15.90, outside Europe £18.15)

Please send me .... copies of David Kinchin's
POST TRAUMATIC STRESS DISORDER: THE INVISIBLE INJURY
at **£15** a copy UK (rest of Europe £16.50, outside Europe £17.50)

Prices include postage & packing. 30-day money-back guarantee.

Name (BLOCK LETTERS) ....

Address ....

....

....

Postcode ....

❏ I enclose sterling cheque payable to "Success Unlimited"
or credit card: Visa ❏   MasterCard ❏   Switch ❏   Solo ❏

Card number ....

Switch/Solo issue number ....

Expiry date ....

Name on card ....

Signature ....

**Send to: Success Unlimited, PO Box 67, Didcot,
Oxfordshire OX11 9YS, UK**
Order online
www.successunlimited.co.uk/books/
Telephone orders: 0700-ACHIEVE (2244383)
Fax orders: 07000-785776   Trade enquiries welcome